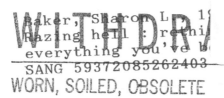

Razing Hell

Razing Hell

Rethinking Everything You've Been Taught about God's Wrath and Judgment

Sharon L. Baker

WESTMINSTER
JOHN KNOX PRESS
LOUISVILLE · KENTUCKY

First edition
Published by Westminster John Knox Press
Louisville, Kentucky

10 11 12 13 14 15 16 17 18 19—10 9 8 7 6 5 4 3 2 1

Book design by Drew Stevens
Cover design by designpointinc.com
Cover art © iStockphoto.com

Library of Congress Cataloging-in-Publication Data

Baker, Sharon L., 1956–
    Razing hell : rethinking everything you've been taught about God's wrath and judgment / Sharon L. Baker.
        p. cm.
    Includes bibliographical references and indexes.
    ISBN 978-0-664-23654-0 (alk. paper)
    1. Hell—Christianity.   2. God (Christianity)—Attributes.   3. Hell—Biblical teaching.
4. God—Biblical teaching.   I. Title.
    BT836.3.B35 2010
    236'.25—dc22

                                                                                2010003675

PRINTED IN THE UNITED STATES OF AMERICA

∞ The paper used in this publication meets the minimum requirements
of the American National Standard for Information Sciences—Permanence
of Paper for Printed Library Materials, ANSI Z39.48-1992.

Westminster John Knox Press advocates the responsible use of our natural resources.
The text paper of this book is made from at least 30% postconsumer waste.

For my sons,
Collin, Nicholas, Kelly, and Graham Baker,
with love

Contents

Acknowledgments

I express heartfelt gratitude to the many colleagues who provided invaluable help by listening to my ruminations, reading the many rough drafts, and exploring the depths of hell with me. I greatly appreciate their hospitable scholarship, their generous attentiveness, and unfailing friendship that stimulated me intellectually and encouraged me personally. They include John D. Caputo, Susanna Caroselli, Lynne Cosby, Michael Cosby, Crystal Downing, Jenell Paris, B. Keith Putt, Eric Seibert, Valerie Smith, Valerie Weaver-Zercher, and Cynthia Wells. I also thank my friend and colleague David Downing. His imaginative talent for inventing titles is evident to all who read the cover of this book.

As is often the case with educators, my students taught me more about hell than I care to admit. Their many questions and thoughtful reflections concerning my reinterpretation of such a classic and stubbornly imbedded Christian doctrine provided important insights that are written into the pages of this book. Although I can't possibly name them all—there are literally hundreds—exceptional thanks go to Bethany Ellis, Robert Holland, Kristina Lewis, Chelsea McInturff, John Michael Pickens, Jared Quesenberry, Jonathan Stoltzfus, and Victoria Yunez. I offer special thanks to my formal conversation partners Brooke, Lisa Stephens, and Eric Gephart: you'll read much more about them in the following pages.

I am very grateful to my agent, Greg Daniels, and editors Daniel Braden and David Dobson, along with all the very helpful people at WJK, for their indefatigable patience, discerning eyes, and professional expertise.

As always, I owe deep gratitude to my mother Helen Crosby, aunts Carol Hester and Mildred Pelrine, mentors Ann MacRitchie and Betty Heisig, and good friend Debbie Pickens for their extravagant grace toward me, their constant prayers, loving care, listening ears, and honest critique. They've all given me a little taste of heaven in the midst of thinking and writing about hell.

Introduction

I think and judge it best for you
to follow me, and I shall guide you, taking
you from this place through an eternal place,
where you shall hear the howls of desperation
and see the ancient spirits in their pain,
as each of them laments his second death.
—Virgil, in Dante's Inferno, Canto 1

Then death and Hades were thrown into
the lake of fire. This is the second death,
the lake of fire.

—Revelation 20:14

When I was twenty-six, I found out I was going to hell. Young, impressionable, and without a strong faith, I listened intently as the pastor of a church I was visiting described in graphic detail the torturous, unquenchable flames that would burn human bodies—including, I presumed, mine—forever and ever. He spoke of worms eating away at decaying flesh, total darkness without the presence of God, and worst of all, no release from those horrors for all eternity. I certainly didn't want to be one of those unfortunate many to feel the flames licking at my feet soon after leaving life in this world. So I took out the proper fire insurance and asked Jesus to save me from my sins and, therefore, from eternal torment in hell. Whew!

That was twenty-five years ago, and hell is still a hot topic. Almost 60 percent of Americans believe in hell. So do 92 percent of those who attend church every week. After that first shocking revelation about hell, I believed the pastor and never questioned its reality, its justice, or its duration. How many of us have grown up hearing about and believing in the existence of hell, a fiery abyss that eternally burns without destroying, tortures without ceasing, punishes without respite, where the only thing that dies is the hope of release or reconciliation? If the number of students and friends who come to me with questions about it serve as an indicator, most of us have cut our teeth on this picture of hell.

Lisa did. We've been good friends for twenty years. We raised our kids together and grew up as Christians side by side. Lisa is one of those friends who often says what no one else dares to say or asks the questions no one else dares to ask. We talk on the phone often, usually about a controversial theological topic, and lately the topic has centered around—you guessed it—hell. An inquisitive and thoughtful student and friend, Brooke, asks troubling questions too. Hell bothers her, yet she lacks alternatives. She was raised in an intellectual and educated environment and thinks about things that normal teenage girls wouldn't give a second thought. Eric, a senior ministry major in college and a very bright student, hates hell too; but he just cannot let go of the ideas he has always been taught. He wants to work as God's servant, furthering the kingdom of God by winning souls to Jesus. And hell, as bothersome as it is to him, tends to make unbelievers listen. He wants to believe differently but fears the consequences.

The idea of hell haunts my friend Lisa and my students Brooke and Eric. Along with many others, they question the justice of it all—eternal punishment for temporal sin. They don't understand how a God, who *is* love, can send so many into eternal torment. They are not alone. As I began to study the Bible for myself all those many years ago, it staggered my senses to think of billions upon billions of people, the majority of all those who have ever lived throughout history's millennia, burning forever and ever in hell.

I teach theology at a Christian liberal arts college in Pennsylvania, and every semester a handful of students struggle with traditional Christian doctrines like hell. Yet other students get upset if they think I am trying to take hell away from them by explaining alternative views. They hate hell, but at the same time they want hell. Or perhaps they need hell to support other beliefs they hold. My mother, who will deny what I am about to say, also objected to tampering with the doctrine of hell. When I asked her why, she said that these traditional doctrines brought her comfort in her old age.

"Comfort?" I asked, a bit astounded. "How can the idea of billions of people engulfed in the flames of eternal torment be a comfort?" She couldn't put her finger on the reason. Now I know that my mother doesn't relish the notion of eternal punishment—at least for most people—and neither do most of us. For some reason, however, we feel that if we start tinkering with one traditional doctrine, our entire belief system may cave in around us. Some of you may feel that the authority of the Bible is at stake. But this doesn't have to be the case. As long as we base our tinkering on sound biblical interpretation, we won't find ourselves sliding into heresy. In fact, we may actually develop theological and biblical ways of thinking that are more consistent with our image of God as a loving creator who desires to liberate us from sin and evil. So together, in conversation with others like Brooke, Lisa, and Eric, we will search for an alternate and biblical view of hell. And we aren't alone in this search. Many others have gone before us who just couldn't harmonize the knowledge of the love of God through Jesus with the image of God as a merciless judge who sends billions of people to hell.

Although no formal doctrine of hell existed in the early church, some of our ancient church fathers sought to correct ideas of eternal punishment with their interpretations of Scripture. Irenaeus, Origen, Clement of Alexandria, and Gregory of Nyssa strenuously and publically objected to notions of hell that depict God as an angry judge, waiting to throw the wicked into eternal torment for temporal sins. They held the work of atonement through Jesus Christ worthy of such high praise and having such significant value that they believed redemption in Jesus' name would continue on to the last judgment and beyond. They couldn't believe that God would limit the opportunity of salvation to the temporal realm, especially if the possibility for repentance remained an option even after the death of the body. For these venerable old saints, eternal hell could not be an option for a God of love, the God who through Jesus Christ died to reconcile *the world* to himself (2 Cor. 5:19).

If the idea of hell haunts your dreams and disturbs your sleep, if you ever wonder at the justice (or injustice) of it all or about the God who deems it necessary to send the majority of humanity, beloved humanity, created in God's image, to burn there forever just because people found themselves raised in the wrong faith or had never heard of Jesus, this book is for you. Or if you grew up in a tradition that either dismissed hell as a malicious myth or did not talk about hell at all, you will resonate deeply with the content of this book. It may open up new ways for you to think about God and what awaits us when this life comes to an end.

Hell should evoke nightmares; it should stir our hearts to abhorrence, plague our minds with questions about its legitimacy; and awaken in us a sense of injustice. It did so for Lisa, Brooke, and Eric, and it does so for me and always has. Hell haunts me deep down inside, where I fear to tread and fail to admit uncertainty lest ripples of doubt disturb my secure little world of faith, lest someone find out and think me less Christian and more heretic. Brooke, eyes wide with apprehension, said, "We don't dare talk about it!" I say it's time we do. We all need a safe space to contemplate tough issues, to consider our questions, and to give heed to our doubts; here is that space. We will talk about our troubles and questions concerning hell, but we will also discuss alternative views, different ways of thinking about hell that are consistent with a God of love, justice, mercy, and compassion, who desires the salvation of all creation (1 Tim. 2:4).

As you read, be assured that I have no intention of doing away with hell. I can't. I have too high a respect for the authority of the Bible as God's Word. And we do find references to fiery judgment and eternal punishment in the Bible; we'll talk about those in detail later. So I am very concerned about remaining faithful to Scripture; but I'm even more concerned about remaining faithful to the God of love, who desires the salvation of all people (1 Tim. 2:4), whose grace is exceedingly abundant beyond all we can think or even ask for (Eph. 3:20), and who loves enemies, even the Hitlers, the Idi Amins, and the Osama bin Ladens of the world (Matt. 5:43–48; 1 John 4:8). Our traditional views of hell as a place of eternal punishment where unbelievers dwell in undying flames contradict this image of God. This concerns me greatly.

I am also concerned about the good news, God's good news, the good news about God's *grace*. Our traditional focus on hell as an evangelistic tool does not genuinely communicate the very heart of the gospel. If we receive Jesus as Savior because we want to escape the eternal fires of hell, we miss the entire point of the good news. What *is* the point, you may ask? We'll discuss it in the last chapter; but suffice it here to say that salvation has almost everything to do with transforming the world for God's glory and little to do with eternal destination for our personal comfort. So in writing this book, I hope to reconsider our image of God and, as a result, to rethink our traditional views of hell and to shift our motivation for evangelism away from avoiding doom and gloom to truly preaching the good news of God's grace and living as an active member in God's kingdom.

The first part of the book discusses the image of God that leads us, or even allows us, to believe in an eternal hell. Chapter 1 traverses the terrain of the historical portrayals of hell. We'll take a look at the origins of the idea of hell, how it developed, and what hell looks like for theologians across the centuries and, thus, for many of us. In chapter 2 we'll look at the images of God that the traditional views of hell require us to hold on to. Although we find most of these images of God in the Bible, they aren't by far the most prevalent. Rather, we find that the Bible emphasizes the image of God as a loving, compassionate provider, who seeks to reconcile and restore God's people. Chapter 3 analyzes the justice of God. Traditional theories of hell lead us to view divine justice as retributive. But is that the only, or even the most common, sense of God's justice in the Bible? Chapter 4 deals with the issue of forgiveness that traditional views of hell lead us to believe, usually without being aware of it. If "God is reconciling the world to himself, *not counting our transgressions against us*" (2 Cor. 5:19 alt.), how do we explain eternal torment for sin? We'll see that often we base our ideas about divine forgiveness on our ideas about divine justice as retributive. But is this really what the Bible teaches?

In the second part of the book we begin to rethink the image, justice, and forgiveness of God in light of Scripture. The biblical witness guides us as we search for the God of love. In chapter 5 we'll discuss the violence of God, looking at doctrines that have contributed to the view of a violent God, and why divine violence is a problem for theology and for Christian living. Chapter 6 searches through Scripture and reveals to us the image of God as love, forgiveness, compassion, justice, and mercy—characteristics of God we have always acknowledged. This chapter confirms that, indeed, above all else, God is love. We will learn what that love entails, how God feels about us, how that love works in the world and in our lives, and why, because of that love, we can hope for a redemptive future. Moreover, if we want to change our views of hell, we must also interpret divine justice through the lens of love. When we try to adjust our minds to the image of God as nonviolent, the first question most of us ask is "What about God's justice?" Traversing the pages of the Bible, chapter 7 gives us an alternative view of divine justice, not as retributive, but as redemptive and restorative. Following that, the next question many of us raise when we rethink divine justice is about the nature of God's forgiveness. Does forgiveness require punishment first, then forgiveness later? Or does God truly forgive without condition? In chapter 8 we'll take a close look at divine forgiveness from a biblical perspective and find answers to these important questions.

Now we arrive at part 3, which describes in detail an alternative view of hell in light of the image of God as love, biblical ideas of justice that reconciles and restores, and divine forgiveness without conditions or prerequisites. In chapter 9 we'll talk about fire in the Bible and what it has to do with hell. Then you will read about an alternative view of hell, what that might look like for the unfortunate hell-bound person, and what such a view tells us about God. In chapter 10 we'll deal with Jesus' sayings on hell, the unquenchable fire, eternal darkness, and worms that live forever. Chapter 11 will answer the question many of us will ask next: "What does Jesus have to do with it?" We'll discuss the meaning and significance of Jesus' work on the cross and how it affects those who stand in the fires of hell. Since theology without practical application profits us nothing, in chapter 12, we'll deal with the ethical question "How then should we live?" We'll also discuss the importance of spreading the gospel message to those in need of redemption, faith, hope, and love. (For those of us who like to know which version of the Bible we're reading, I've used the NASB unless indicated otherwise; see the copyright page, above.)

As I look back at that first time I heard about hell and its horrors, I wonder how many other pastors pounding pulpits across the world have their parishioners running, scared out of their wits and into the kingdom of God, taking out fire insurance as a precaution against the threat of hell. "Who cares?" you might say. "As long as they purchase their policy in time, who cares *why* they buy?" God might. God may desire to save us from the flames in order to spend eternity in loving communion, not by scaring us to death, making our hair stand on end, shaking in our shoes on holy ground, coercing us to surrender or die—but by luring us with divine compassion, urging us gently with a caring hand, pursuing us diligently like Francis Thompson's "Hound of Heaven" until, with love for God in our eyes and Jesus in our hearts, we freely choose to enter God's kingdom—for an eternal relationship with our Creator, not in fear of eternal recompense for sin.

I hope you enjoy reading this book on hell. While you read, I hope to help you find refreshing new ideas that stimulate your mind to think and to consider a picture of a God who loves unconditionally and who abhors evil and violence enough to shatter its power, to extinguish its influence, and to terminate its existence for all eternity. Only through the total obliteration of all evil and violence will the work of Christ find its full effectiveness so that the peace, reconciliation, and restoration God desires for all creation will forever be ours, and everyone's. Let's begin our journey together.

PART 1

Traditional Views of Hell, God's Wrath, and Judgment

1

The Landscape

Through me the way into the suffering city,
Through me the way to the eternal pain,
Through me the way that runs among the lost.
Justice urged on my high artificer;
My maker was divine authority,
The highest wisdom, and the primal love.
Before me nothing but eternal things
Were made, and I endure eternally.
Abandon every hope, who enter here.
              —Sign on the gate into hell, in Dante, *Inferno*, Canto 3

And besides all this, between us and you
there is a great chasm fixed, so
that those who wish to come over
from here to you may not be able, and
that none may cross over from there to us.
—Abraham, in the parable of the Rich Man and Lazarus, Luke 16:26

It's a good thing I love to help struggling students. Within the span of a week, two of my students came to my office to talk about hell. Eric looked a bit despondent as he sat down in the chair near my desk.

"I had a discussion about evangelism with my roommate last night," he said quietly.

"Oh?" I replied, trying to switch my attention from grading Hindu philosophy papers to Christian evangelism.

"Yeah. He thinks that even those who have not heard about Jesus will burn in hell forever." Now he had my attention.

"Really? Do you believe that too?" I asked.

"Well . . . yes, I guess I do. But I don't want to. Doesn't it seem unjust of God to hold someone accountable for believing in a Jesus they've never even heard of? I mean, it's not their fault, is it? Yet during all eternity they suffer for a choice they didn't choose to make."

As the conversation progressed, I couldn't tell which bothered Eric more: the thought of an unjust God sending people to hell for all eternity, the idea of someone who had no control over whether or not they had faith in Jesus yet suffering horrendous eternal torture, or the fear he felt by expressing his doubts and angst over such firmly held doctrines.

All three worried him and left him with the scary feeling of standing on the outside of his comfortable faith community as he questioned the status quo.

A few days later, Brooke knocked on the door. She bounced into my office and threw herself into a chair, obviously excited about something. Before I could expend any mental effort wondering at the cause of her exhilaration, she burst out with "Guess what we talked about in Bible class today!"

"Uh . . . the Bible?" I said.

"Hell!" she blurted out.

"Sorry?" I said, thinking she didn't like my answer.

"No! Hell! We talked about hell in class!"

"Brooke, you've already told me hell bothers you, so why are you so excited about it?"

"Because of what the Bible *doesn't* say about it! Maybe I can think differently about hell after all! Maybe God doesn't really send people into eternal torture and we've been wrong all along!"

Brooke's enthusiasm over the possibility of an alternate view of hell revealed the depth of her discomfort with a God who would exact such pain upon much-loved creatures and with the thought of anyone suffering such endless agony.

I went home thinking about my conversations that week with Eric and Brooke, their problems with traditional views of hell, the struggles they wrestled with, and their very different emotions involved in questioning their traditions—Eric scared about the consequences and Brooke excited about the possibilities, both feelings arising from asking the tough questions. The next morning the phone rang. Lisa sounded agitated on the other end. "I'm so irritated with God right now I could scream," she said.

"Well, what's God done now?"

"My grandmother lies dying in a nursing home, and a friend from church told me she will go to hell if she doesn't receive Christ as her Savior before she dies! What a terrible thing to say at a moment like this! And if she's right, what kind of God would send my sweet old grandma to suffer in hell forever? She's never hurt anyone in her life!"

Hell again! If it were I, I'd be more upset with the friend than with God! But since I knew Lisa believed the same thing about hell that her church friend did, I asked her, "Lisa, you've always believed that God sends unbelievers to hell, too. Why are you all of a sudden so angry about it?"

"Because it's my *grandmother* who's in danger of going there!" was her vehement response. That makes sense. We seem to believe the horrible until it hits too close to home. Lisa and her grandmother were very close, and she couldn't stand the thought that the woman she loved so much, who had shown her so much love, would suffer unendurable punishment forever. The threat of her much-loved grandmother's potential eternal torment drove Lisa to question seriously what she had always believed about hell. Whatever the motive—either Eric's despondency over those who don't know about Jesus, or Brooke's excitement over another view, or Lisa's anguish over loved ones suffering forever—hell intrigues us, plagues us, causes us fearful discomfort, and begs us to think critically and honestly through its implications. With Eric, Lisa, and Brooke as conversation partners, we will do just that. We will search for the "truth" about hell.

THE JOURNEY BEGINS: A TOUR OF TRADITIONAL HELL

Hell has intrigued and attracted Christians for centuries. Fascinated by the mental images the idea evoked in their minds, artists throughout the ages created gruesome portrayals of hell and its wretched inhabitants. They usher us into the fiery pit, eternally aflame with burning putrid flesh. Foul-mouthed demons with malodorous breath devour vile sinners as blood drips from their fangs and human entrails hang grotesquely from clenched claws. We blanch in horror, our terror only eased by the awareness that this infernal fate falls on someone else and not upon us. But how did hell receive such wide press in a community based on Christian love? Theories abound.

Many Christian historians agree that concepts of eternal punishment, burning in a place like "hell," developed for the most part during the time period between the Old and New Testaments as Greek and Persian religious thought infiltrated Jewish literature, culture, and beliefs. The seeds of these concepts developed further, took root in culture, and eventually found their way into the New Testament. We will trace the birth of hell as a place of fiery eternal punishment in chapter 10. For our purposes in this chapter, we know that the early Christian fathers read and interpreted the New Testament through a certain lens and handed down to us Christianity's traditional view of hell.

The entry on hell in the *Westminster Dictionary of Theological Terms* describes it like this: "In Christian theology, the place of the dead after death in which the wicked endure eternal punishment and the total absence of God." This definition is created from centuries of Christian thought on the topic of hell. So before we start talking about alternatives, let's embark upon our tour of hell and see how our early church fathers, medieval theologians, and contemporary thinkers imagined it and how they handed it down to us.

Dante Alighieri wrote a classical piece titled *The Divine Comedy* (1308–21), which he broke down into three parts: *Inferno*, *Purgatorio*, and *Paradiso*. Dante describes the horrors of the inferno as Virgil, the ancient Latin poet, leads him through the nine increasingly evil and torturous circles of hell. During the tour, Virgil allows Dante to speak with hell's inhabitants and to gloat at their dismal desolation. As Virgil leads him, Dante takes his readers along, describing in intricate detail the tortures and terrors he sees on his trip through the dungeons of hell. With that image in mind, let me act as your Virgil as I lead you through the various images of hell as thought and taught by the Christian tradition.

The ancient church fathers paint vivid pictures of what awaits those doomed to eternal fire. One of our earliest church fathers, Justin Martyr (ca. 160), says that hell's inhabitants "will suffer punishment in eternal fire according to the merits of [their] deed" (*1 Apology* 17). Irenaeus (ca. 180), another early church theologian, believed that Scripture clearly reveals that "eternal fire is prepared for the sinner" (*Against Heresies* 2.28.7). The well-known Clement of Alexandria (ca. 195) writes that "all souls are immortal, even those of the wicked. Yet it would be better for them if they were not deathless. For they are punished with the endless vengeance of quenchless fire. Since they do not die, it is impossible for them to have an end put to their misery" (*Fragments* 6.2). Marcus Minucius Felix (ca. 200) agrees with Clement: "There is neither limit nor termination of these torments. There, the intelligent fire burns the limbs and restores them. It feeds on them and nourishes them" (*Octavius* 35). He believes that unceasing punishment in the fires of condemnation await the unrepentant sinner, whose burned body parts regenerate only to be burned off again.

I could quote plenty more, but I think these few excerpts give you a clear picture of the nature of hell as a place of eternal torment according to our tradition's early theologians. As you can see, these men allowed their creative senses to run wild.

Taking their cue from the early church fathers and their interpretation of the Bible, medieval and modern theologians, pastors, and priests picked up the early Christian images of hell and expounded even more vividly on its unending horrors. The famous preacher Jonathan Edwards (1741) spins a verbal image of hell that sizzles with righteous indignation toward those who deserve its torments: "O sinner! Consider the fearful danger you are in: it is a great furnace of wrath, a wide and bottomless pit, full of the fire of wrath, that you are held over in the hand of that God, whose wrath is provoked and incensed as much against you, as against many of the damned in hell. You hang by a slender thread, with the flames of divine wrath flashing about it, and ready every moment to singe it, and burn it asunder."

Edwards describes the experience of hell's torrential fires with diabolical flourish:

> [The wicked] shall forever be full of a quick sense within and without; their heads, their eyes, their tongues, their hands, their feet, their loins and their vitals, shall forever be full of glowing melting fire, fierce enough to melt the very rocks and elements. And also . . . they shall eternally . . . feel the torment, . . . not for one minute, nor for one day, nor for one year, nor for one age, nor for a hundred ages, nor for a million of ages, one after another, but *for ever and ever*, without any end, and never, never be delivered!

Imagine hell in the mind of Fray Luis de Granada (1588) as he describes the sinners' lot: "There will the condemned in cruel rage and despair turn their fury against God and themselves, gnawing their flesh with their mouth, breaking their teeth with gnashing, furiously tearing themselves with their nails, and everlastingly blaspheming against the judge. . . . Oh tortured bodies that will have no refreshment but flames." Even John Wesley (1758), who profoundly experienced and adamantly proclaimed the love of God, wrote:

> The wicked will gnaw their tongues for anguish and pain; they will curse God and look upwards. There the dogs of hell, pride, malice, revenge, rage, horror, despair, continually devour them. . . . Consider that all these torments of body and soul are without intermission. Be their suffering ever so extreme, be their pain ever so intense, there is no possibility of their fainting away, no, not for one moment. (Sermon 15)

Another pastor of God's flock paints a torturous picture of a family scene in the abysmal furnace: "Husbands shall see their wives, parents shall see their children tormented before their eyes. . . . The bodies of the damned shall be crowded together in hell like grapes in a wine-press, which press one another till they burst." This would be a diabolical vintage that one would be loathe to sip or to see others sip!

If you think these heinous representations of hell are horrific, take a look at these equally ghastly portraits of God, the mastermind behind this abysmal abyss. Edwards rants that "the God that holds you over the pit of hell, much as one holds a spider, or some loathsome insect over the fire, abhors you, and is dreadfully provoked: his wrath towards you burns like fire; he looks upon you as worthy of nothing else, but to be cast into the fire." Granted, Edwards inflicts these words upon us only to talk later about God's grace, but in the meantime, he treats us to a tyrannical image of a God whose very nature is supposed to be love. Edwards also argues that the suffering of those in hell will bring God joy: "Can the believing father in Heaven be happy with his unbelieving children in hell? . . . I tell you, yea! Such will be his sense of justice that it will increase rather than diminish his bliss." When speaking of God's response to the souls perpetually burning in the flames of hell, seventeenth-century theologian Richard Baxter says that "the God of mercy himself shall laugh at them. . . . God shall mock them instead of relieving them, . . . and he shall rejoice over them in their calamity." Out of incredulity, I can't resist one more quote, this one by seventeenth-century Vicar Peter Newcome: "The door of mercy will be shut and all bowels of compassion denied, by God, who will laugh at their destruction." This surely is a surprising response from the God who loves sinners with an everlasting love, who so loved the world—even to the point of death—and who desires none to perish but all to be saved! But there's more.

Hell and its hapless inhabitants do not suffer in vain. Their execrable torment enhances the existence of the exulted, righteous minority who bask luxuriously in heaven's splendor. A great cloud of witnesses look on, rubbing their hands together in delight, in anticipation of the tortures to come. Peter Lombard (c. 1100) says that the "elect shall go forth . . . to see the torments of the impious, seeing which they will not be grieved, but will be satiated with joy at the sight of the unutterable calamity of the impious." Andrew Welwood (c. 1744) believes that the saints, looking on from the comforts of their celestial abode, will revel in the torment of the less fortunate and be "overjoyed in beholding the vengeance of God." Seventeenth-century clergyman Samuel Hopkins agrees, stating that "this display of the divine character will be most entertaining to all who love God. It will give them the highest and most ineffable pleasure. Should the fire of this eternal punishment cease, it would in great measure obscure the light of heaven, and put an end to a great part of the happiness and glory of the blessed." Thomas Aquinas, one of the most influential theologians in church history, writes: "In order that the happiness of the saints may be more delightful to them and that they may render more copious thanks to God for it, they are allowed to see perfectly the suffering of the damned. . . . So that they may be urged to more praise God." Remember the old lines attributed to Isaac Watts? They go like this: "What bliss will fill the ransomed souls, / when they in glory dwell, / to see the sinner as he rolls / in quenchless flames of hell." All this from recovering sinners who are exhorted to weep with those who weep, to show the love of Jesus, and to obey the second most important commandment, to love others as they love themselves. Although the fodder for their active imaginations came from their interpretation of Scripture, we will see that the Bible does not speak as consistently or as clearly as do their personal visions of hell, a topic we will discuss in more depth in chapter 10.

TROUBLES WITH THE TRADITIONAL TOUR

This view of hell causes troubling questions to bubble to the surface, even for those who have always believed it. Although once in a while a student will offer a critique of the traditional view of hell in the classroom, most of them make an appointment to come and talk with me in the privacy of my office. Some students who struggle with these questions would go so far as to say that they don't want to worship a mean God who inflicts such strict punishment. They have these types of thoughts and questions in common with Lisa, Brooke, and Eric. Some of you may think, "Okay, so you have trouble with hell. God can do what God wants, and God's ways are higher than our ways, so get over it. After all, justice must be served."

And that's true. We cannot always figure out the ways of God. We all want justice (unless we are the ones getting served our share). At the same time, however, God has created us with the capacity to think, to reason, and to understand our faith. When we think through our beliefs, where they originate, and why we hold on to them, we stand in a long line of faithful Christians who have gone before us.

Anselm, archbishop of Canterbury, a very influential medieval theologian, reminds us that our faith seeks understanding, that when we make the effort to understand our faith and our beliefs, we honor God and we benefit others. So when friends and students come to me with questions about hell that haunt them in the middle of the night, we talk about the theological reasons for a rigorous view of hell. I encourage them to think through their objections, to voice their critiques of the traditional views, and to examine what the Bible says.

I asked Lisa why she clings so tenaciously to our traditional doctrines of hell even though, at the same time, she seriously questions them. We traditionally believe that the God we love and worship loves us first, loves us so deeply that we are worth dying for, yet we also believe that this same God casts innumerable multitudes into flames of punishment, not just for a specific time period with a beginning and an end, but for all eternity. As we discussed this inconsistency, we laughed as we thought back to the television series *Lost in Space*, which we both used to watch as kids. When faced with a conundrum, the robot on the show would say, "Does not compute." Well, the disharmony between a loving God and a vengeful God found in our traditional doctrines of salvation and hell "does not compute." This begs the question "Are we stuck with it?" Do we have to believe in eternal punishment, everlasting torture in a place in which evil perpetually coexists with God's eternal, holy kingdom? Are we heretics if we find hell hard to believe? I don't think so. And after seriously testing the waters of theological reflection, many of my students and friends, like Eric, Brooke, and Lisa, don't think so either.

One of the problems that Lisa finds with constructing an alternate view of hell involves the fear of letting the wrongdoer off the hook too easily, of selling out to a feel-good theology that endorses a "Don't-worry-be-happy-God-loves-you" mentality. She brings up an excellent point. We don't want evildoers simply to "take a walk." So we remind ourselves that we need a solution consistent with a God of love *and* justice *and*, even, wrath. At the same time the solution has to take sin seriously in a way that holds wrongdoers accountable and vindicates their victims. We also want a solution that keeps the hope of redemption alive for loved ones gone before us, that does not allow wickedness to exist eternally in another place, but that instead completely resolves the problem of evil by extinguishing it once and for all.

Many of my students tell me that they dare not ask their pastors and Sunday school teachers about their troubles with eternal punishment. They fear that their teachers would think they were sliding down the slippery slope into heresy. So like a child reading a book in secrecy, hiding under the covers with a flashlight long after being tucked into bed, they walk sheepishly into my office, close the door and, with a big sigh, unload their questions, doubts, fears, and desires for a more compassionate judgment. These students seek answers. And they want those answers from me. Because I too grapple with the idea of an eternal hell, I understand their struggle and strive to discover satisfactory, biblical answers consistent with a loving, powerful God. So when students like Brooke and friends like Lisa come to talk, we begin with the problems that hell raises. I ask them to describe their concerns and to talk about what troubles them. What seems inconsistent, improbable, or unsatisfactory? In the remainder of this chapter, I will discuss seven inconsistencies and problems surrounding the traditional view of hell.

First Trouble: Justifying God (Theodicy)

As believers firmly fixed in the tradition, Lisa and Eric have always believed that hell solves the problem of evil. We have a sin problem. People lie, steal, cheat, kill, gossip, envy, get angry—we all sin, and we call it "evil." Every religion has a theory of some sort that tackles the problem of evil and suffering. For Eastern religions, the solution for evil and sin is karma. For Christianity, the solution lies in hell, where the scales are balanced, the accounts settled, each getting exactly what is deserved, and no less. Yes, finally, the wicked get what's coming to them. Their eternal punishment for sin is justified. Those who have suffered at the hands of the evildoers receive their long-awaited vindication: by throwing the unrepentant into hell for all eternity, God has rid the universe of evil for all time—or so we think.

We might call the construction of a doctrine of hell a "theodicy" of sorts. The word "theodicy" combines two words: "justify" ("dicy" from *dike* in Greek) "God" ("*theos*," which means "God" in Greek). A theodicy, therefore, attempts to justify God in the face of evil and suffering, answering questions such as these: Did God create evil? Is God to blame for evil? Why doesn't God stop evil? How does God solve the problem of evil?

For centuries, theologians and philosophers have tried to defend God's honor in spite of the obvious existence of evil and the suffering it causes. A theodicy is built on the premises that (1) God is all-powerful, and (2) God is all good. The questions these premises raise go like this: If God is all-powerful, why couldn't God create a world without evil? Or why can't God put a stop to evil? If God is all good, why would God create a world that included evil? Or why wouldn't God want to put a stop to all evil? The questions that a theodicy of hell address run along similar lines of thought: If God is all-powerful, why wouldn't God exercise that power to keep people out of the flames of hell? If God is all good, why would God choose to send people into eternal punishment? Put in positive terms, we might say it like this: If God is all-powerful, God can keep people from hell. In fact, God can eliminate the need for hell completely. If God is all good, God does not want anyone tormented in eternal flames but wants to save all people.

Yet by holding on to the doctrine of eternal hell, we in essence hold to the belief that in the end God's will to save all people goes unfulfilled, which puts God's power and goodness in doubt. We also suggest, however inadvertently, that Jesus' life, death, and resurrection were limited, not effective enough to save everyone without condition. According to the Bible, however, God's very purpose is to redeem the world, to reconcile and to restore all creation to God. Second Corinthians (5:19 alt.) says as much: "God in Christ was reconciling the world to Himself, not counting their trespasses against them." Notice it says *the world*! Not just a select few. First Timothy 2:4 (NRSV) also states that God "desires everyone to be saved and to come to the knowledge of the truth." In addition, Peter clearly expresses God's desire for humankind, writing that God "is not slow about his promise, as some count slowness, but is patient toward you, not wishing for any to perish but for all to come to repentance," and therefore, to salvation (2 Pet. 3:9).

Do you see the contradiction? God's good purpose and will is to redeem the world. God has the power to do so. Yet God goes against the divine will to save all and creates, preserves, and populates a place of punishment where the wicked and the unrepentant dwell, unredeemed, unreconciled, and unrestored for all eternity.

Actually, the traditional theory of hell doesn't explain how God deals with evil; it exacerbates evil by keeping the wicked perpetually in existence. If hell exists eternally, so does evil, and so does the suffering of untold numbers of people whom God supposedly loves and desires to redeem. As Eric and Lisa seriously considered these kinds of inconsistencies, they both came to the conclusion that, as a theodicy, hell does not adequately solve the problem of evil. They realized that in order to remain consistent with their doctrines that endorse God as all-powerful (omnipotent) and all good (omnibenevolent), they need to reconsider what they have always believed about hell. But rethinking, reinterpreting, and reconstructing take courage. We don't want to rock our theological boat for fear of capsizing and drowning in a sea of doctrinal relativism and spiritual confusion. So we hold tightly to our conveniently held beliefs, even if they don't make sense.

Second Trouble: Eternal Hopelessness

Hell seems to rule out hope—hope for redemption and hope for the total elimination of evil. Just ask Dante, who believes that an inscription over the gates of hell tells the unfortunate multitudes bound for its depths to "abandon every hope, [all] who enter here!" Traditional theories of hell exclude any hope for redemption, reconciliation, and restoration to God and to others. Once a person dies, that's it. Even if that person never heard the name of Jesus, even if that person rejected the good news without truly knowing what it meant, he can abandon any hope for salvation. Suffering in hell for all eternity means that souls burning there forever will exist without any hope of redemption.

Let's take my grandfather, for example. I loved my grandfather and spoke with him often about the forgiveness of sin through Jesus Christ's life, death, and resurrection. He would listen longingly, but just could not bring himself to believe that life continued on after death. He died an unbeliever. What if, after coming face-to-face with God after death, my grandfather, who truly desired to believe the gospel but just could not, finally believes and desires to receive forgiveness and reconciliation? Traditional theories of hell tell us that he has no hope. He is doomed to suffer eternal punishment even after realizing the significance of his unbelief. Would a loving God, who desires to save every person (2 Tim. 2:4), close the lid on love, compassion, and the hope of restoration? Can't God keep the possibility for redemption open? Or is there some law above God that places a time limit on grace—or worse, an eternal limit?

Think about it. Our traditional beliefs about hell also force us to believe that people we love—people God loves more than we do—are eternally beyond grace. *Eternally beyond grace!* Does that sound like God to you? Now I know that God's ways are higher than our ways, that God works in mysterious ways, that God sees the entire picture while we see only a tiny piece. But God also gives us the Bible, a book that reveals God to us so that we *can* know how God behaves, how God acts toward the world, how God relates to us, and what God desires for most for us. Loss of hope for all eternity doesn't sound like the God of Jesus Christ who desires for all people to be saved and to come to the knowledge of the truth. This is another indication that we may need to rethink a doctrine that makes hopelessness a necessity.

Third Trouble: Eternal Evil

The problem of hope also confronts us when we contemplate the notion of eternal punishment of the wicked in hell. The Bible tells us that, in the end, God will abolish evil. A new heaven and a new earth will take the place of the old. Peace, holiness, and love will reign in God's kingdom, uncontaminated by evil. No more tears, no more death, no more pain, no more suffering, no more evil (Rev. 21:1–4). We hold out hope for a time such as this. Yet if hell exists, evil exists. Somewhere, in the universal expanse of God's perfect peaceful kingdom, evil still survives—eternally. Many souls still suffer, still experience pain, still cry, wishing they could die. What does the eternal existence of the wicked and their evil say about God's power? God's love? God's compassion? The efficacy of Christ's atonement? If we hold to the belief in an eternal hell, we also hold to the belief that God's power is not powerful enough to rid the new heavens and new earth of wickedness and evil completely.

Without being aware of it, we also hold to the belief that God withdraws unconditional love once a person's body dies. God's compassion dies once our body dies if we haven't received Jesus during the short span of a lifetime. Somehow, then, God's love for us is tied to the physical body and the temporal realm, and grace disappears for unbelievers after the physical life is gone. We also believe, albeit unawares, that the work of Jesus for our salvation is no longer effective for those who die without receiving God's grace for salvation in one lifetime. The door leading to grace, forgiveness, and redemption freely offered by Jesus closes forever, shutting out the unrepentant soul after sinning for what amounts to a snap of the fingers in light of eternity.

These theological inconsistencies compel Brooke to look for alternative answers for life after death. Yet Lisa and Eric, who acknowledge the difficulties and don't want to believe in the eternal existence of evil, still can't quite let go of hell. In order to temper the inconsistency of evil existing simultaneously with God's goodness and love, they, like Dante before them, talk about hell as total separation from God, in a place where God is absent. But they know that God's presence extends everywhere. No place, no person, no matter how distant, outdistances God. The psalmist tries but ends up asking the questions, "Where can I go from your spirit? Or where can I flee from your presence?" (Ps. 139:7 NRSV). The answer is obvious: nowhere, no place. So for Lisa and Eric and Dante, God's sovereignty still rules in hell; God still maintains control. They must believe that God, therefore, juggles evil in one sphere and goodness and love in another. God overcomes evil but must still maintain and control its existence. Their faith seeks to understand the inconsistency.

Fourth Trouble: Justice in Opposition to Love

Hiding behind the traditional theories of hell is the ghost of a punitive father, haunting the image of unconditional love and forgiving grace. We unintentionally conjure up a cruel father who demands that unrepentant sinners spend eternity in the flames of hell, finding endless torture an agreeable way to achieve justice—which is a far cry from the God who loves with an everlasting love.

Yet God *is* love. In order to harmonize God's love and justice, we hold to the belief that God must punish unrepentant sinners without end and yet love them at the same time. In doing so, we develop a picture of a God who promotes eternal punishment as positive, as part and parcel of divine love and justice. A paradigm like this causes significant theological difficulties. For one, it creates an artificial tension between love and justice. We try to relieve these tensions by appealing to God's love and mercy on the one hand, and to God's justice and wrath on the other, assigning split personalities to God, as if God were a character like Dr. Jekyll and Mr. Hyde. Such a view of God's love, mercy, justice, and wrath leads to the conclusion that to love is to punish eternally and, therefore, to punish eternally is just. We believe that this form of retributive justice sets all things right and justifies the accompanying violence of punishment.

As she struggled with this tension, Lisa asked, "If God loves even enemies (after all, Christ died for us while we were still enemies), and desires reconciliation with each one, should this fact alone give us cause to think differently about hell? Shouldn't justice look more like love, as in God loving enemies, rather than the retributive justice of eternal punishment?" Although we will continue the discussion on the tension between love and justice in a later chapter, the inconsistency at this point made Lisa, Eric, and Brooke uncomfortable enough to continue the search for alternative answers.

Fifth Trouble: Eternal Divine Violence

Furthermore, our three discussion partners have trouble with hell because its violence—eternal torment and endless suffering in the fiery abyss—gives us a picture of God as a violent, merciless judge. Traditional theories of hell not only keep evil in eternal existence; they also keep the cycle of violence in motion for all eternity. Through loving every enemy, through the life and resurrection of Jesus, God interrupts and, I believe, eventually ends the cycle of violence with that love. But not if we hold to our traditional views of hell.

And we are called to imitate this God, to "be perfect" as God "is perfect" (Matt. 5:48). Through its justification, the cycle of violence continues unabated as we take on "God's job" as militant guardians of the world's moral order and spiritual condition as evidenced throughout Christian history. God as a punishing God, as a violent God who demands a pound of flesh in order to balance the scales of justice, as a God who requires eternal punishment to restore offended honor, who exacts retribution rather than restoration—all this leaches into the structures of the world's governments, courts of law, and familial relations. We can easily blame the centuries of war and bloodshed on the Christian concept of God as violent, whose anger destroys nations and punishes the disobedient without mercy. We give the world the idea that the Christian God is the friend of cruelty. By believing in a God who uses violent measures to accomplish the divine purpose, we justify violence and evil committed in God's name.

That violent behavior has permeated our humanity. Society continues to inflict a cruelty (through the penal system, through war, and through abusive family structures) that is validated by Christianity, specifically by God's penal actions seen in the passion of Christ and in our theories of eternal suffering. We will talk about the problem of divine violence in another chapter, but for now suffice it to say that God's violence directly opposes and contradicts God's love and justice. Thinking about the opposition and contradiction carrying through for all eternity brings to the surface all kinds of mental and emotional conflict.

Sixth Trouble: Retributive Justice and the Bible

After much discussion, Lisa, Brooke, and Eric wondered if theories of God's retributive justice found in our ideas about hell contradict the message of restorative or reconciling justice found in the Bible. We have to admit that we often read the Bible through a more retributive lens; thus our notions of hell portray God as retributive rather than restorative. Instead of endorsing retributive readings of the New Testament, in which the wicked suffer for all eternity, we more often see a theology of divine protest against violence and a divine movement toward restoration and reconciliation. "God was in Christ reconciling the world to Himself," so that all people might be reconciled to God through the cross, having by the cross put to death the enmity between God and humanity. While we were still *enemies* of God, as opponents, still steeped in our sin, still unrepentant, deserving nothing but evil in return for our rebellion (retributive justice), God reached out to reconcile us through Jesus (restorative justice). Now this *is* justice!

The heartbeat of the New Testament witness circulates the good news of reconciliation more so than retribution. Rather than eternal punishment that finally satisfies an offended God, the gospel message speaks of mercy, reconciliation, and restoration as God's justice. A theory of hell based upon restorative justice and reconciliation harmonizes more effectively with God's love. It focuses on the restoration of a broken relationship rather than on forms of retribution that require suffering for all eternity, without hope of redemption.

Seventh Trouble: Justice and Eternal Punishment for Temporal Sin

This last trouble concerns people more than all the previous ones. Is eternal punishment for temporal sin just? In other words, does sin committed during one short, temporary life span deserve an eternity of punishment? Even in our own society, we strive to make the punishment fit the crime. We make laws, elect judges, appoint juries, hold court sessions, and try offenders in order to "prove" guilt and pass sentence on a just punishment for the guilty. In contrast to this, we cling to traditional views of hell, in which our loving God exacts eternal punishment for temporal sin—an extreme case of the punishment *not* fitting the crime—and we consider this to be "justice."

Again we will discuss the biblical view of justice and how it should influence our views of hell in later chapters. But at this point in our search for answers, you can imagine that Brooke, in her desire to think differently, Lisa, in her struggle with her dying grandmother, and Eric,

---

Some Terms We'll Use throughout the Book

Temporal sin   Temporal sin refers to time rather than to eternity. Temporal sin, then, is sin committed within the fleeting boundaries of a human lifetime.

Retributive justice   Any form of justice that puts things right through punishment or payback: an eye for an eye. The wrong must be set right through action of some sort against the wrongdoer.

Restorative justice   A theory of justice that focuses on repairing a harm or offense so that the relationship between victim and offender can be restored.

---

in his concern over the world's lost, were ready to hear more. I hope you are ready to read more!

To many people, including a large number of my students, the violent doctrine of hell that Christendom holds dear amounts to very bad news indeed. In fact, hell ought to be as bad a news flash to Christians as it is to those we believe are going there. Hell should be such bad news to us that it should so disturb our sense of justice and raise so many theological red flags in our minds that we attempt to reinterpret it, to turn the bad news of hell into the good news of salvation—or, in other words, to communicate the good news as the good news it really is.

I hope that after reading what theologians have said about the horrors of hell and the way those horrors portray God, we will experience a sense of dismay, disbelief, and even a bit of cognitive dissonance. As a result, I hope we will be more open to asking the tough questions and to hearing an alternative interpretation of what hell might be. I believe that there is a view of hell that lines up with Scripture, that gives possible solutions to the troubles above, and that weaves "hell" into the fabric of a loving, compassionate God who never forsakes us—the human race, who never abandons us—all humanity, and who seeks to reconcile us with God now and for all eternity.

2

The Image of God

O vengeance of the Lord, how you should be
dreaded by everyone who now can read
whatever was made manifest to me!
                          —Dante, *Inferno*, Canto 14

A fire is kindled in My anger,
and burns to the lowest part of Sheol,
and consumes the earth with its yield,
and sets on fire the foundations of the mountains.
                          —The LORD, in Deuteronomy 32.22

Projections of the divine character as gleefully wrathful and vindictive may shock many of us. After reading the previous chapter, Lisa called me on the phone. "I can't believe how horrible God looks in these images our tradition paints!" she said. "This doesn't sound like a God of love! Why have we bought into this horrific doctrine? Is it biblical, really?"

Hardly taking a breath, she continued on in this vein: "I have been a Christian for a long time and have heard sermon after sermon preached about God's love for all creatures. On the other hand, however, I have also heard sermon after sermon preached about God sending people to hell for eternal torture. Until recently, I never thought about the contradiction. I always held both images of God in my mind without question. I want to maintain my theological integrity and present an accurate picture of God to my children and friends. How do I harmonize these two disparate images of God?"

I sympathize with her desire and struggle with the same issue. In the Bible we see God characterized as retributive and violent alongside characterizations of God as loving and forgiving—a seeming major contradiction. When I met with Brooke, she brought up similar concerns. We were out eating sushi, talking about the traditional images of hell sketched in the last chapter. She put her hands on either side of her head dramatically and with her usual humor said, "It sounds like a bad horror flick, like *Texas Chainsaw Massacre*, with God as the one wielding the chainsaw! Even the government considers torture a criminal action! How can we condone it just because God is doing it?"

She does have a way with words, doesn't she? But there's some truth to what Brooke says. Theologians, pastors, laypeople, people of faith, and people of no faith wonder how a loving God can damn anyone to infinite, conscious torment for sins committed during a finite lifetime. Even in human lawcourts, juries, lawyers, and judges ostensibly work to fit the punishment to the crime. Often sentences are commuted through the possibility of parole. The exercise of the courts to establish a verdict, to indict a criminal, and to assign a fitting sentence is what we call "justice." We have created the judicial system in order to serve justice, so that our citizens receive fair treatment, so that the punishments fit the crimes. Yet when we create doctrines in which God inflicts eternal punishment for temporal sin, we invoke "divine justice" as our justification. But is this justice?

Lisa and Brooke aren't alone in their concern for divine justice and the image of God. Eric took part in a class discussion about traditional depictions of hell. He, along with most of his classmates, hoped to soften the implications of an eternal hell and a God who would require such an unorthodox punishment. After much discussion, no one had come up with a satisfactory rationalization for it all. But isn't that just what we have tried to do? We try to come up with good reasons for why God is justified in sending people to eternal torment even though God went to a lot of trouble and heartache to save them by sending Jesus. But in spite of our attempts (and our good intentions), our hellish exposés do not serve justice or portray God accurately. They may actually serve to cheapen the extravagant grace of God. The thought that a loving God would allow hell, a graceless place of meaningless torture, to exist eternally contradicts God's overflowing grace, desire, and ability to save all people. It diminishes the extent and effectiveness of Jesus—his life, death, and resurrection—to reconcile all people to God.

WHERE DOES IT COME FROM?

After a class discussion on hell, Eric came into my office and asked, "Where does the image of God as a violent tyrant come from? Why do we find it possible to believe such things of a God who, as we are also taught, loves every person who ever lived?"

Countless students and reflective adults tell me that they are turned off by Christianity mainly because of the violent images of God invoked in our doctrine of hell, which depicts God as mean-spirited, who delightfully metes out eternal torment to those unfortunate enough to find themselves on the wrong side of faith. In one breath we lure the unrepentant with tales of the forgiveness and love of God revealed in Jesus, and in the next moment we terrorize them with threats of the wrath and punishment of God executed by eternal torture in hell. We don't just pull these conflicting images from thin air, however. Let's take a look at Scripture and try to discover where these images come from.

Old Testament

We receive most of our images of God as violent and retributive from the Old Testament, whereas the New Testament typically portrays God as peace-loving and reconciling. In fact, the character of God described in the Old Testament seems quite different from the one drawn for us in the New Testament. Throughout the centuries of Christian thought, some have criticized this seeming discrepancy even to the point of suggesting that the Christian community omit the Old Testament from their Scriptures. Thus Marcion of Sinope, an early second-century theologian, believed that the God of Jesus couldn't possibly be the same God as YHWH in the Old Testament—the one a God of peace and love, the other of violence and retribution. Unfortunately, views like Marcion's also led to terrible anti-Semitism and persecution of the Jews. Those who supported that idea were quickly proclaimed heretics, and the community made sure that our Bible contains both Old and New Testaments! But what do we do with the vastly different images of God characterized in the two Testaments? We'll discuss alternative (and faithful) ways to interpret them in another chapter. For now, however, we want to see where our ideas about divine violence originate and how we typically try to harmonize them with the loving and compassionate images of God found in many other passages of Scripture.

Many of us read stories from the Old Testament, see the violence that God requires or causes or condones, and think nothing of it. Others of us read these stories and wonder how a loving God can commit such extreme injustices. Either way, these texts help to form our ideas about God's character, how God behaves, and how God deals with people. Because of the formative nature of these images, it is important to examine them in more detail. We can find one of the stories that most disturbed Brooke, Lisa, and Eric in 2 Samuel 6. In this narrative, David gathers a few thousand Israelites together so that they can move the ark of the covenant from the house of Abinadab into Jerusalem. The men put the ark on a cart pulled by oxen. Somehow, the oxen disturbed the cart, and to keep it from falling off onto the ground, Uzzah reached out his hand to steady it. Without warning, God struck Uzzah dead for touching the ark! God gave poor Uzzah no time to explain himself and no time to repent for touching the ark. Although touching the ark was considered an act of irreverence, I can imagine Uzzah thinking that allowing the ark to fall on the ground would be a more egregious act of disrespect. Yet God executes him—in an instant—for saving the ark, for an act of goodwill!

In Genesis, God destroys all the inhabitants of Sodom and Gomorrah without a fair trial (Gen. 19). In Exodus 12, God kills *all* the firstborn of the Egyptians—babies, children, adults, and even animals—regardless of guilt or innocence. In 2 Samuel 24, God sends a pestilence in which seventy thousand innocent people die. Why? Because *David* had sinned by taking a census of the population living in the land! In 1 Samuel 15, God commands Saul to kill the Amalekites, not just the military men of the community, but *everybody*—men, women, children, and animals—genocide for sure! When we compare these mass killings with contemporary examples, the Holocaust, the genocides in Bosnia, Rwanda, and other places, or even the terrorist attacks of September 11, 2001, come to mind. Though these more-contemporary mass murders often invoke the name of God as justification, we still consider them to be heinous criminal acts.

But there's more, a lot more. I'll mention just a few. In Genesis 12, for example, God punishes Pharaoh for Abraham's deception about Sarah. Abraham lied, not Pharaoh. Why didn't God punish Abraham instead? In 1 Kings 22, God sends a lying spirit to entice Ahab to go to war so that he and his army will die at the hands of the enemy. In this case God works the divine will by asking a spirit to lie and deceive. At the same time, in other passages of Scripture, God condemns deception. In fact, one of God's Ten Commandments prohibits lying (Exod. 20:16; Deut. 5:20). In Numbers 16, the man Korah rebels against Moses. God responds not with forgiveness in hopes of reconciliation, but by killing all of Korah's descendants, servants, and possessions with horror-show theatrics: the ground splits open and buries them all alive.

In Deuteronomy 7:2, God promises to "utterly destroy" the inhabitants of Canaan so that the Hebrew people can possess it for their own. I wonder how many innocent people died at God's command as a result.

To many readers and thinkers, these stories present God as unjust. God kills thousands without a trial, without allowing the people to repent of their sins or to explain their actions. We watch without flinching as God commits horrendous acts of genocide, deception, and execution.

In my mind, however, one story tops the violence of all the others. We are all familiar with it. In fact, when I started shopping to decorate the nursery for my first son, I contemplated buying wallpaper with cute little pastel drawings of Noah's ark scattered around in whimsical fashion. Go into any children's department in any major retail store, or type "Noah's ark" into an Internet search engine, and you'll find an almost unlimited number of fanciful toys, cute little stuffed animals, framed pictures, action figures, children's videos, and art deco clothing depicting the story of the flood. Since we are so incredibly immune to the horrific nature of the story, we don't realize that we are decorating our children's bedrooms, the places where we hope they spend their nights in peaceful slumber, with a story describing the murder of nearly the entire human and animal population! A large-scale mass murder committed by *God*!

While living in Texas for twelve years, I heard stories and saw live footage on the news stations of people becoming stranded in flash floods, often losing their lives. I warned my sons not to drive through sections of road overflowing with water during a rainstorm for fear of the same fate befalling them. We sit at home and watch in tearful-eyed sympathy as mothers and spouses weep on camera, mourning the loss of their drowned loved one. We may even hear them cry out to God, asking why God let this happen to them, not thinking that the walls of our children's bedrooms might be covered with scenes from an even nastier and excessively more deadly flood brought upon someone else's (everyone else's) loved ones by that same God.

JUSTIFYING GOD

Why do we protest against most forms of violence in our own age, culture, and personal lives yet seem oblivious to the gruesome violence of God in our Scriptures? Varying theories abound. So let's discuss a few of them and see if we recognize our own rationalizations for accepting divine violence in any of them.

Divine Immunity

First, some of us believe that God is immune to human systems of justice, that human justice has no purchase with divine justice. Everything God does is just because God does it, whether or not those actions contradict God's own law and commandments. Those of us who hold to this view believe that, because our understanding is limited, God is above human critique and questioning. Now, I agree that God is shrouded in mystery, and we will never plumb the divine depths with full understanding. This approach, however, contradicts many other passages of Scripture in which God commands us to love our enemies, to forgive those who have sinned against us, to take care of widows and orphans and oppressed people. In addition, views that appeal to God's mystery immediately close off further discussion. I strongly believe that we can find more plausible answers and images of God in Scripture that reveal God's true character. After all, this view does not glorify God in the least. It even dishonors God by portraying God as a tyrant, behaving in ways that contradict the nature of God as love.

Higher Reasons

Second, many of us resort to interpreting these difficult texts by arguing that God has good reasons for acting in certain ways. God has a just cause for wreaking violence on enemies. In many cases, God punishes the wicked for their evil actions. These punitive measures make sense to us. After all, we want to see the wicked punished for their deeds, right? In the days before the flood, for instance, all the earth was filled with violence and corruption, so God's flooding the earth seems justified. But even if we believe that all the adults committed evil and deserved to die, think of all the innocent children who drowned, children who never even had a chance to sin! So even though we may question God's actions and wonder about the justice of killing, say, 185,000 Assyrians in one fell swoop (2 Kings 19:35), or millions in a worldwide flood, we rationalize, believing that God has different standards of justice and good reasons for killing that we just can't understand.

I remember asking a Sunday school teacher years ago how God could order the murder of cities full of people during the conquest of Canaan and still be just. He told me that archaeologists found that the bones of those murdered, even the bones of the children, contained evidence of venereal disease, which would have infected the Israelites and thus the lineage of the Messiah. So God ordered them all killed in order to preserve the bloodline that would produce Jesus. That explanation might make sense to some, but there isn't any evidence, first of all, that the people living in the cities during the conquest of Canaan had STDs, and second, that a connection exists between STDs and God's command to kill everyone, men, women, and children. But to explain what we consider to be horrific actions, we try to justify God with irrational "rationalizations." This approach closes off discussion; even worse, it leaves us with the idea that sometimes violence and killing are acceptable if executed in the name of the God who, with divine reasoning, advocates such actions.

Greater Good

Third, we may try to justify God's actions by believing that God works toward a greater good, that we do not see the big picture. One of my Bible study teachers in church compared this greater-good image with another image, that of a tapestry. While embroidering a tapestry, we see the back of it, with its tangled webs of floss crisscrossing chaotically, with loose threads hanging, knots showing, and no evidence of the beautiful picture developing on the other side of the cloth. But when we look at the right side of the finished product, we see the whole picture perfectly sewn into the fabric.

While the relevance of this metaphor may resonate with many of us, I'm not sure we can apply it to God's violent actions in our Bible stories. For instance, the threads that go into sewing a tapestry must intertwine in such a way that they fashion a certain picture. If I am embroidering a tapestry of the beautiful Pennsylvania farmlands in the springtime, I will use colors that correspond to the countryside. I would not embroider the green rolling hills with pink and purple polka dots or the clear blue sky with lime-green and red stripes. Not only would the back side of the tapestry be a total mess, but also the front, the picture itself, would not in any form resemble the Pennsylvania farmlands. In the same way, we need to be sure we are weaving an image of God that will resemble a God who has compassion, who forgives sin, who loves even enemies. I am convinced that the picture we have embroidered of a violent God is comparable to pink and purple polka-dot hills! Violence, even divine violence committed for a greater good, doesn't fit the picture.

In his book *Disturbing Divine Behavior*, Eric Seibert points out that even divine violence committed for the purpose of preventing a greater evil leaves us with major problems. For instance, when God led the children of Israel out of Egypt, he killed all the firstborn males of every family, herd, and flock of the Egyptians. That's a lot of sons, fathers, grandfathers, uncles, brothers, and pets! If we rationalize God's actions with the greater-good approach, we might say that God used violence against the Egyptians in order to save the Israelites from Egyptian violence. According to this view, God uses violence only for redemptive purposes. Seibert points out, however, that this approach depends entirely upon a myth, the myth of redemptive violence. This myth supports the idea that violence is justified as long as it ultimately brings about a greater good. In actuality, historical events have proved that evil only brings about more evil, that violence only causes more violence. We end up caught in a vicious cycle, believing that in the end violence will bring about peace. But is this true? And do the ends always justify the means? Do we do evil that good may come or that grace might increase? Paul declares, "May it never be!" (Rom. 6:1–2). If we hold God to a higher standard, how can we approve of evil that kills so many innocent people? I also wonder how eager we would be to champion "redemptive violence" if it were our loved ones, instead of an anonymous "other," who were suffering the violence of death. It seems, then, that the greater-good approach to God's violence only leads to no good.

Progressive Revelation

To explain and to justify divine violence in the Bible, we often resort to an approach that scholars call "progressive revelation." There are varying ways to do progressive revelation, but basically it looks something like this: God reveals only what the people of that day and time can understand; and throughout the millennia, God changes the way God deals with humanity and sin. Consequently, we could say that the Bible progressively reveals the character of God, but because the people could only understand little bits about God at a time, God had to deal with people patiently and differently as time progressed. As cultures develop and worldviews change, understanding of God develops and changes as well. We could also say that God dealt with Israel in one way and with the church in another way. As a result, God's character and behavior seem quite diverse and even in opposition at times.

For example, some scholars point to the sacrificial system initiated by Moses, believing that as far back as that age God began to reveal the divine plan of salvation through Jesus Christ by requiring them to sacrifice animals (we'll discuss this more in another chapter). Because the societies surrounding the Israelites during that time all practiced sacrificial rituals of some sort, God used what the people were familiar with, something they could understand in order to reveal the divine character and will. As the society progressed and the people were able to understand a bit more about divine actions, God revealed more to them by sending prophets. They explained that the true sacrifice is an internal one of the heart rather than an external one of animals. In time, and at the right time, God sent Jesus, who revealed God more fully through his way of living and through his final sacrifice so that finally all people can know and understand God's plan for the world.

The progressive revelation approach to interpreting the Old Testament might be one of the most plausible. Yet there are many problems with it. The most glaring one is that scholars cannot be sure of the time period in which most of the biblical texts were written. If we hold to the view of progressive revelation, we have to have an exact order for each portion of the revelatory text. We must be able to show the step-by-step progression of each book of the Bible throughout history. Since we can't calculate the progression with any amount of certainty, we can't construct and count on a theory of how God acts in the world based upon progressive revelation.

IN THE NEW TESTAMENT

But before we come down too hard on the Old Testament, one story in particular in the New Testament gives us an image of God that we have traditionally interpreted as redemptive divine violence, a story in which God requires violence in order to redeem humanity. It is our founding story, the passion of Christ, his death on the cross.

We love the cross. We center our liturgy around it. We sing about it, talk about it, write books about it, and even wear it around our necks. But at the same time, there's something quite disturbing about our interpretation of the cross, in the way it portrays God. I was first made aware of the disquieting nature of the cross when my Aunt Millie decided to leave the Catholic Church and eventually the Christian church altogether. She just couldn't with good conscience believe in a God who required the death of an innocent man in order to forgive the guilty. According to our Christian tradition, God not only required the violence of the cross, but God also, according to some views, brought about the violent death of Jesus, the beloved Son of God. In other words, in order to save us, God required and desired the horrific and violent death of an innocent man. And we call that violence good—a violence necessary in order to redeem. What image of God does this leave us with? One of an angry father who must severely punish one child before he can forgive the others? Or one of a vengeful and unjust judge who must see someone take the hit for sin even if that someone never sinned?

This would never fly in our judicial system. We just don't execute an innocent man on purpose. These traditional views of atonement perpetuate the myth of redemptive violence; but worse, they make God complicit with something we would normally consider very unjust. Hold that thought, though. We'll talk more about Jesus and the cross in chapter 11. The point I am trying to make here is that the divinely required violence of the cross adds to an image of God as violent. It helps us to accept and advocate not only God's violence but also our own.

No matter how we try to deal with the difficult Bible stories in which God wipes out thousands of people at one time, or in which God strikes one person down for an honest mistake, these stories serve to characterize God as mean, vindictive, unfair, and out to get us at the slightest provocation or mistake. When we try to justify God's behavior, we do so in ways that present violence in a positive light. And throughout Christian history, we have often and unjustifiably taken the next step: we use these stories and this image of God to justify our own violence. If these stories provide the structure for our image of God, we imagine we can behave in similar ways as children of God. God's fight becomes our fight. God's just anger becomes our just anger. God's violence becomes our violence, and innocent people get hurt. Yet we cannot deny the biblical stories, those that portray God as violent along with those that reveal a God of infinite love, forgiveness, and mercy. And if we believe that the most accurate image of God, the one that takes precedence over all the other images we see in Scripture, is the image of love, we must rethink some of our preciously held traditional views of God and especially of hell. Tied up with the image of God and our beliefs about hell are the notions of divine justice and forgiveness. Does God's justice require recompense, a tit for a tat, a balancing of the scales, before releasing someone from the debt of sin and therefore from the fires of hell? As a place of punishment, is hell just? Does God forgive only if this type of justice is served? If we answer "yes" to these questions what does this say about God's justice and forgiveness? We'll discuss this last question in the next few chapters.

3

The Justice of God

"If I take the Old Testament as the definitive source for insight into the
nature and character of God, then not only must I believe that God acts
violently; I must also believe that God's justice is retributive, right?"

That from Brooke. And she's sounding more like a college student!
Not surprisingly, Brooke continues to struggle with the inconsistency
between retributive justice seen in the Old Testament and the obvious
desire of God for restorative justice through forgiveness revealed by
Jesus in the New Testament.

Along the same line of thought, after I had a lengthy conversation
with Lisa over the chapter on the image of God, she wondered the
same thing and wrote me an e-mail: "I don't like retributive justice.
It seems to keep the cycle of violence going indefinitely. I don't think
that would be God's will; but if I continue to believe in eternal punishment in hell, retributive justice must be God's will, right? I mean,
what's more retributive than hell—that's like, eternal retribution! Is
that scriptural?"

Well, the Bible does give us a picture of God as retributive in some
passages. In fact, we get our own notions of righteous retribution from
those same Scriptures. If we make them the focus in determining how
we view God, we too will see justice as retributive. Let's look at some
of these passages describing divine retribution and talk a bit about
justice.

DIVINE JUSTICE IN THE BIBLE

Moses, communicating the words of God to the people in Deuteronomy 28, furnishes us with one of the Bible's clearest pictures of retributive justice. First, he sets forth all the blessings the people will receive if they obey their God. They have wonderful things to look forward to if they walk in God's ways! From fertile crops, herds, flocks, and wives to victory in battle, prosperous real estate gains, timely rains, and cupboards overflowing with good things to eat; if they do what God says, God showers them with blessings, fourteen whole verses filled with them. You can almost hear the people asking next, "What happens if we mess up, if we don't do exactly what God says?" They don't have to read far for their answer.

On the opposite side of the coin, if the people disregard God's rules, they have fifty-three verses of curses to endure! They won't have food for their tables, but that's the least of it. God will smite them with disease. They will lose their wars, and their dead will be eaten by birds and beasts. Their wives will cheat on them, and their herds and flocks will be given to their enemies. Their gardens will be infested with worms and weeds; from the top of their heads to the bottoms of their feet, God will strike them with oozing sores that will never heal. They will turn into blind and insane cannibals who cannot defend themselves, and enemy armies will conquer them. The message is clear: love and obey God or pay the price! Real tit-for-tat theology here, retributive justice at its worst. Even then, it all seems a bit uneven—fourteen verses of blessings compared to fifty-three verses of curses! As Brooke said, "That's retribution on steroids!"

The book of Jeremiah immerses us in the theme of divine retribution—at least if those are the passages we concentrate on, which is what we'll do for now. God rants and raves against the nations, against Israel, and against all who stand in opposition. At one point, God even tells Jeremiah *not* to pray for the people—this from a God who indicates elsewhere that we are to pray for our enemies, and even to pray without ceasing! I took a class on Jeremiah while working on my first seminary degree. The professor, an older Southern Baptist man near retirement, stood in front of the class week after week, hammering away about the caliber of God's wrath, condemnation, and vengeance. Looking back at it now, this class and the professor's fixation on divine wrath profoundly affected me. His take on Jeremiah did not at all mesh with the God whom I worshiped, who had "brought me up out the pit of destruction, . . . set my feet upon a rock," and "put a new song of praise into my mouth" (Ps. 40:1–3). So I raised my hand and asked, "But what about all the verses that say God is love, God's loving-kindness never fails, God's mercies are new every morning, and loving enemies?"

The professor became red in the face, took at step forward, and with his finger pointed at my face said, "God is a God of WRATH and VENGEANCE [he spoke these words in all capital letters, I'm sure of it, and probably bolded too]! He will DESTROY the wicked! I'm tired of hearing about love! Love has no place here! And if you can't get on board, you can drop the course!" Oops. There goes my GPA.

In the story of Sodom and Gomorrah, God rains fire and brimstone down on both cities, incinerating all the inhabitants, including women and children. Why? As retribution for their sin. God didn't even give them a chance to repent and change their ways. Nineveh got a better deal than that from God.

And we can't forget the flood! We see divine retributive justice at work in the flood story. The earth, filled with violence and corruption, suffered the annihilation of all its inhabitants—men, women, children, animals, and plants—all destroyed by God. Why? Because "the earth is filled with violence because of them" (Gen. 6:11–13 NRSV). So God returns violence for violence and wipes them all out, "from man to animals to creeping things and to birds of the sky" (7:23). It seems that throughout history we have followed God's example of returning violence in response to violence! But we'll discuss our violence later.

Yet our conversation about divine retribution wouldn't be complete without hell! In the first and second chapters we talked plenty about the retributive nature of hell and the image of God that leaves us with. But if we add together all the instances of "earthly" divine retribution in the Bible, those instances don't even come close to the horrifically harrowing nature of hell, wrought by the vengeance of God as punishment for sin. If we continue to hold on to our traditional views of hell as a place of eternal torment, we also must accept a God who would create and require that kind of hell, a God whose anger, vengeance, and vindictiveness endure forever without hope of mercy.

MAKING SENSE OF IT ALL

But something about this retributive God just doesn't make sense. God is angry, violent, and relentlessly vengeful in one passage, yet compassionate, forgiving, and generously merciful in the next. For instance, after outlining the horrific curses in Deuteronomy 28, God again speaks through Moses with words of love, faithfulness, and redemption in Deuteronomy 32. In Jeremiah, God rails against the world, promising famine and destruction, violence and vengeance. Then in the next breath, God pledges undying love and promises boundless mercy and incalculable forgiveness. Without warning them, God completely destroys two cities filled with people because of their sin, yet in the same book (Genesis), God receives credit for a beautiful story of grace and forgiveness that saves an entire people from destruction. Furthermore, with our traditional views of hell in mind, we teach about God as retributive, unmerciful, and unforgiving, as an eternal tormentor bent on the unending torture of most of the world's population from time immemorial. Yet, in the same breath, we preach and praise a God of love, whose loving-kindness never ceases, who forgives without calculation, who loves without condition, and who desires the redemption of all people and of all creation. What's up with that? How do we so easily live with these theological inconsistencies? Some scholars who work with victims of abuse have actually compared God to an abusive spouse or parent who acts with violence one minute and professes deep love the next.

The Traditional Sense of the Atonement

Ironically, even our most treasured story—and the basis for our salvation, as traditionally thought—encourages an image of God as retributive. The conversation on images of divine retributive justice wouldn't be complete without talking about what happened to Jesus on the cross and the metaphors and images that the event of atonement evokes. Typically, traditional theories of atonement project retributive justice into our theology of unconditional grace and forgiveness. Embedded in the traditional interpretations of the passion story of Jesus, the same story in which God lovingly bestows grace upon undeserving sinners, we discover a harsh and unjust retributive act. The very act of God that responded peacefully in the face of inordinate violence, that reversed the human concept of justice from one of retribution to one of forgiveness, that revealed unprecedented, unconditional love for all people, and that presented to us an unsurpassed, divine example of how to live justly and with mercy—that act of God was somehow turned into a basis for violence. A violent God punishes an innocent man for the world's sin!

> **Atonement**   The word literally means "at one," coined by William Tyndale in the 16th c. Now refers to doctrines of reconciliation between God and humans.

We sing about it in hymns and choruses; we hear it preached in sermons and taught in Bible study groups. God cannot forgive unless someone, in this case an innocent someone, pays the price for sin. Think about the words to some of our favorite hymns. We all love "Jesus paid it all." We express with joy what Jesus did on the cross when we lift our voices, singing, "Sing, oh sing, of my Redeemer, / with His blood, He purchased me. / On the cross, He sealed my pardon, / paid the debt, and made me free." Or this one: "O victory in Jesus, my Savior, forever. / He sought me and bought me with His redeeming blood." I could go on and on quoting hymns chock full of atonement theology expressing a retributive form of justice, which most of us are so used to hearing that we don't even think about it. I would like to raise our awareness of what we have believed not only most of our lives but also for much of Christian history after the emperor Constantine. So let's dig a bit deeper into the theories of atonement we have all grown to treasure, theology that we sing, preach, and teach.

Throughout the centuries, since Constantine made Christianity acceptable, atonement theology and its varying motifs have focused on the cross and Jesus' violent death. The passion of Christ has been described in metaphors that align with the historical context of the time. These metaphors vary, ranging from images of the temple, to the battlefield, the lawcourt, slave market, feudal law, courtly love, and account keeping, to family life. Most of the traditional theories, however, have been those that reduce the passion to an equation, formulated by a divine mathematician so that a special death is necessary to balance the cosmic accounts, to administer the quid pro quo (the crux of retributive justice) so that God can forgive sin. That special death is provided by Jesus Christ.

Throughout history, theologians have taken the many metaphors in Scripture and molded them into one theory or another to help us understand the cross. For example, the medieval theologian Anselm of Canterbury developed what he called the "satisfaction" theory of atonement, in which Jesus' death satisfies God's offended honor and pays our debt for sin. It also provides a restoration of order akin to the feudal system of his day. For Peter Abelard, another medieval theologian, Christ suffered and died in obedience to God in order to reveal the extent of divine love. For Thomas Aquinas, the passion effected salvation through satisfaction so that God was pleased with Christ's offering of himself for humanity, in payment for a debt owed to God. For Reformation theologian John Calvin and his penal substitutionary theory of atonement, the passion of Christ vindicates the law that proceeds from God's righteousness, echoing the structure of criminal law common in his time and ever since. Martin Luther's theory of atonement uses the language of satisfaction, in which Christ takes our place in a human-to-divine transfer of punishment for sin.

Although each of these atonement theories entertains various nuances more complex than I have indicated in this brief summary, one thing remains clear and common to all: God would not simply wipe our slate clean of sin by forgiving it. God would not write off the loss of honor or debt owed or love corrupted. God must either make satisfaction, inflict punishment, or assume punishment. In these theories, we can receive salvation only through some economy of quid pro quo. They are based upon the notion of retributive justice. Lurking behind these theories is the ghost of a punitive father, haunting the image of forgiving grace, a cruel father who demands the blood of an innocent person in retribution for sin, finding the death of his own son an agreeable way to save the world.

Some biblical scholars and theologians hold that doctrines of atonement advocating penal or satisfaction theories are not true to the biblical witness. Rather than endorsing retributive readings of the New Testament (in which an angry father inflicts punishment or requires satisfaction at the expense of the suffering of his innocent and loving son), we should see a theology of divine protest against violence and a divine movement toward restoration and reconciliation. "God was in Christ reconciling the world to Himself," so that all people might be reconciled to God through the cross, having by the cross put to death the enmity between God and humanity. Rather than retribution, the heart of the New Testament witness seems to indicate reconciliation and restoration as justice and mercy, not punishment or satisfying an offended deity. The Bible reveals that God in Christ freely offered forgiveness of sin rather than forgiveness forged by payback. But in a later chapter we'll discuss atonement and ways to think about it more in line with restorative justice.

Our Traditional Sense

We may wonder why our views of divine justice are important. What difference does it make? We may believe that God saves us and that's the only thing to concern ourselves with. After his Bible class one afternoon, Eric sauntered into my office with a dismal look on his face. The class had just discussed biblical justice, and much to Eric's dismay, most of his classmates were bent on retribution, based upon some of the biblical texts they read. Reflective student that he is, he asked an astute series of questions. "How should we handle the violent texts? Should we really make these passages our focus when so many other passages negate retributive justice in favor of restorative justice? I mean, is it really that important to see justice in a different light?"

"Wonderful thinking," I replied. "Those questions are exactly the ones you should ask!"

Medieval theologian Thomas Aquinas offered his students an answer for interpreting these difficult texts. Basically, he believed that any of the Scriptures that sounded revolting to us still include some spiritual meaning that help us live the spiritual life and gain a holy character. He instructed his readers to draw meaning from the difficult passages congruent with the building up of our love for God and our love for our neighbor. Even if we interpret wrongly, we really can't go wrong when we use God's love and desire for redemption as our lens. It sounds simple. And since Jesus summed up the entire Old Testament law, including the retributive-sounding bits, with "You shall love the Lord your God with all your heart, and with all your soul, and with all your strength, and with all your mind and your neighbor as yourself" (Luke 10:26), we can't be too far off the mark if we focus on that love when we read, interpret, and apply the Bible to our lives.

But that's not usually the case! Historically, Christians have *not* leaned toward love, neither toward God's love for all creation nor toward our love for one another in our biblical interpretations, from which we gather our instruction, correction, and training in righteousness (2 Tim. 3:16). For good or for bad, our interpretation of the Bible usually dictates how we behave. Let me give you some examples that deal with our interpretation of biblical justice and our corresponding thoughts, actions, and words.

While researching for essays on divine justice, I came across a sermon written and delivered by a pastor. The catch line, meant to lure prospective church attenders, said this: "God's anger has been kindled, and judgment is on the way." He went on to say that the gem of truth concerning this sermon is that these are God's delightful words! This pastor preaches about an angry God, steadfast in fiery fury to execute judgment and retribution—and these are God's delightful words! The same sermon stated that "God is love, but one part of love is hate"—not the type of "hate" spoken of in Luke 14:26, in which we put God before all others, but real honest-to-"goodness" hate! Now, I don't know what Bible the pastor of that church reads, but search as I did, I couldn't find that verse in my Bible. Why? Because it doesn't say that! This pastor projected his own perception of God onto his interpretation of the biblical texts. We all do it. And we can't completely avoid projecting our context into our understanding of the Bible. But we can listen with an open mind to other ideas and interpretations that may bring our own prejudices and presuppositions to the surface, where we can be aware of them.

Shortly after the September 11, 2001, terror attacks, the evangelist Jerry Falwell (died 2007) made a number of outrageous statements that revealed his underlying view of God and God's justice as retributive. He offered this as an explanation and, worse, a rationalization for the murder of thousands of innocent people, many of whom probably loved God: "[The ACLU has been] throwing God out successfully with the help of the federal court system, throwing God out of the public square, out of the schools. The abortionists have got to bear some burden for this because God will not be mocked. And when we destroy 40 million little innocent babies, we make God mad. I really believe that the pagans, and the abortionists, and the feminists, and the gays and the lesbians who are actively trying to make that an alternative lifestyle, the ACLU, People For the American Way—all of them who have tried to secularize America—I point the finger in their face and say 'you helped this happen.'" In other words, out of anger and a sense of retributive justice, God made religious devotees (whose own distorted beliefs about God significantly dictated their behavior) fly airplanes into tall buildings as punishment/retribution for America's sins.

Surely the entire rationale for this type of violence defies logic: God kills thousands of innocent people as punishment for our murderous ways in order to motivate us to stop killing innocent people! Yet we've all heard the same rationale applied to hurricane Katrina, the 2004 tsunami in Asia that killed hundreds of thousands, the AIDS epidemic, and more. I cannot state it strongly enough: *the image of God we hold in our heads and hearts matters* because that image dictates our behavior. It enables us to condone, justify, or even engage in violent acts against our "neighbors." Seeing God as a violent judge, who throws multitudes of people into the eternal fires of hell for punishment without end, contributes to our own behavior. Some of us may begin to think that if God can mete out such horrific punishment for sin for all eternity, then we certainly can judge and punish others with violent means. Our view of divine justice profoundly affects the way we think and live. So let's be open to rethinking, reevaluating, and maybe even revising our conceptions of God so that we imitate God's love and desire for reconciliation—even with our enemies.

4

The Forgiveness of God

. . . But I would
not have you, reader, be deflected from
our good resolve by hearing from me now
how God would have us pay the debt we owe.
Don't dwell upon the form of punishment:
consider what comes after that; at worst
it cannot last beyond the final judgment.

—Dante, *Purgatorio*, Canto 10

For I, the LORD your God, am a jealous
God, visiting the iniquity of the fathers on
the children, on the third and fourth
generations of those who hate Me.

—Exodus 20:5

The son will not bear the punishment
for the father's iniquity, nor with the father
bear the punishment for the son's iniquity.

—Ezekiel 18:20

I picked up Brooke one Saturday afternoon to take her to practice her parallel parking. She jumped into the driver's seat and started the engine before broaching the subject. "I'm reading Dante on purgatory."

"Oh? Well, what do you think about it?"

"I don't like purgatory at all!"

"I don't think anybody Dante meets there likes it, although it sure beats the inferno. Why don't you like it?"

"Well, if God forgives sin, why does God still require all those poor souls to suffer for their sin before they go to heaven? Does Christian theology and the Bible support suffering for sin even though God has already forgiven it? I mean, if forgiving means that we are pardoned, we don't have to pay a penalty for our sin in addition to it, right?"

Brooke is right to question the apparent inconsistencies surrounding forgiveness, punishment, and even (or especially) the doctrine of purgatory. Does God require our punishment as compensation for the blessing of divine forgiveness? If so, then even forgiveness carries with it notions of retribution. It's as if God says, "Okay, I'll forgive your sin but only if you let me punish you for it first." That's retribution rather than genuine forgiveness, which lets an offender go free without charge.

No one narrates a more seductive, albeit troubling, tale of retributive "forgiveness" than Dante in his *Purgatorio*. It truly is a page-turner. We journey through the levels of purgatory with Dante and Virgil, where countless unfortunate Christian souls suffer in misery for sins committed during their earthly lives. In purgatory, those guilty of the sin of pride labor under large boulders that bring them low to the ground. Those guilty of envy sit cradled in each other's arms with their eyes sewn shut—they can't covet what they don't see (Cain, because of envy for Abel's acceptable sacrifice, is still there!). Those guilty of anger live constantly enveloped in impenetrable, smelly, dark smoke—indicative of their smoldering anger while on earth. Those guilty of sloth run around in constant activity to make up for past laziness. Those guilty of greed lie tied face down to the ground, constantly reminded that they lived their lives looking to the glory of earthly treasures rather than to the glory of heavenly ones. Those guilty of gluttony live in purgatory, starving and thirsting until they have satisfied God enough to be set free. Those guilty of burning lust walk endlessly through a blazing fire until their lust burns only after God. These thousands upon thousands of Christians spend just as many months enduring terrible torments until at last they redeem themselves enough to receive God's mercy and entry into heaven. As he journeys through the levels of purgatory, shades of those who once lived confront Dante, begging him to enlist the prayers of saints still living so that their punishment for sin may be hastened, so that they can more quickly gain full pardon and paradise.

In many respects, Dante's writings reflect traditional Christian theology. God withholds total forgiveness until we "pay up" somehow. Either through remorse, repentance, confession, penance, tears of contrition, righting the wrong, or even forgiving others, divine forgiveness is conditioned rather than unconditional—at least according to Dante and the major streams of our tradition. Indeed, forgiveness with accompanying notions of some sort of retribution is built into the theology of the church. Many of our church traditions require repentance and penance before pardon is bestowed. Others insist that in order to receive forgiveness, we must confess our sin. I had a friend in Florida who believed that if she cursed while driving her car and then got into an accident and died before she had time to confess for cursing, she would go to hell. A pastor told another friend that God would not forgive her sin, any sin, if she held anger in her heart toward anyone. In fact, he said that God would not hear her prayers at all!

Does true forgiveness require a prior condition on the part of the one forgiven? If we think so, and if we think that God requires something from us as recompense in order to forgive, is that really forgiveness? Then how would we explain Romans 5:10, which tells us that while we were still *enemies*, God reached out in forgiveness to reconcile us to God? What about the Prodigal Son, who received his father's forgiveness before he had a chance to confess or tell of his repentance (Luke 15)? More important, what does a retributive notion of forgiveness tell us about God? And what do these beliefs communicate about the character of God to unbelievers?

FORGIVENESS AND MATTHEW

We may misinterpret forgiveness as conditioned and often as an economic exchange. This notion may come from a certain reading of Matthew 18:21–35. In this parable Jesus tells his disciples to forgive seventy times seven but then seems to undo that notion by telling the story of the unforgiving servant. The king forgives the servant his large debt. The servant then goes out and instead of forgiving a fellow servant a small debt, he has him thrown into prison so he can repay every cent (notice here that repayment or economic exchange or punishment is the opposite of forgiveness). When the king finds out about it, he throws the servant he had forgiven into prison. Jesus brings this home for us by saying: "So my heavenly Father will also do to you, if each of you does not forgive your brother or sister from your heart" (18:35 NRSV). In Matthew, after praying, "forgive us our sins as we forgive those who sin against us," Jesus goes on to tell his disciples and us, "If you do not forgive others, then your Father will not forgive your transgressions" (6:15). This is an economy of retributive forgiveness if there ever was one!

Some Christian communities take these words of Jesus very literally. Most of us remember the horrible tragedy at an Amish school in Nickel Mines, Pennsylvania, in 2006. Charles Roberts, a man well-known to the community, walked into a schoolhouse and shot ten little girls, killing five of them. In the aftermath of the shooting, the Amish community responded not with anger and cries for retribution, but with love and forgiveness. With astonishment news stations around the country reported the unprecedented response from the Amish community, including the parents of the children who had died.

Be certain that I am not diminishing the extravagance of grace and the gravity of the sacrifice involved in the act of this heartfelt, genuine forgiveness offered by the Amish. But what motivated them to forgive with such abandon harks back to what we have been talking about as our traditional view of forgiveness. In the book *Amish Grace*, written by my colleague David Weaver Zercher, Donald Kraybill, and Steven Nolt, a number of the Amish of Nickel Mines tell their story and the reasons behind forgiving Roberts so quickly. Over and over again they say that they must forgive so that God will forgive them of their sin. While explaining the importance of the Lord's Prayer in Matthew 5, one man said, "the Lord's Prayer plays a big part in our forgiveness. If we can't forgive, then we won't be forgiven" (91).

Well, we say, that's what the Bible tells us. And it does. But are there other ways to interpret, other lenses through which to look that will help us understand forgiveness? Can we view it not as an economic exchange (as in "If I do this, I'll get that in return"), but as what it really is—an extravagant, compassionate gift that requires and expects nothing in return, a true sacrifice that sets the guilty party free from debt? I believe that the Amish truly did forgive Charles Roberts in that way. But it doesn't change the fact that we usually think of divine forgiveness as being in some sense conditioned. In so doing, we construct an image of a vindictive God who can't forgive without gain, effectively hindering the magnitude of sacrifice and the abundance of grace in the very act of forgiveness.

I remember sitting in the dining room of our family home on Sacandaga Lake in New York State one summer evening, playing gin rummy with my cousins. We always have a great time whenever we get together but, on this night, the zeal of my newfound Christian faith impelled me to tell my cousins about the salvation we can all have through Jesus. My evangelistic attempts angered one of my cousins, who shouted out, "God is a mean ***!" In total shock at such an irreverent outburst, I asked him why he thought such a thing. I told him that God loves us all, that God loves him. He explained that if God truly loved everyone, then forgiveness would come freely and easily without all the religious bustle and brouhaha, all the jumping through hoops to pacify an angry deity. At that point I didn't have an answer for him. But right or wrong, I do now. Hopefully he'll read this book and try to think differently about God. The point remains, however, that the meaning of forgiveness or pardon is to set the guilty party free from punishment, from any debt, to let go of the offense without conditions attached. If we require punishment or recompense in any way, then we haven't forgiven—we've been compensated, the injury from the offense has been satisfied, and there's no need to forgive. Such a view contaminates the nature of true forgiveness and diminishes the work of Jesus. We'll discuss this and an alternate interpretation of the verses in Matthew 6:14–15 in another chapter, but first I want to talk a bit more about where our ideas of retributive forgiveness come from.

FORGIVENESS AND ATONEMENT

I sat in my office, going over the material for my next class on Hindu gods, when Eric came to the door with a perplexed look on his face. "What's up? Why that *look* on your face?"

"I just came out of my theology class, and we were talking about the atonement. First of all, I didn't realize there were so many different ways to explain what Jesus did on the cross. Second, don't these traditional theories mess with forgiveness somehow? If God needed someone to pay the debt for sin, what was left to forgive? I mean, if Jesus satisfied the debt, there wasn't a debt left to forgive, right?"

I love my smart students. I actually love all of my students. But the smart ones really make my day sometimes. And Eric is one of those. And he's right. Let's look at a couple of atonement theories just to see what he is talking about.

Christus Victor Theory

When theologians discuss the cross of Jesus, they speak in terms of "atonement" or of theories of atonement. Although many of these theories help us to articulate how the life, death, and resurrection of Jesus saves us, we can take the main theories most popular in our tradition and boil them down to four: *Christus Victor*, satisfaction, moral exemplar, and penal substitution. Throughout the centuries, theologians tweak and mold these theories into those that fit their own personal belief system, and they also speak about more than just these four. But for our purposes we need only deal with the ones I have named above.

These theories stem from varying interpretations of verses found in the New Testament that describe what happened when Jesus died on the cross and rose again. The first theory appeared in Christendom quite early and was the favorite of the persecuted church between the first and fourth centuries. The *Christus Victor* (Christ the Victor) theory emphasized, as its name implies, the victory Jesus won over death, sin, and evil. For example, Colossians 1:13 tells us that God "rescued us from the domain of darkness, and transferred us to the kingdom of His beloved Son," and 2:15 talks about God disarming "the rulers and authorities," making "a public display of them, having triumphed over them through [Jesus]." Early believers interpreted these verses to describe the victory of Jesus in making atonement for sin by conquering the devil and death—killing death and destroying Satan, so to speak. Ephesians 2:14–16; Hebrews 2:14–15; and 1 Corinthians 15:54–57 (for example) also speak of this victory. If you watched the film *The Passion of the Christ* (2004), the scene immediately after the resurrection illustrates the story behind *Christus Victor*. The camera makes a long shot down into a dark pit. As it pans closer to the bottom of the pit, we finally see the devil figure, face contorted with rage, screaming and shaking "her" body at the camera. Christ won the victory for our souls. The devil lost, and boy, is she mad as hell! Whether you hold to this theory or not (and most of us combine these theories to explain what we believe about Jesus), it still requires that someone give something in return for salvation, some sort of exchange in order for God to forgive sin (although the *Christus Victor* doesn't focus on forgiveness per se). And this is what someone gave: Jesus gave his life. He had to die in order to defeat the devil and conquer sin and death: *then and only then* does God forgive. A useful theory, but still fraught with retributive ideas of forgiveness.

Satisfaction Theory

Medieval theologian Anselm of Canterbury formally developed the satisfaction theory of atonement in the twelfth century. Anselm pictured God much like the feudal lords who ruled towns and cities in his day. When humans sinned, they fouled up the perfect order of the divinely created universe and offended God's honor. So God had to restore the order of the universe either by punishing sin to restore God's offended honor, or by requiring someone to satisfy the debt owed to the injured divine honor. The problem lies in the fact that sin so greatly dishonored

God that all the human beings working together could never satisfy the debt; and no person could ever suffer the enormous amount of punishment it would take. Only God could pay the debt. But then, since *they* were the ones who sinned, only humans should pay the debt for God's lost honor. God's answer? Jesus, the God-man. Problem solved: Jesus came, died on the cross for sin (the wages of sin are death, after all), and made more than sufficient satisfaction for it. In so doing, he restored God's honor. Only after God's honor was restored and the order of the universe put once more as it should be, would God forgive us our sins. Although many Bible verses may be used indirectly to support this theory, we can interpret Hebrews 1:3 as evidence for the satisfaction theory of atonement: "when [Jesus] made purification of sins, He sat down at the right hand of the Majesty on high." Again, as with the *Christus Victor* theory, the satisfaction theory still requires the fulfilling of certain economic conditions before God will forgive sin.

Moral Exemplar Theory

Medieval theologian Peter Abelard reacted against Anselm's satisfaction theory, constructing what we call the moral exemplar theory instead. According to Abelard, a God of love would never, ever require the death of God's own Son as satisfaction. He believed that throughout his life and death, Jesus revealed most profoundly the love of God through his own example. After all, "no one has greater love than this, to lay down one's life for one's friends" (John 15:13 NRSV). And that's what Jesus did. When we look upon the cross and see Love, embodied in Jesus, hanging there in pain for our benefit, our hearts become so infused with love for God that the Holy Spirit comes and indwells us at the moment. *Then* God forgives us. Again, God grants forgiveness only after Jesus fulfills the conditions for it on our behalf: he dies for our sin in order to reveal God's love, and we look on and love God in return. Here is the economic exchange all over again!

Penal Substitutionary Theory

In the fifth century, Augustine of Hippo first spoke about Jesus taking our punishment for sin. But it wasn't until the sixteenth century that reformer John Calvin formally developed the theory of penal substitution to describe the atonement. According to Calvin, God punished (penalized) Jesus for sin in our place (substitution). Although many Bible scholars do not believe we can find biblical support for this theory, if we read Hebrews 7:26–27 and 9:11–12 through the lens of a punishing God, we can interpret them as support for this model of atonement. Biblical or not, the fact remains that built into all these theories is some system of economic exchange: Jesus wins the victory or satisfies God's honor or with great love provides the perfect example or suffers the punishment for sin in our place—all before God will forgive sin. According to these views and the mainstream thought in our tradition, God will not forgive unless God first receives some sort of compensation for sin. Is this, then, truly genuine forgiveness? Let's put the question and its answer in terms more familiar to us.

Summing Up: The Theories' Cons in Common Terms

According to my calculations, if Eric owes me $100 and I make him pay me back and then say, "Now I forgive you your debt," he'd think I was nuts! The debt was paid when he gave me the money. I had nothing to forgive; I had been paid back. If someone else pays me the $100 for Eric's debt and I say to him, "Thanks. I forgive the debt," the same logic carries through. The debt was paid no matter who paid it! There wasn't anything left of the debt to forgive. But our traditional theories of atonement keep us in this economy of exchange in which God forgives sin only because Jesus somehow pays the debt it incurred. Jesus satisfies the debt either by punishment or ransom paid or by paying it with his blood. In all of these cases, God has nothing left to forgive because Jesus through his death has balanced the cosmic accounts.

When doing theology, we must always ask: Why is this important? Does it really matter whether or not the death of Jesus evened the scales or paid a debt in an economic exchange? The answer? Yes! It matters! For starters, ideas of God that champion divine violence as seen in penal and satisfaction theories of atonement promote the idea of suffering love as masochistic so much so that our highest ideas of love seem close to perversion. Consequently, to love is to punish, to punish is just, retributive justice sets all things right, and hence, violence is justified. Ephesians 5:1 tells us to "be imitators of God, as beloved children." Unfortunately our understandings of forgiveness in these terms so permeate our lives, actions, and ideas that our forgiveness takes on the image of God's forgiveness as retributive. If we believe that God's forgiveness trades in exchange, we will imitate it and withhold grace from those we are commanded to love. But on the other hand, true love, genuine love, loves and forgives while the offender is still an enemy. No exchange is involved there! We take a risk and extend grace where none is deserved, just as God did through Jesus (Rom. 5:8, 10; Matt. 5:44). But what, then, does it mean to forgive? What does forgiveness involve, and who receives it? How *does* God forgive us? And are some conditions attached? We'll explore these questions and more in part 2.

PART 2

An Alternative to Hell, God's Wrath, and Judgment

5

Rethinking the Violence of God

Those who have died here beneath the wrath of God,
all these assemble here from every country.
— Dante, *Inferno*, Canto 3

In violence we forget who we are.
— Mary McCarthy, *On the Contrary*

His name will be called
Wonderful Counselor, Mighty God,
Eternal Father, Prince of Peace.

— Isaiah 9:6

I spoke with Lisa on the phone for a long time last night. She's really struggling over her grandmother's illness and imminent death. To make things worse, her church friends keep telling her that her grandmother will go to hell if Lisa fails to lead her to Jesus. I think that's why she would like to rethink forgiveness and justice a bit. She said to me: "God's justice and forgiveness given without condition sounds right to me, especially in light of what I've always been taught about God's love. But then, why do we find it so easy to buy into the violence of hell when Jesus told us to love our enemies? Sometimes we even seem to take a certain satisfaction in the thought that God will be violent toward sinners and send them into eternal punishment. I just don't get it. Why do we want to hold on to hell, and why do we feel justified in doing so? We don't seem to think about how horrible it makes God look."

I understand Lisa's concerns, and I've given them a lot of thought lately. We all want to feel like we belong, and we sometimes get a sense of satisfaction when we belong to the "right" club and others don't. Now, I know that most Christians do not take delight in the thought that someone will burn in hell forever. And many of us hope, pray, and evangelize in order to bring more people into the kingdom of God. But still, we carry an attitude of smugness about us: *we* have the right answers and you don't; *we* are going to heaven and you're not. Even our pity and sadness over the fate of unbelievers comes off as arrogance in the eyes of those we don't admit to our exclusive club of heaven-bounders. I think some of this acceptance of hell and of the violence it perpetuates eternally on the unfortunate sinners who dwell there comes from our interpretation of divine violence in the Bible.

Our interpretation of the Old and New Testaments not only produce our violent theories of atonement, but also our violent doctrines of eternal hell. In the name of God, we assign unfathomable numbers of sinners to the fires of hell for all eternity! Just try to get rid of hell, and see what happens. I have friends mad at me for trying to reconsider the fate of the unbelieving hell-bound unfortunates. I have to assure my students that I am not trying to take hell away from them—and I'm not, honest. You'll see. And some students every semester, albeit kicking and screaming, start to realize the good sense in reinterpreting hell in light of a God of love who desires to reconcile with us. But how can we do that when the Bible seems to advocate such violence? We can't ignore the Old Testament.

INTERPRETING THE VIOLENCE

We do have to take the passages describing divine violence seriously. We can't just eliminate them from our Scriptures. Since we can't ignore the Old Testament "texts of terror" we need to use responsible methods for interpreting them. We can help ourselves do that by looking at the culture in which the Hebrew people lived, where their perspectives came from, how they interpreted the world around them, how they viewed the events they lived through, and the actions they took. So let's do that briefly.

First of all, the cultures around the Middle East, where Old Testament events take place, functioned according to the strict tribal rules of retribution or retaliation. If you lived back in those days and a person killed your brother, you would have the right to kill the brother of the murderer and would lose face if you let the man off the hook. If a person injured one of your cows, you could injure one of his as retribution. This "law of retribution" governed the way people lived and helped to form their perspectives of right and wrong. It became such a part of the fabric of their lives that they were unaware of any other way. In fact, this way of thinking so permeated their understanding of the order of the world that they naturally applied the same perception to God.

In addition, the people of those times and culture attributed everything that happened as coming directly from the hands of God. If it rained, it was because God sent the rain. If it didn't rain, it was because

God withheld it. If the crops grew well, they grew because God caused them to. If a woman had a child, God got the credit for opening the womb. If a woman couldn't bear a child, God had closed the womb. If the army won a battle, God had won it for them. If they lost, God prevented their victory. Everything—and I mean everything—happened or didn't happen due to the will, the power, and the action of God.

So the way the Hebrew people understood God and the world they lived in governed their interpretation of the events in their lives. For them, therefore, the law of retribution, coupled with their perceptions of God's involvement in every aspect of life, resulted in an image of God as completely controlling and justifiably retributive. We may say, then, that the Hebrew people understood God as a divine warrior who exacted retribution, who killed or ordered the killing of guilty parties, including entire nations of people. For them, God behaved in the same way that one of their tribal leaders would behave. They also understood themselves as God's warriors on earth, interpreting all their violent actions as coming from the hand of God. To take it one step further, they believed that anything at all that happened—plagues that killed thousands, earthquakes where the ground opened up to swallow people whole, the death of a child, tornadoes that destroyed property and took lives, or any other calamity you can think of—came from God's hands.

Christian writers Steve Chalke and Alan Mann, authors of *The Lost Message of Jesus*, write about the Israelite concept of divine power and God's dealings with the nations. Those ancient peoples, true to the cultures around them, believed that any event or activity that revealed a show of power ultimately found its source in God. The Scriptures citing God in wars, massacres, executions, famine, and natural disasters expressed their belief that God was intimately involved in every event and every circumstance of their lives. The very expression of faith found in the stories of the Old Testament implicated God in their violence. God continually tried to demonstrate divine love to the people. But for the Israelites, who were "saturated in a worldview that saw him as power, this was going to be a slow uphill struggle" (49). Chalke and Mann continue on to say that "having a god of power on your side helped justify cruel acts of revenge towards those who had wronged you. That is why, if we focus in on individual Old Testament verses and stories, it is easy to fall into the trap of seeing God as a vengeful despot" (49). Many scholars believe that, influenced by the cultural religions around them, Israel fell into that trap.

The question we need to ask is this: Did their cultural perspectives and, therefore, their preconceived ideas about God get projected into the Old Testament texts? We don't know for sure. But if the Bible, as God's written word, is a divinely inspired book written by humans who lived in a particular context, we might conclude that the possibility exists. Because they wrote from within a specific context and world-view, they may indeed have written their own perceptions of God into the text—unless we believe that every writer and editor of the Old Testament went into some sort of trance and wrote only what God dictated to them. But seeing the texts that depict God as a violent, rage-filled deity as part and parcel of the ancient cultural perspective in no way compromises the truth of God's Word. In fact, understanding the stories through the eyes of those who told them and eventually put them into writing gives us a beautiful glimpse into the faith journey of those who walked with the same God we love and trust.

BIBLICAL EXAMPLES

Although we want to understand Israel's faith as Israel understood it, we still don't have to interpret our Bible through the lens of a violent God. The Bible actually gives us evidence leading us to believe that violence does not please God, that violence is a sin. Let's look at some examples.

In the beginning God created the heavens and the earth by speaking them into being. We're so used to hearing our own creation story that we don't realize how unusual it is. Every culture and religious tradition has its own story. Hundreds of myths, from hundreds of ancient cultures, tell a story of exactly how this world came to exist. With the exception of the very ancient Sumerian myth, which has much in common with ours, most of the creation stories from other cultures describe great fights and violence between deities, in which a god's body parts are divided up to form land and sea and sky. Other stories chronicle the sacrificial death of a god whose body parts make up portions of the creation. Each story not only sheds light on the creation of the universe; it also reveals the character and nature of the God who created it all.

But our story is different in a very significant way: God creates the universe not through murder or sacrificial killing, but through peaceful means. God simply speaks. No bloodshed, no infighting between gods, no sacrificial death, and no divine body parts formed into planets strewn across the universe. So from the very beginning, through the manner in which God created the cosmos, God discloses the divine character as one of peace rather than violence.

In Genesis 4 the Bible's first act of violence occurs. Cain kills his brother, Abel. Rather than killing Cain in a fit of vengeance according to the laws of retribution in those ancient days, God sends him away. But not before God stamps a mark on him that hopefully will serve to prevent others from murdering him. God seems to know that violence begets more violence and so seeks to prevent it from happening. As we move through Genesis, we come to chapter 6, in which God repents from creating the earth. What God created *in* peace and *for* peace, we humans corrupted with violence. Genesis 6:11–12 tells us that "the earth was corrupt in the sight of God, and the earth was filled with violence. God looked on the earth, and behold, it was corrupt; for all flesh had corrupted their way upon the earth." The flood happened because God found that we were consumed with sin. Interestingly, the only sin mentioned in the text is violence! Now, granted, the story continues with great violence wreaked by God, and we can't ignore that. But we can dig beneath the text for the message of truth contained within. We'll talk more about that at the end of this chapter.

In Ezekiel 22:1–27, God's people are again accused of and condemned for being violent, guilty of horrific bloodshed. The prophet Ezekiel even calls their town a bloody city, one that sheds blood prolifically. Their violence is considered wicked, and their injustices bring their doom. Ezekiel also warns the people that they will soon pay the consequences for their sin. Why? Because "violence has grown up into a rod of wickedness" (7:10–11). In Isaiah 59:2–7, the peoples' "hands are defiled with blood," and their sins multiply because of their violence toward one another. Violence is their sin. And because of their violence, God judges them by allowing them to suffer the consequences for their sin. Thus we see that violence puts into motion a cycle that begets violence in return. Hosea 4:1–2 speaks about this endless cycle of violence, telling the people that God has a bone to pick with them over their unrighteous behavior. They swear, lie, kill, steal, commit adultery, and then he says, "They employ violence, so that bloodshed follows bloodshed." Micah also speaks the word of God and criticizes the people for their violent ways: "The godly person has perished from the earth, and there is no upright person among men: All of them lie in wait for bloodshed" (7:2). Murder and waiting around to shed blood indicate the violence of the people. Manasseh, one of the worst kings of Judah, was considered to be very wicked, not only because he reinstituted idol worship, causing Israel to sin, but also because "he shed very much innocent blood" (2 Kgs. 21:16). He was a violent ruler and, therefore, considered wicked by God.

Throughout the prophets, God condemns nation after nation because of their violence, terrorization, affliction, and discord. The valley of sacrifice that God condemns in Jeremiah 19:2–6 and 7:30–32 is the valley called Gehenna. God speaks out against the people because they have filled the valley with the blood of innocent people as a sacrifice to their idols. Named the "valley of Slaughter," it represents a place of violence, torture, and revolt against God and against divine righteousness, justice, and mercy. The people shed blood and thought they were doing so to please God! Yet Psalm 5:6 clearly states that God abhors those who do violence by shedding blood. Can we believe that God ever condones or unleashes violence if God loathes the very violence that we believe God commits? How can we harmonize the seeming God of violence with the God who hates it?

Although the Old Testament seems to sanction divine war and violence, the prophets proclaimed the way of peace. We see significant hints of a new message in Micah 4:3 and Isaiah 4:2, in which the people "will beat their swords into plowshares and their spears into pruning hooks. Nation will not lift up sword against nation, never again will they learn war." The "wolf will dwell with the lamb," and little children will not have to fear deadly snakes (Isa. 11:6–9).

If we take the entire of message of God given not only to the Israelites but also to the entire known world, we see God communicating love through the calling of Abraham and Sarah, the covenant promises of loving-kindness, the rescue of the people from the oppression of Egypt, the temple filled with the Shekinah glory of God's continual presence, the promises of unending compassion and faithfulness spoken through the prophets, and the bountiful salvation available to those who have ears to hear. This message applies to the Israelites so very long ago, and it applies to us today, communicating the good news of God's salvation through Jesus our Lord to all who read and hear.

TO HARMONIZE OR NOT TO HARMONIZE— THAT IS THE QUESTION

One day after a class discussion on alternate ways to read the Old Testament, Eric caught me in the hallway and said, "I've noticed that the Old Testament seems to promote nonviolence and especially the nonviolence of God in certain passages. But how do we harmonize the peace passages with those that say the opposite?"

Eric is right to ask that question, but I'm not sure that we should try to "harmonize" these opposing passages of Scripture. Any attempt to smooth out the difficulties in the appearance of divine violence will inevitably create new wrinkles. We just can't reconcile the differences between a God who exacts justice through violence and a God of peace whose loving-kindnesses never cease, who loves all people, and who desires a restored relationship with them. And if the thought that the ancient cultural perspective gets assimilated into the text clashes with your own perceptions of Scripture, we do have another answer. We can still decide which texts we will focus upon, which image of God we will use as a basis for our own behavior.

Determining the Main Message

Passages of judgment and violence do fill pages of Scripture, but we can also see that judgment and violence are not God's final words. In fact, God's main message and purpose for giving us the Bible have nothing whatever to do with violence and judgment. We can ascertain God's main message by identifying the reason for the Bible. A quick search for the purpose of Scripture leads us to a couple of verses in the New Testament. John 20:31 tells us that "these [things] have been written that you may believe Jesus is the Christ, the Son of God; and that believing you may have life in His name." The purpose for the Bible? Reconciliation with God through faith in Jesus Christ. In addition, 1 John 1:4 says that "these things we write, so that our joy may be made complete." God gives us Scripture for our joy, the joy we find in the Lord, through knowing Jesus, and for finding salvation from sin.

There's more. Now that we have reconciled with God, 2 Timothy 3:16–17 gives us insight into the purpose of Scripture for our lives in Christ. It says that "all Scripture is God-breathed and profitable for teaching, for reproof, for correction, for training in righteousness" (NIV). Why? "So that the person of God may be adequate, equipped for every *good* work" (3:17 alt.). And what is the good work of God that the Bible equips us for? To serve in the "ministry of reconciliation," as "ambassadors for Christ," and as a sweet-smelling "aroma" of Christ "in every place" (2 Cor. 5:18–20; 2:14). God gives us the Bible, then, for our salvation, its consequent joy, and instruction on how to live our lives as Jesus lived his. God's main message is one of forgiveness, reconciliation, restoration, and peace.

This main message of reconciliation comes through loud and clear in the Old Testament as well. Even though judgment occurs, whether from God directly or as a consequence of sin, the message of Scripture reveals God's desire to redeem. In Isaiah 54:7–8 the prophet warns the people that they will suffer for a brief time, that God will hide the divine face from them only for a moment. Isaiah, as the mouthpiece of God, goes on to say that "'with everlasting loving-kindness I will have compassion on you,' says the LORD your Redeemer." God hides the divine face from them so that they will realize the error of their ways and turn back to God. The purpose is to reconcile the people to God. The main message of the Psalms communicates God's rescue and redemption. The people may fight and kill and sin against God, but God's actions aim toward a reign of peace, justice, and love. God promises to deliver the people without the aid of swords, arrows, battles, or mighty horsepower, but with love and forgiveness instead. In other words, rather than using violence to conquer evil, God uses peaceful means to redeem humankind, including God's enemies. I could list hundreds of verses that first speak of judgment and finish with God's promises to redeem instead of to condemn, to give joy instead of tears, and to bring gladness instead of sorrow, because of God's loving-kindness, compassion, and mercy—the divine desire to reconcile and save. When God finishes this work of love, "all the ends of the earth shall remember and turn to the LORD; and all the families of the nations shall worship before him. For dominion belongs to the LORD, and he rules over the nations" (Ps. 22:27–28 NRSV).

If the Old Testament doesn't convince us of God's main message and purpose, we turn to the New Testament and interpret God's desire for us through the lens of Jesus. Think about it. If Jesus fully embodies God, as Christian tradition claims, then Jesus also fully reveals God to us. If we want to know how God behaves, we look at how Jesus behaved. If we want to know what God would do in a certain situation, we look at what Jesus did. I think that's why WWJD paraphernalia has such widespread popularity in some Christian circles. What would Jesus do when confronted with an enemy (and the Bible makes it clear that an enemy is one who rejects God and lives according to human desire rather than divine purpose)? We don't see Jesus destroying those who reject God, swinging his sword, chopping off heads, spilling blood in a fit of anger, hell-bent on vengeance. In fact, as he hung on the cross, we see the opposite: he prayed for our forgiveness instead. In the Sermon on the Mount in Matthew, Jesus reverses the law of retaliation and exhorts his followers to turn the other cheek, to pray for their enemies, and even to love their enemies—our enemies (Matt. 5).

On the first day of a class titled "Theology of Violence and Nonviolence," John-Michael, one of my students, wore a T-shirt with this printed on the front: "When Jesus told us to love our enemies, he probably didn't mean kill them." Violence that destroys the enemy and love that redeems the enemy do not go hand in hand. If Jesus commands us to love peacefully, to reconcile unconditionally, wouldn't we expect God to do the same?

The Jesus Lens

An interesting passage, Luke 4:16–21, covertly yet poignantly counteracts the idea of divine retribution and vengeance. Jesus enters the synagogue in Nazareth and begins to read from the Scriptures: "The Spirit of the Lord is upon me, because he has anointed me to preach the gospel to the poor. He has sent me to proclaim release to the captives, and recovery of sight to the blind, to set free those who are oppressed, to proclaim the favorable year of the Lord." He then *closes the book and sits down.*

Jesus communicates three significant points here. First, quoting from Isaiah 61:1–2, Jesus stops quoting and closes the book immediately before the next line, which says, "and the day of vengeance of our God." He omits that line from his reading of Isaiah—a very important omission for sure! Second, by omitting vengeance, Jesus reveals to us the lens through which he interprets his Bible: the lens of peace and redemption rather than violence and vengeance. Third, when he finishes reading, he closes the book and sits down. Everyone seeing and hearing Jesus would have known that as soon as the book closes and the leader sits down, the scriptural message has been delivered, in this case, minus the last phrase.

The significance of the omission of "the day of God's vengeance," the closing of the book, and the sitting down is this: Jesus reinterprets the message of the Old Testament. Through Jesus, God will bring not a sword but salvation, not revenge but redemption, not the violence of force but the compassion of forgiveness. All throughout the New Testament, we see Jesus, by word and deed, exhorting us to live in peace by loving enemies, reconciling with those who have something against us, healing the sick, and taking care of the poor—all ingredients in the

Bible's main message. In spite of our sin and rebellion, God remains faithful to the divine purpose to redeem, and that is the main message and purpose of the Bible. Shouldn't we then interpret Scripture through that lens, the same lens that Jesus used and exemplified? We can call it "the Jesus lens."

Reading our Bible through the "Jesus lens" helps us see that God in Christ interrupted the cycle of violence with divine love, seeking to reconcile and restore rather than to punish and retaliate. God in Christ worked to tear down structures of violence and to redeem the world with love and forgiveness. The teachings and example of Jesus reveal to us that God does not prefer violent means to gain what God desires. Christ reveals to us that God's justice is mercy in the form of restoration, reconciliation, and redemption from the strong powers of the world. Where reconciliation is the focus, violence is cut short. Where restoration of relationship is foremost in theories of hell (and atonement), violence is excluded from the divine character. Where violence is seen as a human act free from any connection with God's way of acting or redeeming humanity, "legitimate" use of coercive power no longer holds sway over society, governments, or families. If through our theology we break the cycle of divine violence, the breaking of the human cycle of violence, at least for us, can follow.

BUT THAT'S NOT HOW IT IS

When I teach Islam, many of my students come to class knowing only what they hear in the media. Many of them actually take the course, they tell me, just so they can understand why Islam is so violent. What they don't realize is that the God of our Old Testament orders far more killings than does the God of the Qur'an! Religions, no matter which one we talk about, have a violent history. They do violence in the name of God even though most of the religions of the world teach peace, love, and compassion for others.

Normally, however, what does the concept of religion, especially Christianity, bring to mind? Piety, prayer, sacrifice, sacrament, the sacred, God, love of the neighbor—all these ideas and the practice of them have significant meaning in our faith tradition. Christianity is a credible, honest, and respectful affair. Most respectable, peace-loving people view it as worthy and valuable for character building, for transforming the world, and for future assurance of eternal life. But it doesn't always work that way. What we fail to realize about religion can hurt us and our loved ones.

Throughout the ages, Christianity has generated violence and abuse beyond measure. Over the centuries, vast and horrible massacres, murders, and untold abuses lay the blame for their atrocities at Christianity's door. The Inquisition, the many Crusades, and the various genocidal wars, all fought under the sign of the cross, in the name of Christ, and by the presumed command of God—these atrocities have left millions of innocent people dead. Because these "holy" warriors marched to the drumbeat of a violent God, the ones whom Christ longed to liberate were instead tied up and tortured; those whom Christ sought to love and save were instead slaughtered in hate. Across the centuries, perceptions of God as an advocate, instigator, or engineer of violence have incited the abuse of women and children, disguising its abuse under a spiritual facade of obedience, personal sacrifice, endurance, and perseverance. As a result, innocent victims of these misperceptions remain prisoners of their own tradition, oppressed, abused, and victimized by the very faith that promises to love, liberate, and save them. Countless others, Christian and non-Christian, have suffered horrific deaths in supposedly divinely ordained bloodbaths. Why do these atrocities occur? What motivates such misguided oppression, dutiful killing, and vengeful doctrines?

I realize that most of us look back on the Inquisition and the Crusades with horror and shame. Maybe God didn't ordain violence of that magnitude, even though the church at that time thought so. We may think, "Certainly things are different today." I don't think so. Let me give you some contemporary examples of violence or the possibility of violence that we advocate today in the name of our Lord.

From our nation's conception, Christian preachers have filled our minds with the notion that we Americans are God's new Israel, God's chosen nation, God's light to the world. As a result, we believe that our causes are God's causes, our wars God's wars. We conquered the land just as the Israelites did, by waging war with Native Americans. Using the Bible, we supported slavery. In the United States' war against the Philippines from 1899 to 1902, during which as many as 250,000 Filipino soldiers and citizens died, devout Christian Senator Albert Beveridge explained that not only was the war moral and right, but also that "God had marked the American people as his chosen nation to finally lead in the redemption of the world" (Hughes, *Christian America*, 29). Killing a quarter of a million people in the name of God in order to redeem the world?

In 1979 the Moral Majority, under the direction of Jerry Falwell, lobbied against reducing U.S. nuclear arms, advocated for American dominance in the world, and pushed for violence and war. Why? Because they believed it was in line with the biblical message and God's will for America. I will never forget Jerry Falwell's comment during a CNN interview after the terror attacks of 9/11. Speaking of the terrorists, he said we should "blow them all away in the name of the Lord." *In the name of the Lord!* Sounds like a contemporary crusade to me!

In his book *Christian America and the Kingdom of God*, historian Richard Hughes writes that when American Christians "advocate the deployment of nuclear weapons on the grounds that God will use those weapons in the final battle of Armageddon, they violate the most fundamental teachings of the Christian faith and invite catastrophic consequences" (18). Just think about the violence we have condoned, using our faith and our God as rationales—contrary to God's command to love our enemies.

The government and many Christians appealed to the same logic for the invasion of Iraq in 2003. In fact, our most conservative and Bible-conscious denominations believed along these lines. Polls showed that 77 percent of America's evangelicals supported the war in Iraq compared to 62 percent of the Catholics and mainline Protestants. Jesus predicted this kind of killing in the name of God. He said to his disciples, "Indeed, an hour is coming when those who kill you will think that by doing so they are offering worship to God" (John 16:2 NRSV). Though this verse refers to nonbelievers killing believers in the name of God, the killing itself, on both sides of the coin, is offered as a service to God.

Not only do we blame *present* violence on the edict of God; we also handily blame any *future* violence on God's will. Professor Merrill Unger completely buys into the violence of God both present and future, writing that "if God permits men to use atomic warfare, it will be to accomplish His purpose and to glorify His name." Horrific violence that kills millions of innocent people used *to glorify God's name?* Charles Jones, a Baptist minister, believes that "some day we may blow ourselves up with all the bombs. . . . But I still believe God's going to be in control. . . . If He chooses to use nuclear war, then who am I to argue with that?" During the Reagan administration, Defense Secretary Caspar Weinberger said, "I have read the Book of Revelation and yes, I believe the world is going to end—by an act of God, I hope—but every day I think the time is running out" (25, 29).

Look at one of our tradition's all-time favorites, "The Battle Hymn of the Republic." One of its phrases goes like this: "Let us die to make men free, while God is marching on." It implies that, as we fight and kill, *God*, through us, through our actions, is marching on! Is this the same God who tells us to love our enemies? The same God who, out of a loving desire to conquer evil, sent Jesus to show us the way of love and died for us *while we were still God's enemies*? Yet we continue to justify our own acts of violence against other nations and peoples by rationalizing that God would have us commit cold-blooded murder by waging war, killing innocent people, calling it collateral damage, and providing arms to other military outfits in the name of keeping God's peace. Our image of God, the way we conceive of God as violent, punitive, and warmongering, allows us to countenance such horrendous acts. With this mentality, we can unleash all sorts of violence, killing whomever we please, whenever we think it necessary, because God ordains it all. And as God's chosen nation, God's light to the world, we have free rein! Please! God help us all: Kyrie eleison (Lord, have mercy).

Where do we get these ideas? One reader of the *Harrisburg Patriot News* provided an answer to that question. She responded to an editorial on October 19, 2004, concerning the inconsistency (and irony) involved in Christian support for the Iraqi war, which kills thousands of men and women, while at the same time advocating opposition to killing thousands of unborn fetuses. The reader invoked the image of Americans as God's chosen people and wrote: "You never mentioned the OT where God led the Israelites into battle on many occasions. He wanted Israel to stamp out sin so it would not lead their sons and daughters astray. . . . When they obeyed Him in going to war, he always provided the victory" (29). She comments next about the character of Jesus at his second coming: "He is angry and powerful, and will wage war" (96). The content of this comment could have been made by any number of Christians, by both pastors and laypersons. It makes it obvious that we get our ideas of justified violence from the image of God we carry around with us, which we develop out of our traditional interpretations of the Old and New Testaments.

Ironically, when we read the Old Testament, however, God does not escape the accusation of violence. Actually God seems most mighty when striking down nations of sinners in judgment. The theme of God's violent judgment occurs more often in the Old Testament than the theme of human violence. Almost a thousand pages of the Old Testament describe God's violent, blazing anger, punishments, destructions, annihilations, and retributive actions against people of every nation and tribe.

The theme of divine retribution against evil permeates the Old Testament texts. As we saw in a previous chapter, God gets hurt and angry and exacts retribution on the guilty. Sometimes God seems to get lost in a fit of irrational wrath and wipes out thousands in one fell swoop. At other times God hands the guilty over to human murderers, delivering them like lambs to the slaughter. Then, most commonly, God allows the evil to take its course and leaves the guilty to suffer the consequences of their own sin. They fall into the fires they themselves have started (Isa. 50:11). The violence they have wrought will multiply and reproduce itself in their own lives: what goes around comes around (Ps. 7:16). In other passages, God delivers them into the hand of their own iniquities and hides his face from them or removes the divine blessing from their lives (Isa. 64:7). In Psalm 81:11–12, God gives the guilty over to the stubbornness of their own hearts because they did not listen to God's voice.

What we see, whether from God directly or indirectly, is that the way the people of those times interpreted life was through the lens of their own worldview, the one held by the cultures around them. In the ancient mind, whatever happens, good or bad, comes from the hands of the gods. In the case of the Hebrew people, the God of Abraham, Isaac, and Jacob gave and took away, gave victory in war or manipulated defeat, answered prayer or hid the divine face, provided rain for crops or brought drought, opened the womb or closed it. And now this same God of the Bible is our God, too. Thankfully, however, we have other ways to interpret Scripture, an alternative lens through which to read these difficult texts. We have our "Jesus lens." And through the lens of Jesus, we can focus on the image of God he revealed to us: a nonviolent image of love, compassion, and mercy. And it's very hard to believe, hook, line, and sinker, that the God revealed to us through Jesus would ever agree to throw sinners into eternal punishment in the unquenchable fires of hell.

"Hold it!" Brooke interjected one evening over sushi, after I had explained to her the biblical evidence for God's abhorrence of violence and the case for interpreting these texts through the lens of Jesus' life and teachings. With her brow wrinkled in confusion, she asked, "It doesn't seem like we have constructed our ideas about hell through the lens of Jesus at all! But we don't want to give up hell. Why is that? Why is it so easy for us to designate who we think will end up there? Almost with a sick sort of pleasure, we point our fingers at other people and never at ourselves; we take the role of God's righteous prosecutors and condemn others to suffer for all eternity in the flames of hell. Why does that comfort us so—even if we don't admit it?"

HELL? WHY?

Actually, I've often wondered the same thing as Brooke. Literary scholar René Girard offers a theory that sheds some light on why so many Christians hold the traditional doctrines of hell so dear. He explains that every community, especially religious ones, develop myths that tell the story of how a community gets rid of evil in its midst. According to Girard, the community brings forth a scapegoat. A scapegoat takes the blame for evil, separating the sheep from the (scape)goats, so to speak—the good guys from the bad guys. Keep in mind that the scapegoat can take the form of an entire community of people, much as the Jews were under Hitler's reign. The community bands together in unity and destroys the scapegoat in order to purge the people of sin and to establish peace. They then construct a story around the event. These stories (or myths) justify the violence of the community as a necessity for social solidarity and purity. They communicate that the violence of the community is good and the evil of the scapegoat is bad. The scapegoat is considered guilty; the violence against it justified and therefore condoned. The myths camouflage the gravity of the violence against a community by taking the side of the murderers against the victims. Illegitimate violence is reframed as legitimate. The persecutor's stories seem convincing, and as generations pass, they become the truth.

Not only do myths justify violence in order to preserve a community intact from uncontrolled vengeance and outbursts of violent behavior; they also tell the story from the perspective of the ones who do the killing, the ones who benefit the most from the violence through the preservation of social harmony. The scapegoat's own voice is silenced so that even those closest to it, carried away by the intoxicating power of the violence and its "redemptive" quality, do not recognize the evil of the violence. It all seems so righteous, this violence for a good cause.

In this way, myths make us blind and mute to the illegitimate violence that lies within the collective violence of the scapegoating process. Indeed, the Greek word for myth, *muthos*, indicates the blindness they cause. *Muthos*, from the root *muo*, means to "close" or "keep secret," to close the eyes or mouth and to remain silent. The myths' silencing of the scapegoat and the unjust violence committed against it traps believers into trusting the myth to keep community peace through "legitimated" violence at the scapegoat's expense. The mythmakers are completely unaware of the true nature of the violence and the unjust treatment of the scapegoat. As long as we keep on believing the myths and their legitimation of violence, they remain in effect and we hold on to them, believing in their purifying power. The problem with the myth and its legitimation of violence, however, is that only violence maintains the peace. The notion that violence creates peace is mythic (untrue) all on its own. We know that violence only escalates and increases violence. According to peace activist Mahatma Gandhi, the good that violence does is only temporary, but the evil it does is permanent.

I believe that the traditional hell myth—the wicked are cast out of the community of the righteous into eternal damnation in the fires of hell—fits rather well into Girard's mythmaking template. We believe that hell, with its eternal violence, is necessary to protect the community, God's community, from violence and unrighteousness. The hell myth exists as the very fabric of our perspective on God's last judgment. Its thread is woven into the tapestry of our theories of salvation. Worse, we insist that God designed it all, that behind all the torment and torture lies God, the very God who loves enemies! We have made hell part and parcel of the good news! We believe that the victims—those thrown into hell, our scapegoats—pervert our Christian community and deserve the punishment they receive. They are the weeds among the tares and the chaff among the wheat, the dross that needs to be blown or burned away. They must be destroyed for their wickedness, and we must keep the violence burning and brewing for all eternity as we look on in harmonious solidarity, singing, "Good news! The wicked ones are suffering eternally!"

But when is anyone's eternal torment good news? Eternal suffering for temporal sin seems, at best, unjust. Don't we implicate ourselves and, worse, God, when we conquer evil with evil? Paul puts the question to us like this: "Shall we go on sinning so that grace may increase? By no means!" (Rom. 6:1–2 NIV). "God forbid." Those who perpetuate the hell myth also perpetuate the existence of eternal evil and suffering in God's ostensibly redeemed universe. Although souls will still exist, albeit in endless torture, the possibility for redemption, for reconciliation, and for restoration with God will be closed off forever. Do we truly understand what we advocate when we believe in the traditional doctrine of hell? Do we so passionately need a corporate scapegoat to prove our righteousness and goodness, to feel as though we have a handle on how to abolish and punish evil, to feel peace about our own eternal destination? Are we so ready to believe something that contradicts the main message of the Bible, as we have seen above? We hate evil, yet at the same time we believe and advocate the unmitigated evil of a divinely ordained place of eternal punishment for those unfortunate enough to believe the "wrong" thing, not at the wrong time, but in time, in temporality. Father, if that is the case, please forgive us, for we know not what we are believing. Deliver us from this doctrine of death!

Only when the power of the myth begins to weaken is the scapegoat mechanism fully revealed to the community. Once doubt is thrown on the validity of a myth, the community can no longer retain a positive attitude toward the unjustified violence. The blinders are stripped off, their tongues are loosed, and the myth loses its power. Any myth, theory, or doctrine that accommodates divine and human violence, especially on an eternal level, and most especially issuing from a God who is love, should drive us to continue the search for an alternative view of hell more in line with the God revealed in Jesus Christ. As a result, believing in the traditional hell myth may well indicate that we need our blinders removed. Maybe the theories of justified violence implicit in the myth need to be rejected, rethought, and rearticulated so that hell's victims await not a theology of hell but a theology of hope.

Instead of viewing God as the one who commands the killing of entire nations of people, including men, women, children, and animals, let's peer through the ministry of Jesus, who taught that God did not send him to condemn the world but to save the world. Instead of interpreting God's wrath as violence loosed against enemies, let's hold Jesus up as our interpretive lens and conclude that God loves enemies as well as friends. Instead of concluding that God rubs divine hands together in delight at the thought of inflicting eternal punishment in the bottomless pit for lost souls, let's envision Jesus, who weeps over Jerusalem, longing for souls to say "yes" to the offer of bottomless love. Even Paul, who knew something about the message of Christ, tells us that God doesn't want anyone to perish, but instead, for all to be saved (1 Tim. 2:4). He said that through Jesus, God went about the business of reconciling the world to God's self. The world—the whole world! The bottomless pit is crossed out through the bottomless love of God. Now that is good news!

Look at the broader vision of the Bible, God's purpose, not just our favorite verses. We see that God's plan is that all be saved and come to the knowledge of the truth, that not one should go to hell but all have eternal life, that in Christ all—the whole world—be reconciled to God. The ministry that God gives us is to be ministers of reconciliation. We are not told to judge the world. We are not told to hold everyone in the world to God's standards. We are not told to scare sinners with the threat of their going straight to hell. God does not tell us to stand as the world's moral barometer or gatekeepers at heaven's gate. God tells us to be ministers of reconciliation, a sweet aroma of Christ in every place, an aroma of love. Only by this will others know that we belong to God. That is the message of the Bible, both Old and New Testaments. So what does this message of hope and love tell us about the image of God? We'll find out in the next chapter.

6

Rethinking the Image of God

Turn our vision to the Primal Love,
that, gazing at Him, you may penetrate—
as far as that can be—His radiance.

—Dante, *Paradiso*, Canto 32

The one who does not love does not know God,
for God is love.

—1 John 4:8

I woke up to the sound of my phone beeping, not my alarm, but a text message from Brooke. Strange . . . too early for her, I thought.

"Can we talk about God this weekend, when I get home?" she wrote. I texted her back,

"Sure, what's up?"

"I have to write a paper on God, and lately we've been talking more about a hellish God. I want to write about a compassionate God."

Brooke isn't alone. Eric, too, wanted a break from what he called the "mean God." One day before class, his concern for evangelism led him to ask, "I know the stereotypical image of the fire-and-brimstone preacher, pounding the pulpit, sweat flying from his face as he threatens rapt churchgoers with tales of eternal torment if they don't come to Jesus. But I don't want to be one of those kinds of preachers. I think people will more likely want to 'come to Jesus' if I preach about God as love and compassion. Love rather than wrath attracts. So can we build a case for the image of a loving God rather than of an angry God?"

I'm glad that both Brooke and Eric want to concentrate on the character of God as love. And one of the first steps we can take in developing an alternate theory of hell is to reexamine our image of God. As I pointed out earlier, traditional doctrines of hell (and of atonement) that depict God as an angry tyrant litter the landscape of Christian history. The Old Testament tells the exciting, beautiful, and sometimes messy story of a community's walk with its God. The experiences and life situations of this community weave a tapestry that reveals the character of their God (and ours). The same holds true for the New Testament. The difference, however, is that in the New Testament we have a person who, as our tradition claims, perfectly reveals God to us. As we discussed in the last chapter, Jesus reveals God so that the way Jesus acts is the way God acts. The way Jesus thinks is the way God thinks. What Jesus says is what God says. So it makes sense to look at the Old Testament, where we usually get our violent images of God, in light of Jesus and how Jesus reveals God. If we see God primarily through the lens of Jesus, through his life and message, his actions and teachings, an alternative scenario comes into view, one that does not harmonize with an angry, vengeful God. So let's go first to the Old Testament and read and interpret it through our Jesus-colored lenses.

THE OLD TESTAMENT AND JESUS-COLORED GLASSES

The loving, merciful God of Abraham, Isaac, Jacob, and Moses differed from the fickle, cantankerous gods of the surrounding cultures in a very significant way. Rather than dwelling under a tree or on a mountaintop, YHWH, the Hebrew God, traveled with the people. Wherever Abraham went, God went with him. When Moses led the people out of Egypt, God accompanied them, leading the way with a pillar of fire by night and a pillar of cloud by day. This God, unlike the other gods, desired loving relationships, mutuality, and reciprocity—all the components of a good "marriage." This God ate dinner with Abraham, wrestled with Jacob, called Samuel from his bed, spoke with Moses face-to-face, came to Elijah as a gentle breeze, and hounded the psalmist until he cried out in wonder (and maybe a bit of frustration), "Where can I go from Your Spirit? Or where can I flee from Your presence? If I ascend to heaven, You are there; if I make my bed in Sheol, behold You are there. If I take the wings of the dawn, if I dwell in the remotest part of the sea, even there your hand will lead me" (Ps. 139:7–10). The relational God goes where we go—even to the point of emptying himself into the form of a mere human being, a humble servant, loving us to the point of death and beyond (Phil. 2:5–8).

As we discussed before, we can see that the Hebrew community understood their God not only as one who wreaks violence and vengeance against the disobedient, but also as one who rescues them from those who do violence. For them, their God is the rescuer of those oppressed by violence. Over and over again the psalmists cry out to God for deliverance from their own personal abysses. They lament over the dire situations they find themselves in and, mirabile dictu, God hears and comes to the rescue.

One of my personal favorites, Psalm 40:1–2, is attributed to King David, who takes us to his private prayer room, where we hear his lament and his heartfelt plea for deliverance. David beautifully describes God's redemption and sings a song of praise for God's greatness: "I waited patiently for the LORD; and he inclined to me, and heard my cry. He brought me up out of the pit of destruction, out of the miry clay, and he set my feet upon a rock making my footsteps firm. He put a new song in my mouth, a song of praise to our God; many will see and fear and will trust in the LORD." In another, Psalm 46:1–3, we learn that we can run to God for all of our troubles and find refuge for our souls and peace for our hearts: "God is our refuge and strength, a very present help in trouble. Therefore we will not fear, though the earth give way, though the mountains fall into the heart of the sea; though its waters roar and foam, and the mountains quake with their surging" (NIV). Repeatedly the psalmists cry out to God to rescue them from danger, from enemies, and from oppression. No other gods in the surrounding cultures have a God that they can count on to rescue them in times of trouble.

If we read further, we also catch a glimpse of God's attitude toward the violence from which we seek rescue: "He makes wars to cease to the end of the earth; He breaks the bow and cuts the spear in two; He burns the [war] chariots with fire. 'Cease striving and know that I am God; I will be exalted above the nations, I will be exalted in the earth.' The LORD of hosts is with us; the God of Jacob our stronghold" (Ps. 46:9–10). I could quote hundreds of verses to show you the character of God as rescuer and redeemer in the Old Testament, but I think you catch the point.

Keeping our lens in mind, we know that Jesus also comes to our rescue, even while we are still sinners (Rom. 5:8–10). From the New Testament we know that Jesus is exalted above the nations and all the earth (Phil. 2:9). We know that through Jesus comes the salvation of the world (2 Cor. 5:19). And we know that Jesus came to usher in the kingdom of God and bring peace on earth and goodwill among all people (Matt. 3:2; Luke 2:14). The Old Testament also paints an image for us of God's enduring love and compassion. Exodus 19:5–6 expresses this divine love (see also Deut. 7:6–8; 1 Pet. 2:9). God calls the people God's own possession or special treasure, which gives us a beautiful picture in the Hebrew language.

When my sons were quite young, they each had a small box in which they kept their private little treasures, things that were special to them, things they wanted kept safe. They put money in their boxes, pretty or strange-shaped rocks they had found on the beach, dead bugs, and as they grew older, they put love letters from their girlfriends in there (it was difficult for me to keep my hands and eyes out of their boxes, but I succeeded . . . well, mostly). These things were very precious to my boys. My fondest memories of my grandmother are the times she would pull out *her* little treasure box, held shut with a red rubber band, filled with all her precious jewelry. She didn't have much, but what she had she treasured deeply. She always kept her tiny gold box near the chair where she sat, and every once in a while I could convince her to show me the small, shiny rings, pendants, and brooches. Even though it was only made of glass, I loved the pink solitaire ring the best. When she died, I inherited that ring. Now I keep it in a small box, in a safe place, and sometimes I pull it out and think of my kind and gentle grandmother and her little box of special treasures and her delight in showing it to me.

God, too, thinks of us as special. God lovingly possesses us as a special treasure and hides us in the recesses of the divine heart. God wants to protect us, to set us aside for God's pleasure, to love and to enjoy and to treasure always. Jesus reveals to us just how precious we all are to God. So precious that he showed the greatest kind of love by laying down his life for us (John 15:13).

Isaiah 30:18, another one of my favorites, reveals the image of God as a lover longing to give us gifts of grace: "The LORD longs to be gracious to you, and therefore He waits on high to have compassion on you." Again, if we understand the Hebrew language, we glimpse an image of God as sitting on the edge of the divine throne, looking down at the earth, longing (this is a strong word in the Hebrew), thirsting with a strong craving, to bestow upon us grace and compassion. God strongly and emphatically desires to give all of us every good thing. God loves us and treasures us.

Zephaniah 3:17 presents us with an image of God as a smitten dancing partner: "The LORD your God is in your midst, mighty to save. He will exult over you with joy, he will be quiet in his love, He will rejoice over you with shouts of joy" (NASB/NIV). Again, we lose the impact of this verse by its translation into English. If we could videotape God acting out this verse in light of its meaning in the Hebrew, we'd see God dancing circles around us (yes, God dances!), and shouting and singing and laughing with joy. Then in quiet love, God stops, encircles us in the protective safety of the divine arms, and looks at us in wonder. I remember looking at my own babies like that. I'd hold them in my arms and just gaze at them in love. I'd fondle their little fingers and toes, amazed at their perfection. I'd run my hand gently down their tiny soft heads, smelling their sweetness, meditating on their beauty, smiling at them as they looked up at me in trusting innocence. That's the image we get of God when Zephaniah says that "He will be quiet in his love." God contemplates us in quiet loving embrace. Then all of a sudden, out of sheer joy and exhilarating love, God jumps up and once more dances around us, jumping and leaping and singing and shouting for joy over us!

We bring God such joy; God loves us so much; God desires to grace us with all the heavenly treasures so strongly; God works to rescue us from our own pits of destruction so avidly that God made the sacrifice and sent Jesus as the bearer of those gifts and as the one who satisfied those longings. What a beautiful, loving image! And so inconsistent with the God we spoke about in the first few chapters—but fitting with the God Jesus reveals to us.

THREE WORDS—THREE IMAGES

If, for the sake of simplicity, we want to consolidate the most significant images of God according to the revelation of God through Jesus, we can do so with three words. Compassion (or love), peace, and faithfulness.

One of the most significant images of God in the Old Testament, also supported by the life and teachings of Jesus, finds its expression in the Hebrew word *rāham,* which we usually translate "compassion" or "mercy." We find it scattered throughout the Old Testament in verses like Lamentations 3:22: "The steadfast love of the LORD never ceases, and his mercies [*rāham*] never come to an end" (NRSV). In fact, the writer of Lamentations continues on to say that God's mercies [*rāhamim*] are new every morning—every morning God desires to show us mercy (3:23). In Joel we can almost see God weeping in sorrow over the disobedience of the people, beseeching them to return: "Yet even now . . . return to me with all your heart, and with fasting, weeping, and mourning; and rend your heart and not your garments." Next Joel sheds some light on why God longs to forgive: "For He [God] is gracious and compassionate [*rāham*], slow to anger, abounding in lovingkindness and relenting of evil" (2:12–13). Through Isaiah, God communicates the depth of the divine compassion for us: "The LORD longs to be gracious to you, and therefore He waits on high to have compassion [*rāḥam*] on you. How blessed are all those who long for him" (Isa. 30:18). This verse explains that God longs for us and desires to bless us with compassion. God delights in showering us, and the whole earth actually, with *rāḥam*.

Interestingly, the word *rāḥam* comes from the Hebrew word for "womb" or "uterus," and evokes for us a beautiful image of God's deeply felt compassion and tender love, just as the love between a mother and the child she carries in her womb. Although most of the times the word appears in the Old Testament it refers to God and God's loving compassion, we do see it used to describe a mother's love for her child in 1 Kings 3:16–27.

You remember the story. Two women in the same house each give birth to a baby, one born dead and the other born alive. The woman whose baby was born dead takes the living baby and says it is hers. The other mother, knowing the baby is hers, vehemently contests the other woman's claim. Unable to solve the problem on their own, the two women come before King Solomon, seeking his wisdom in order to settle the issue. After they each present their case, Solomon orders the newborn baby cut in half so that each woman can have a half of the child. One woman agrees and the other woman, out of compassion (a form of *rāḥam*) for the child, cries out to Solomon, "Oh, my lord, give her the living child, and by no means kill him!" (3:26). Now which woman is the mother of that child? Right. The one whose heart burns with compassion, so much so that she is willing to give up the rights to her baby so that he may live (some Jewish versions of the text translate the word *rāḥam* as "her *womb yearned* for the child"). God has the same kind of compassion for all God's children, the compassion that a mother has for her babies. Not only is this a profoundly feminine image of God in Scripture; it also communicates to us an image quite different from the warrior God we see in other passages in the Old Testament. This image, however, coheres with the image of God that Jesus portrays. In fact, we see that same kind of loving compassion in Jesus as he sits weeping on the Mount of Olives, looking over the city of Jerusalem (the city of peace). His heart's desire was to gather them together as a mother hen gathers her chicks, but they were completely unwilling. They rejected Jesus' love and compassion, and it broke his heart (Luke 13:34).

The meaning of another word, *shalom*, closely related to the idea of compassion in the Old Testament, moves like a gently flowing current throughout the entire Bible. Many Bible scholars would sum up the central message of both Old and New Testaments as God's desire, determination, and diligence to bring *shalom* on earth. That's why God took the formless void of primordial chaos and made it into a peaceful creation (chaos is the opposite of *shalom*). The desire for *shalom* moved God to make covenants with the people of earth, and eventually to send Jesus to save the world and usher in the kingdom of *shalom*, God's peaceable kingdom on earth.

Although *shalom* most often gets translated as "peace," its meaning encompasses the entire range of what peace means, a state of harmony among God and all of creation, a total wholeness, completeness, and well-being that infiltrates every aspect of life on every level: moral, ethical, emotional, relational, and spiritual. *The Theological Wordbook of the Old Testament* defines *shalom* as "entering into a state of wholeness and unity, a restored relationship," and asserts that it is "among the most important words in the OT." The word, as expressed in the entirety of its meaning, has God as its source. *Shalom* not only issues from God; it also reveals to us a significant characteristic of God's nature. Again, if we read the Bible through the lens of Jesus, we see that the Prince of Peace corresponds perfectly to the Old Testament image of God as the source, initiator, and sustainer of *shalom* in every sense of the word.

Let's look at the third word before we move on: "faithfulness." Deuteronomy 32:4 beautifully paints an image of God as a faithful rock, one who cannot be moved, who stands steadfastly, invincibly, and firmly rooted in loving-kindness and mercy: "The Rock, his work is perfect, and all his ways are just. A faithful God, without deceit, just and upright is he" (NRSV). Psalm 119:90 tells us that God's "faithfulness continues throughout all generations"; it never fails. In Psalm 36:5 we also read that God's "lovingkindness extends to the heavens" and God's "faithfulness reaches to the skies." As we surely know it from the song by Thomas O. Chrisholm, Jeremiah, in contemplating the wonders of God, proclaims for all to hear (and read): "Great is Your faithfulness!" (Lam. 3:23). In other words, God's faithfulness to all on earth is infinite, never ending, and unchanging. Jesus embodied God's faithfulness in so many ways. He indicated his great faithfulness, saying he would never leave us or forsake us (Heb. 13:5). As the author and perfector of our own faith, his faith must be of the utmost perfection. And importantly, God through Jesus faithfully, always, forgives our sins—and we take that on faith, our faith in God's faithfulness seen in Jesus.

So by focusing on a few of the characteristics of God that are consistent with what we see in the life and teachings of Jesus, we can draw a significantly different image of God than one of an angry, vengeful divinity determined to punish the world for every last shred of sin. Instead of a God who angrily unleashes calamity upon the nations, we see a God who lovingly pours forth compassion upon the earth. Instead of a God who comes swinging the divine sword, we see a God who comes spreading the divine *shalom*. Instead of a fitful God, whose moods swing as violently as his sword, we see a faithful God, whose steadfast love never ceases.

PICKING AND CHOOSING—JESUS

"Okay, I like this," Lisa said after we talked about the Jesus-colored glasses. "But how do we pick and choose? How do we know which Old Testament passages refer to the image of God as consistent with God's character and which ones the community projected into the text due to their worldview?"

Most of my students, with brows knit in consternation, ask the same question—as they should. Whether we want to admit it or not, we all put more weight on some Bible verses and passages than on others. In that regard, I'm no different from everyone else. The 1963 Baptist Faith and Message, a confessional statement of the Southern Baptist Convention, declares that one guideline should dictate how we interpret all of Scripture: "The criterion by which the Bible is to be interpreted is Jesus Christ." In other words, up until the year 2000, when the leadership unfortunately took that statement out of the document, the SBC churches read the Bible through Jesus-colored glasses. And as we construct an alternate view of hell and read the Bible through one specific lens, we will choose to pay more attention to verses that more consistently harmonize with the life and teachings of Jesus.

As we discussed before, no matter what we believe about the divinity of Jesus, we Christians interpret through this lens because we believe that Jesus most perfectly reveals God to us. Because this is true, the behavior of Jesus mirrors the behavior of God. Jesus tells us himself that if we see him, we see the Father (John 14:6, 9). He also discloses to us that his actions and behaviors are identical to God's; whatever God does, Jesus does the same (5:19). So how can we do anything other than read and interpret the Bible through Jesus-colored glasses—if we want to know God's character and behavior, that is? In order to understand God, we must understand Jesus. In order to develop an accurate picture of the image of God, we need to examine the image of Jesus that the Bible draws for us.

The Sermon on the Mount in Matthew 5–7 is one of the first places we meet Jesus teaching the ways of God in the kingdom. Although Jesus' interpretation of the law moves it from the realm of external rule-keeping into the realm of internal love and obedience, he allows us to glimpse the heart of God. Here Jesus exhorts his listeners to be peacemakers, to turn the other cheek, to go the extra mile, to love their enemies, to pray for those who treat them badly, to forgive others unconditionally, and then he sums it all up by telling them why. Because in this they find perfection (or holiness), just like the perfection of God. That's right—the exhortation to be holy as God is holy falls in the context of loving others. To love as God loves is to be holy as God is holy. By acting in the way Jesus preaches in the Sermon on the Mount, we most aptly imitate the holiness of God (5:48). We become perfect from the same actions that make up God's perfection.

From the very beginning of Jesus' life, we see the purpose of his coming. The angels tell us: "Glory to God in the highest, and on earth peace, goodwill toward all people" (Luke 2:14 KJV alt.). Not only do the angels connect Jesus to God's work on earth; they also link peace on earth and goodwill toward all people to bringing God glory. Peace and goodwill bring God glory, and Jesus lived (and died) to make sure we knew that. We see Jesus' revealing God to us when he says, "Come to Me, all who are weary and heavy-laden, and I will give you rest. Take My yoke upon you and learn from Me, *for I am gentle and humble in heart*; and you will find rest for your souls" (Matt. 11:28–29, emphasis added). If Jesus has such compassion for the people, if Jesus is gentle and humble, then so is God.

All throughout the Gospels, Jesus heals the sick, raises the dead, loves his enemies, liberates the oppressed, and submits peacefully to death despite our sin, evil, and violence against him. We gaze further into the heart and mind of God as Jesus tells us his purpose, what he came to accomplish during his lifetime, and what God would accomplish if God were walking the earth: "The Spirit of the Lord is upon me, because he has anointed me to preach the good news to the poor. He has sent me to proclaim release to the captives, and recovery of sight to the blind, to let the oppressed go free, to proclaim the year of the Lord's favor" (Luke 4:18–19 NRSV). Leaving out the next sentence that speaks of the day of God's vengeance, he closes the book and sits down, emphasizing the divine significance of his calling. Because God sent Jesus to do those things, we realize that God operates in the same way, for the same purpose.

Jesus also reveals to us that God forgives unconditionally. When the disciples ask Jesus how many times they should forgive a person, Jesus gives them an astounding answer: seventy times seven. Though we might want to stick to the letter of the law and calculate this to mean we should forgive someone 490 times, the disciples would have considered this number so outrageously high that Jesus must be telling them to forgive over and over again, always (Matt. 18:22).

With his message to turn the other cheek and to go the extra mile, Jesus confronted the cultural and Jewish laws of retributive justice with the radical message of the kingdom of God: by forgiving, Jesus revealed God's image as forgiving rather than retributive. The people were caught in the nets of retributive justice as a way of life. Some theologians claim that the ethics of God's kingdom confront and reverse the law of retribution and establish the law of grace. Jesus gives us the ultimate example of this reversal when, from the cross, he asked God to forgive us (Luke 23:34; cf. Acts 7:60). By exposing the law of retribution, Jesus exposed himself to the consequences of those who break community with the status quo, who disturb the traditional sense of law and order with the radical message of God's kingdom of peace and love and redemption—redemption, not retribution; restoration rather than revenge. So they killed him. And Jesus let them—another important insight into the nature of God as nonviolent, peaceloving, and peacekeeping.

THE KINGDOM HAS COME

Jesus preached that God's kingdom had arrived, here and now. But what does God's kingdom look like? Because our tradition typically interprets certain passages in Isaiah as glimpses into the future when the kingdom of God comes to earth, we can turn there and glean images from these verses. From Isaiah 9:6–7, we see that peace will rule the kingdom. In fact, peace is the major characteristic of God's kingdom.

> For a child will be born to us, a son will be given to us; and the government will rest on His shoulders; and His name will be called

Wonderful Counselor, Mighty God, Eternal Father, Prince of Peace. There will be no end to the increase of His government or of peace, on the throne of David and over his kingdom, to establish it and to uphold it with justice and righteousness from then on and forevermore.

Now think about it. Do we ever see Jesus—or Paul, for that matter—advocating violence or retribution in the Gospels? No! Violence and retribution do not fit into the gospel message or into the ethics of God's kingdom. How, then, could it be part of God's ethics or God's eternal plan? How can the violence and evil of an eternal hell be part of God's plan for anyone? With the alternative image of God we have gained by looking through the Jesus lens, we really don't have much of a choice. We're going to have to rethink our ideas about divine justice and divine forgiveness. We'll especially have to rethink our notion of hell.

7

Rethinking the Justice of God

I know indeed that, though God's justice has
another realm in heaven as its mirror,
you here do not perceive it through a veil.

—Dante, *Paradiso*, Canto 19

Righteousness and justice
are the foundation of Your throne;
lovingkindness and truth
go before You.

—Psalm 89:14

THE QUESTION OF JUSTICE

After our discussion on retributive justice, Brooke, Eric, and Lisa all voiced concern about it. As usual, Lisa kept me on my toes with her emphasis on biblical accuracy. She cited a couple of verses that talk about God exacting justice on the wicked. A bit hesitantly she added, "As much as I don't want to believe it, God's justice looks and sounds rather retributive to me. I'm not sure we can reason our way out of that just to make God seem more loving, even though I want to try!"

Eric aimed his concern at the guilty. He experienced uneasiness about what he calls "soft" justice, or "letting the guilty get away with murder." "I guess it wouldn't be fair for God to let the wicked just take a walk. In some way they have to answer for the terrible things they've done. At the same time, however, if God is love, wouldn't God *want* to save these wicked people?" he wondered.

On the other side of the coin, Brooke, true to her heritage and with typical Anabaptist concern for marginalized people, thought that the victims of abuse and oppression would endure further abuse if those who mistreat them don't suffer any consequences. "Sometimes," she pointed out, "the conviction that God will hold the guilty accountable for their crimes gives victims enough hope to hang on to life, to hang in there, to keep fighting for their lives. The victims need to know that God looks out for them too, right?"

As Eric and Brooke pointed out, we don't want a milksop God who lets brutal murderers off the hook without any consequences. We don't want victims to remain eternally without restitution. A friend of mine who works extensively with victims of political abuse in South America made this clear. During a discussion about hell, he said that sometimes the only thing that keeps oppressed people going day to day is the hope that God's justice will prevail in the end. Victims need justice. But must that justice necessitate eternal punishment in hell? Must divine justice be retributive?

TYPES OF JUSTICE

There are many kinds of justice, but for our purposes we've focused on two. The first type is what I've been calling "retributive justice." It simply means any form of justice that puts things right through punishment or payback, an eye for an eye. The wrong must be set right through action of some sort against the wrongdoer. Retributive justice does not require forgiveness, and if forgiveness later occurs, it is meaningless because the offense has already been set right through the retributive measures. The other type of justice is what I am calling restorative or reconciling justice. It is justice served by reconciling with the guilty and restoring the relationship. This form of justice requires forgiveness.

The discomfort of Lisa, Brooke, and Eric reveals that all of them, whether they intend to or not, view justice as retributive. They, and probably most of us, have been taught to believe that the only way to vindicate the innocent and to hold the guilty accountable is through some method of retributive justice, as in our traditional views of hell. As we saw in chapter 3, traditional theories of hell emphasize God's justice as retributive in nature. As legitimate as retributive justice seems, its legitimacy does not rule out thinking differently about justice, yet still thinking biblically. I believe that the Bible, especially surrounding the life and teachings of Jesus, sheds light on a different kind of justice, one more in line with a God of love. This is the second type of justice we've been talking about, called restorative or reconciling justice. If we are to think differently about hell, we must first pinpoint the nature of divine justice. If God resorts to retributive justice as the prominent way of dealing with sinners, then the traditional views of hell make sense. But if God seeks to reconcile with sinners through restorative justice, then we must rethink our views of hell.

THE SEARCH FOR BIBLICAL JUSTICE

The Biblicality of Beliefs

According to contemporary historian Howard Zehr, whether or not biblical justice focuses on retribution or restoration remains an important issue, one that lies at the heart of our understanding about God's nature, character, and actions in salvation history. The way we interpret the Bible always arises from our own presuppositions, personal history, and social context. What we have always been taught, whether right or wrong, examined or unexamined, dictates how we think about God and God's actions in the world, especially actions toward the guilty.

A conversation with Lisa demonstrates a case of believing what we have always been taught. On the phone a couple of days ago, Lisa declared with certainty that "God cannot look upon sin, cannot be around sin." I asked her to show me in the Bible where it says that. Now the Bible does tell us that God abhors sin (Ps. 45:7; Prov. 6:16–19), that God seeks to conquer and to redeem sin (à la Jesus and in Isa. 44:22; Rev. 1:5), and that God will forgive sin (New Testament). One verse in Habakkuk tells us that God cannot look upon sin *with favor*, which means that God cannot look at sinful ways and *approve of them*, but it never says that God *cannot look upon sin at all* (Hab. 1:13). If that were the case, how could God look upon the world?

We know that God looked upon the sin of the world in Genesis 6:5. How can God see to answer prayer without looking upon sin? More important, how can God come as a human being and not just walk among sinners, but also eat with them, sleep among them, and allow himself to be put to death by them? If we say that God can't look upon sin, we also have to say, then, that Jesus is less than God or that Jesus could handle sin better than God. I don't think many of us are prepared to believe that. I suppose we could say that Jesus' compassion outweighs God's so that he can suffer what God cannot. But then what does that say about the Trinity and the "one God" theory? It separates God from God to the point where we have two Gods, one who could look at sin and one who could not.

Where do we get these kinds of ideas, that God cannot look upon sin, or that God's justice is chiefly retributive, or the existence of an eternal hell? They become such a part of our belief system that we think they are scriptural. But often they don't come from the Bible at all. They come from our contexts, our communities of discourse, our friends and pastors and parents and Sunday school teachers. Upon closer examination, however, we find that the Bible teaches something quite different from what we have always believed. Retributive justice as a central aspect of God's nature might be one of those ideas. For a minute let's try to set aside our context, what we have always been taught, and explore this further.

The way we view justice often stems from our own interpretations of God. If we interpret Scripture as mainly describing God as a God of wrath and a punisher of sin, we will likely interpret justice as more retributive. That's why this book contains two chapters on the image of God. I cannot emphasize strongly enough the importance of how we conceive of God, the image of God we hold dearest.

Lisa and Eric inherit most of their theology from a church that preaches and teaches hellfire and brimstone and that emphasizes God's angry, punitive nature. As a result, their views of a God who demands eternal flames of hell as punishment for temporal sin seem natural. Neither one of them questioned it until recently. And for that reason this study has been a bit more difficult for them to attempt with an open mind.

If our view of God places greater focus on divine love and grace, our views of justice will likely be reconciling and restorative. Brooke, unlike Lisa and Eric, was brought up in an environment that emphasizes God as a loving, merciful, forgiving peacemaker. Her Anabaptist tradition focuses on the God revealed in Jesus Christ, who as God in the flesh came to seek and to save the lost, to reconcile them to God, to make peace between God and humanity. As a result, she has always questioned the traditional views of hell as a place where God throws sinners into eternal punishment. She finds it easier to think differently about hell because of her context (community of discourse) and theological "training." In fact, in a conversation with Brooke last night, she admitted that her generation finds it easier to think differently about hell because they are willing to emphasize God's love and desire for reconciliation. They see divinely mandated eternal punishment for mere temporal sin as a horrendous injustice. So for Brooke and her peers, restorative justice must come into play even in their views on hell.

Eric, Lisa, and Brooke find support for their ideas about justice in Scripture. But what does the Bible emphasize most about divine justice? And where do we see God's justice most effectively at work?

Characteristics of Divine Justice

When trying to rethink closely held doctrines, like divine justice, it's always hard to know where to start. So with Bible, commentaries, and my Greek and Hebrew in hand, I have outlined my plan of attack. I thought I'd start with the premise that "God is love." If I found this first premise true, I would move on to the question of divine justice. What does divine justice look like, and how does it act in light of the fact that God is love? On the one hand, if God's justice responds to human sin retributively, exacting vengeance in equal measure, then my search is over and I will be stuck with hell. (Although, think about it: In the case of hell, God punishes in unequal measure, requiring an eternity of punishment for one short lifetime of sin. So even according to the rules of retributive justice, a tit for a tat, God's justice under this scenario isn't very just.) On the other hand, if God appears to respond to sin and wickedness in a redemptive, restorative manner, I know the search is still on since there's nothing redemptive or restorative about hell.

What I find in Scripture, however, leads me to the conclusion that we have lost much of the true meaning of divine justice due to our context or to the teachings most familiar to us. The Bible has so much to say about God's justice, most of it scattered throughout its pages in no particular order. So to prevent confusion, I have boiled down my findings into seven characteristics of divine justice. This list of seven is not exhaustive, of course. But these characteristics condense what the Bible most emphasizes about God's justice, the kind of justice that comes from God's very character.

Justice as Nonviolence

First, in the biblical texts, justice is often opposed to violence. In Isaiah 5:7, God "expected justice [from Israel], but saw bloodshed" instead (NRSV). Isaiah 59:3–4 begins with the violent, wicked actions of the people, stating that "your hands are defiled with blood, and your fingers with iniquity; your lips have spoken lies, your tongue utters wickedness. No one brings suit justly, no one goes to law honestly" (NRSV). Because of these unjust, violent actions "justice is far from [them]" (59:9). If we compare that passage to Isaiah 16:4–5, it indicates that once oppression and violence are gone, justice is established. From these verses we see that justice and violence have nothing in common. In other words, where there's violence, justice is absent. We may even be able to say that justice and violence stand as opposites so that one cancels out the other. The absence of justice in acts of violence begs this question: If justice is not present in violence, how then can we conceive of a God who executes justice through violence, especially the eternal violence of hell as we have traditionally thought it?

Justice as Righteousness

Second, justice almost always has a parallel relationship to righteousness; when we see justice, we also see righteousness, both expressed in the form of action. Proverbs 8:20 tells us how these two actions work together: "I walk in the way of righteousness, along the paths of justice" (NRSV). Justice, like righteousness, is a way or a path. The word "way" or "path" in the ancient Middle Eastern culture (the culture the Bible comes from) speaks of a collection of right actions, an active *doing*, a certain way of walking through life. In Hebrew the word "righteous" actually means "a collection of right actions," again implying *doing* rather than just an abstract condition of the heart and mind. Often the words "righteousness" and "justice" are paired with the Hebrew verb *'asah*, meaning "to do," indicating that both justice and righteousness are action words: we *do* justice and we *do* righteousness. In other words, justice and righteousness in the Bible don't point to a state of being, something we *are*; they point out something we *do*, actions we take as we live our lives.

Isaiah 56:1 gives us God's take on this parallelism: "Thus says the LORD: Maintain justice, and do what is right, for soon my salvation will come, and my deliverance be revealed" (NRSV). Maintaining justice and doing what is right also brings divine salvation and deliverance, quite an important connection to God's redemptive action in the world.

So we see that justice and righteousness in the Bible are not abstract ideas that remain hidden in the heavenly places, hoped for and prayed for but never quite arriving. They happen because specific actions make them happen. For example, justice and righteousness acted out, according to Scripture, include loving compassion for others, taking care of the oppressed, the poor, the outcast, and the enemy. God's righteousness, God's carrying out right actions, is an extension of God's justice, which does not include violence, but instead indicates a loving compassion even for the enemy.

Justice as Mercy

Third, justice is expressed through acts of mercy. Justice and mercy appear in parallel in the well-known verse Micah 6:8: "What does the LORD require of you but to do justice, and to love kindness [mercy], and to walk humbly with your God?" "Justice" and "mercy" are also often paired with the verb that means "to do." In another passage, the words of God come to Zechariah, again coupling the actions of justice and mercy, by exhorting Zechariah to "render true judgments, show kindness and mercy to one another" (7:9 NRSV). In the next verse the text explains how true judgment or justice is to be accomplished through merciful actions: "do not oppress the widow, the orphan, the alien, or the poor; and do not devise evil in your hearts against one another" (NRSV).

We see then that mercy describes the nature of justice. As such, it includes maintaining the cause of the needy (Ps. 140:12; Ezek. 34:16), giving food to the hungry (Ps. 146:7), rescuing the oppressed (Isa. 1:17; Jer. 22:3), and peacemaking (Isa. 42:1–4; Jer. 22:3). In these verses and in others, mercy and justice complement each other so that in doing mercy, we also do justice. In other words, justice stimulates mercy, and mercy serves and establishes justice.

Justice as Redemptive

Fourth, doing justice is redemptive. Isaiah 1:27 asserts that "Zion shall be redeemed by justice" (NRSV). In another text, the psalmist begs for deliverance and redemption according to God's justice (Ps. 119:153–56). God also promises Jeremiah that the day will come when God will *do* justice and redeem the people (Jer. 23:5–6; 33:15). Isaiah makes the connection between justice and redemption, implying that no justice equals no redemption. He says, "We wait for justice, but there is none; for salvation, but it is far from us" (59:11 NRSV). Consequently, it appears that redemption is the result of doing justice. To redeem, therefore, is to *do* justice.

In addition, the biblical text uses the imagery of flowing streams of fresh water to describe justice (Amos 5:24). Water is a rare and precious commodity in the communities of the Middle East. Particularly rare, almost nonexistent, are streams that continually flow through the arid land. Water imparts life and ensures that it will continue: no water, no life. Justice, like water, is pro-life! Water, especially in the imagery of Amos as a perennial, ever-flowing stream, restores dry ground and parched throats to life, satisfying the longing of the land and of the thirsty inhabitants. In other words, the imagery of justice as a stream continually flowing over the land imposes upon us a beautiful picture of something redemptive, restorative, and life-giving that satisfies the longing of those in need. God's justice, therefore, acts like a stream that flows continually, repeating over and over again redemptive life-giving activity, a repetition of justice flowing along like water over the land.

Justice as a Great Light

Fifth, justice is seen as a great light that drives away the blindness imposed by darkness. Isaiah perceptively expresses this metaphor:

> Therefore justice is far from us,
>   and righteousness does not reach us;
> we wait for light, and lo! there is darkness;
>   and for brightness, but we walk in gloom.
> We grope like the blind along a wall,
>   groping like those who have no eyes;
> we stumble at noon as in the twilight,
>   among the vigorous as though we were dead. . . .
> We wait for justice, but there is none;
>   for salvation, but it is far from us.
>   (Isa 59:9–11 NRSV)

As we can see, without justice, darkness prevails, and we grope around as blind people, separated from the light of divine justice. From a divine point of view, injustice is blind to the path of justice. God's justice heals that blindness and penetrates the darkness with sight.

With that knowledge in mind, think about this: the image of justice expressed in the structures of our government and civil judicial systems is portrayed by an unseeing, blindfolded woman. In this case, the human concept of justice is blind, not sighted; it is represented by darkness, not light. If the *biblical* notion of justice coincides with righteousness and with seeing a divine light, implying that injustice is blind, could it be that the human notion of justice represented as blind is actually injustice in God's eyes? Do the empires of the world have their eyes blindfolded to justice so that injustice, under the guise of justice, reigns? As retributive and punitive, blindfolded human justice exacted by the world's governments does not appear to offer redemption or restoration. But God's justice, on the other hand, does.

Justice as Satisfaction

Sixth, divine justice satisfies God. Proverbs 21:3 actually gives expression to this statement: "To do righteousness and justice is more *acceptable* to the LORD than sacrifice" (NRSV, emphasis added). The passage then proceeds to explain what justice and righteousness look like in practice. Doing righteousness and justice are acceptable and—dare we say?—satisfying to God, more satisfying than the Hebrews' blood sacrifices offered on the altar. The words of God spoken in Jeremiah 9:24 shed more light on justice that satisfies God, who says, "I act with steadfast love, justice, and righteousness in the earth, for in these things I *delight*" (NRSV, emphasis added). In other words, God is delighted or (we can say) satisfied by love, justice, and righteousness worked out practically on earth. Matthew, quoting Isaiah, provides us with further insight into the antiviolent, restorative nature of the justice that satisfies God. Talking about Jesus he says:

> Here is my servant, whom I have chosen,
>   my beloved, with whom my soul is well *pleased*.
> I will put my spirit upon him,
>   and he will proclaim justice to the Gentiles.
> He will not wrangle or cry aloud,
>   nor will anyone hear his voice in the streets.
> He will not break a bruised reed
>   or quench a smoldering wick
> until he brings justice to victory.
>   (Isa. 42:1–3 as quoted in Matt. 12:18–20
>   NRSV, emphasis added)

In this passage, the Spirit of God empowers Jesus to proclaim divine justice, not through offensive hollering and yelling in the streets or through coercive force, but through nonviolent, nonretributive actions. As a result, God is pleased, or satisfied, with Jesus and his actions that bring justice to victory by peaceably, without retribution, restoring us to God. God was displeased, unsatisfied, therefore, that justice could not be found in the land. We can conclude from these passages that restorative justice forged through Christ's actions during his life, death, and resurrection satisfied God.

Justice as Seen in Jesus

Seventh, the justice as expressed in the biblical texts resonates with the justice that Jesus preached and modeled for us. Jesus and the redemption and restoration brought to us through his acts of justice and righteousness appear as a light shining in the darkness. Forgiving enemies, breaking down boundaries between Jew and Greek, slave and free, male and female—all reveal divine justice at work in Jesus Christ. Seeing it as nonviolent, as *doing* righteousness and mercy, as redemptive and restorative, reveals justice in a new light—a redemptive light that breaks through the darkness of violence and oppression, retribution and vengeance.

Interpreting divine justice through the lens of Jesus, his life, teachings, death, and resurrection, challenges retribution and paints a picture of justice that reconciles and restores people to God and to others. For instance, Jesus specifically rejects retributive justice in Matthew 5: he instructs us to turn the other cheek, to go the extra mile, and to love our enemies. In fact, if we take the exhortation to love our enemies (5:43–48) in context, we see that to be holy just as God is holy *is* to love our enemies! Jesus always seems to "err" on the side of grace, serving justice not by exacting retribution or tit-for-tat exchanges, but by sacrificing the exchange, the payment in kind, in order to reveal a different kind of justice that gives freely out of love. In proclaiming the kingdom of God, Jesus preached justice. He revealed to us his distrust of the religious power of the scribes and Pharisees, exerting all of his energies, his entire life, death, and resurrection, into remedying social injustice, into standing on the side of justice by standing on the side of the marginalized, the widow, the orphan, the diseased, and the social outcast.

In other words, Jesus gives us a picture of God's justice as restorative rather than retributive. The God of Jesus does not demand the proverbial eye-for-an-eye form of justice. Instead of strengthening the bars that hold us captive to violence and the cycle of retributive justice, God opens the way for peace and restoration through unlimited, boundless divine love, forgiveness, and reconciliation.

Summing Up the Seven

Let's summarize the study on justice so far. We have seen that the Bible characterizes justice in these ways:

1. To do justice means to bring peace, not violence.
2. To do justice means to do righteous acts.
3. To do justice means to be merciful.
4. To do justice means to redeem.
5. To do justice means to expose the darkness to light, to remove the blindfold in favor of sight.
6. To do justice means to satisfy and please God.
7. To do justice means to live the way Jesus lived and taught.

When Lisa saw these seven characteristics of biblical justice, she said, "I don't see hell as nonviolent, righteous, merciful, redemptive, exposing darkness to God's light, or satisfying to God. If God is love, then even in the end justice must be all those things. Can't we harmonize God's love with God's justice so that even hell is just?" Good question. I am not sure we can harmonize the retributive form of justice inherent in hell with the restorative nature of God's love.

LOVE AND JUSTICE IN HARMONY

Our typical image of God as loving on the one hand and retributive on the other puts justice and love in tension as opposites. We have a God with a split personality. In one instance, God demands retribution for sin; in the next, we see God showing mercy and forgiving sin. But when we read and interpret the Bible from the perspective of divine love (and through our Jesus lens), we see that the standards of justice are driven by a desire for restoration, relationship, and harmony with God and others. In other words, divine reconciling justice is love in action that seeks to make things right, to reconcile with God and others.

In the Bible

The Bible supports the connection of love to justice in many passages, many of which we've already discussed. A couple of passages in particular come to mind, however, in our attempt to harmonize justice and love. Leviticus 19:17–18 exhorts the faithful to love their neighbors by forgoing vengeance and bearing grudges and to forgive them instead. In Deuteronomy 10:18, God serves justice by loving the alien. In a profoundly beautiful passage (Isa. 30:18), God waits on high, longingly, lovingly, and like a spurned lover, aching to shower graciousness upon us—*because God is a God of justice.* The justice of God takes place as an event of hospitality shown to the stranger, as love offered freely without expectation of return, as forgiveness shown even to those who do not deserve it, as the transformation of lives that experience the healing touch of God.

In the New Testament we see evidence of a movement away from the pursuit of retribution, vengeance, and retaliation. Instead, we see a movement toward a pursuit of forgiveness, restoration of relationship, and new life together in the community of God. In the words of Paul: "In Christ God was reconciling the world to himself, *not counting their trespasses against them*" (2 Cor. 5:19 NRSV, emphasis added). If we combine the Old Testament portrait of divine justice with the actions of Jesus, who reveals God to us, we have a more-complete picture of God's justice at work to forgive and to redeem, to repair and to restore.

Through the actions of Jesus during his lifetime and in his passion, we gain an understanding of the divine response to retributive violence and conceptions of human justice. Rather than shouting threats of retaliation in the name of God, Jesus set in motion the ultimate expression of divine justice and its restorative character by asking God to forgive us in a moment that may instead have provoked vengeance and retribution. As revealed in the Christ event, the process of forgiveness, reconciliation, and restoration without retaliation demonstrates the deepest, most profound level of justice—to love and therefore to forgive.

In the Tradition

Medieval theologian Peter Abelard speaks of justice in harmony with mercy and with love. He says that "justified [forgiven] for free means that you are justified, not because of your outstanding achievements or gains, but thanks to God's mercy who was the first to love us." And "In the time of mercy it is God's justice that he gives us and through which we are justified, and the name for it is love." For Abelard, the justice of God, through love and in mercy, results in the forgiveness of sin without condition.

In his book *What Saint Paul Really Said,* Professor N. T. Wright rightly professes that "God's love is the driving force of [God's] justice" (110). In *God and Empire,* John Dominic Crossan, another well-known biblical scholar, uses the analogy of the body to explain the relationship of love to justice: "Justice is the body of love, love the soul of justice. Justice is the flesh and love, love is the spirit of justice. When they are separated, we have a moral corpse. Justice without love is brutality."

A painting in the courtroom of the Pennsylvania State Capitol Building illustrates for us an image that will help us to understand and to reinterpret it in a manner that brings us more closely in touch with the reality of divine justice as loving justice. The painting *Divine Law*, by Violet Oakley, does not depict a scale of balances held by a blindfolded woman, which typically represents justice, but instead presents us with a musical scale played by a celestial harpist. An *L* adorns the left edge of the painting, with the letters LOVE running down the vertical leg of the *L*. The middle of the painting portrays an *A* above a *W*, spelling out the word LAW. This symbolizes the artist's representation of the divine harmony between LOVE and LAW, both working together for the good and peace of all people. Consequently, in a room where justice is served hangs a painting suggesting a form of justice that expresses the purpose of the law: to mediate justice in love and thus to fulfill the law. Violet Oakley's portrayal of justice as a musical scale plays not a dirge but a doxology of justice tempered with love, and served through mercy. Rather than a blindfolded justice, one that does not see, Oakley presents us with a concept of justice that has its eyes wide open, that sees the offenses through the eyes of love and mercy. The justice of love, revealed by the law of love, seeks to overcome condemnation with mercy; after all, mercy triumphs over judgment. So as we look at God through the eyes of love *and* justice as harmonious, working together to redeem creation, the problems of God as a split personality disappear.

AN EXAMPLE OF THE HARMONY
BETWEEN JUSTICE AND LOVE

Doesn't it seem to you that restorative rather than retributive justice is more effective and complete? Take, by way of illustration, an event in the life of Peter the Great (died 1725). In an attempt to squelch the Streltsy revolt, many men and women who betrayed the Tsar were imprisoned and tortured in order to exact a confession of guilt and bring forth repentance. After suffering horrendous pain through the infliction of various tortures, one such prisoner still remained silent. No amount of punishment or pain drew a confession from him. In fact, the torture seemed to harden his resolve to keep silent. Having heard of the prisoner's cold determination, Peter released him from torture, embraced the man, kissed him, and promised that he would not only pardon him, but would also make him a colonel in the Tsar's army. Robert Massie, Peter's biographer, writes that "this unorthodox approach so unnerved and moved the prisoner that he took the Tsar in his arms and said, 'For me, this is the greatest torture of all. There is no other way you could have made me speak.'" The prisoner confessed all and repented. As promised beforehand, he was pardoned and admitted into Peter's army as a colonel, serving Peter faithfully for the remainder of his days.

Brought face-to-face with unexpected love and grace, the man realized the full extent of his betrayal. He repented and was restored to the Tsar. In the face of such love, remorse for his betrayal took the place of his hardened heart. The man suffered great pain for his sin, not from the pain of punishment, but from the realization of the magnitude of his sin. When confronted with the extravagance of love (not punishment), the prisoner saw the depth of his wrongdoing against the Tsar and repented. Justice in harmony with love brought about redemption and restoration where punishment could not. Was justice served? I think yes.

Peter's act of mercy that resulted in the restoration of relationship may have something in common with God's form of justice. Unselfish love seeks to redeem and restore; punishment (typically conceived as justice) seeks revenge and retribution. In order for divine justice to work in harmony with divine love, mercy, and forgiveness, shouldn't it be redemptive and restorative at the same time? How does eternal damnation, burning forever in unquenchable fire, redeem and restore? Is it possible that divine justice *is* the path of mercy and forgiveness?

I hear Brooke's voice in my head saying, "But he gets to walk away, and that's it?" No, justice does not mean "getting let off the hook," or "getting away with murder" (or worse). It means coming face-to-face with the shameful depravity of personal sin by coming face-to-face with the one who has the right and the power to punish but who instead loves and forgives. Love and forgiveness instead of anger and punishment bring repentance and redemption, and in this manner, justice is served.

We'll talk more about the justice of love in chapter 9. I'll even give you an illustration to clarify the point. But for now, we see that divine justice harmonizes with a love that seeks to restore a relationship in spite of an offense. Justice and love work together with one purpose, to reconcile us to God. If justice and love coexist in harmonious, mutual relationship; if to love means to do justice, the kind of justice that reconciles and restores; then "judgment," a word closely connected with justice, must also include reconciliation and restoration. With divine restorative justice in mind, we can move toward the next step in constructing an alternative view of hell: divine forgiveness.

8

Rethinking the Forgiveness of God

Love those by whom you have been hurt.
> —Dante, *Purgatorio*, Canto 13

The weak can never forgive.
Forgiveness is the attribute of the strong.
> —Mahatma Gandhi

The retribution for an injury is an equal injury,
but those who forgive the injury and make reconciliation
will be rewarded by God.
> —The Qur'an 42.40

For you, Lord, are good and ready to forgive.
> —Psalm 86:5

After our discussion about the last chapter, Lisa agreed that divine restorative justice lines up more consistently with the sayings of the prophets and with the life, teachings, and work of Jesus. "If Jesus reveals God to us, then God's primary sense of justice must be restorative. God's goal to redeem us shows us that restorative justice is God's MO [modus operandi, or mode of operating]. But what does God do? Just forgive and forget? Doesn't forgiveness require something on our part, like punishment first or repentance first? God can't just up and forgive without recompense or payment first."

Brooke, on the other hand, was uncomfortable with the thought that God's couldn't or wouldn't forgive without some sort of payback first. She loved the thought of God forgiving freely, as part and parcel of restorative justice. So let's look at the nature of forgiveness and at what the Bible says about it before we go any further into the discussion.

WHAT IS FORGIVENESS?

If biblical justice seeks to make things right, to reconcile and then to restore relationships, forgiveness works *with* justice to move us toward that goal. Without forgiveness, we couldn't reconcile with God and enjoy a restored relationship. Sin stands between us, hinders our relationship, and keeps us apart. So if the goal of justice is to reconcile and restore a relationship—ours with God, in this case—forgiveness of sin becomes essential. But what does forgiveness entail exactly?

The Jewish notion of sin gives us a picture of shackles, something that binds us, that paralyzes us, that demands punishment through payback, and that locks us up in bondage to a debt. Forgiveness of sin, therefore, is the opposite of retribution. It means to "release," "to break the shackles of sin," much like a crippled person is healed and released from illness. When Jesus told the crippled man lowered through the roof that his sins were forgiven, he meant that he was healthy again, not crippled, not held down or impaired with the shackles that locked him up in his handicap. When Jesus said, "Your sins are forgiven" (Mark 2:5), the gates to his paralytic prison were unlocked. Because the text leads us to believe that his illness was due to sin, we could consider his paralysis retribution for that sin. When Jesus forgave him, he was released from the bondage of sin and the burden of suffering. He could walk in God's forgiving justice. The paralytic did not ask Jesus to forgive him; he didn't receive twenty lashes before Jesus forgave him; he didn't do anything other than receive forgiveness and walk away. In the same way, through forgiveness, God releases us from the endless rhythm of suffering a tit for a tat.

In English, the word "forgive" means "to give away," "to release" something we have on someone else. In serving *retributive* justice, the offense would be held on to tightly, not forgiven unless and until the offender balanced the accounts through payback of some kind. In that case, there would be nothing to give away, nothing to release, nothing to forgive; the debt incurred by the offense would have been paid. Instead, we give away the debt by forgiving it; we release someone from the debt that we have a right to collect. We sacrifice the balancing of accounts for the sake of the relationship. Jesus was just such a forgiver and healer of bodies and souls. By his potent form of forgiving, by giving away the debt of sin, by not collecting the payment, he shocked and scandalized those intent on payback, who did not want to let sinners take a walk.

THE BIBLICAL SUPPORT OF FORGIVENESS

We see a beautiful example of forgiveness freely given, without payment or punishment, in the story of Jesus and the woman caught in adultery (John 8:1–11). As she stands before the religious rulers awaiting her sentence, she must know that she is doomed. Everyone knows what happens to an adulterer—death by stoning. Before the scribes and Pharisees can condemn her, Jesus speaks up: "[Whoever] is without sin among you, let him be the first to throw stone at her," he says (8:7 NIV). Even the Pharisees are not without sin; so no one steps up to cast the first stone, which would set in motion a whole volley of stones from the crowd. After everyone else has sidled away from the scene, Jesus tells the woman that he will not demand that she suffer punishment. Instead, we are led to believe that she walks away, free and forgiven. Jesus did not say to her, "You must suffer your punishment before I can forgive you," or "Let me throw the first stone, and then God will forgive you." He simply forgives her and tells her to live in that forgiveness by sinning no more. Because of this, she no longer stands condemned, and the possibility exists that she can reconcile with her community, restore injured relationships, and live in peace.

John the evangelist and Paul the apostle support the idea that God forgives without condition, without our making things right first. John asserts that God first loved and then forgave (1 John 4:9–10; John 3:16). According to Paul, love motivated God to forgive humankind even while we were still enemies—quite a deconstruction of retributive justice (Rom. 5:8, 10). Love unleashed fosters forgiveness, and forgiveness looses us from slavery to sin and sets us free to enter into relationship with God.

The biblical message pinpoints forgiveness of sin as the way to enter into the kingdom of heaven. For instance, in the Old Testament, deeply influenced by the conception of a God impassioned with loving-kindness, who is always ready and willing to forgive, and who delights in mercy, the Hebrew people testify to the extravagance of divine forgiveness. The pages of the book of Psalms practically drip with the tears of those who freely beseech God for forgiveness; and they receive it. Isaiah, Jeremiah, Amos, and Hosea sing the praises of a God who is slow to anger and abounding in loving-kindness, whose mercies are new every morning, who generously forgives transgressions and redeems the undeserving. The New Testament as well testifies to the centrality of forgiveness, giving us a glimpse into the lives of Zacchaeus, the woman at the well, the paralytic lowered through the roof, the woman caught in adultery—freely given forgiveness, all in opposition to the legalistic interpretation of the law that freely rendered retribution. Throughout his ministry, and even as he hangs on the cross, Jesus looses human beings from the bondage of sin and with forgiveness opens up the gates to heaven to all peoples and nations.

The words of Jesus from the cross provide a clue to the importance of forgiveness. Struggling in the throes of death, he utters a brief prayer to God: "Father, forgive them, for they do not know what they are doing" (Luke 23:34). Then to the thief on cross next to him, he scandalizes righteous eavesdroppers by saying, "Truly I say to you, today you shall be with Me in Paradise" (23:43). The thief experiences the closing of the door on earthly existence while at the same time, through love and forgiveness, Jesus opens the door leading to life with God. In the teaching of Jesus, we are exhorted, through forgiveness, to break the cycle of retribution, an eye for an eye, of getting even. We are to dismiss our debtors by forgiving those who offend us, by releasing them from any requirement to right the wrong or from the threat of punishment.

Jesus does not ask us to forgive unconditionally only one time. He multiplies forgiveness in an unending cycle, asking us repeatedly to forgive seventy times seven, which literally means over and over again, without calculation or limit. In these instances and others, Jesus breaks into human history and with forgiveness brings the kingdom of God from heaven to earth. Forgiveness unlocks and opens, it unbinds and loosens. Forgiveness liberates us from the prison of an otherwise irreversible past and transforms the future from one of condemnation and retribution to an open future of redemption and reconciliation.

THE RESULTS OF FORGIVENESS

Repentance

Nonretaliatory forgiveness may have profound consequences for the one released from sin with such sacrificial abandon. As in the case of Zacchaeus, genuine forgiveness often leads to repentance that proves just as costly. When a person is brought face-to-face with his or her sins and experiences the unexpected grace of forgiveness rather than the expected retributive punishment, real repentance may occur. In his book *Violence Unveiled*, theologian Gil Bailie writes, "Jesus seems to have understood that the only real and lasting contrition occurs, not when one is confronted with one's sin, but when one experiences the gust of grace that makes a loving and forgiving God plausible" (208–9). Forgiveness wins a person over through the love inherent in the act. It elicits the good from deep within the person who expects and deserves retribution, but receives redemption through forgiveness instead. Forgiveness calls to the offender with love, summoning the offender to take responsibility for the offense and to repent. Forgiveness doesn't come *after* repentance; it *leads to* repentance.

Repairing the Past

Forgiveness leading to repentance also repairs the past. It turns us around and opens us up to what is called *metanoia*, a thinking back, a change of mind, often translated "repentance." Forgiveness requires that we change our minds about demanding retributive justice, that we give up the offense and its restitution. The unlocking of *metanoia* transforms offense into healing. We relinquish the power of retribution with the power of forgiveness. Consequently, in order to forgive, we must contemplate the past with a desire to transform it, change our minds, unlock the door keeping guard over our grudge and let the offense go, release the offender from the prison of retained injury, forgive him, in the same way we also want to be released from debt and forgiven.

Forgiveness does not annul the past or condone a sin. Instead, it transforms and heals the past. If God were merely to annul the sin of the past, then the offender would be innocent. God would also annul the need for forgiveness for there would not be anything left to forgive. Consequently, the sin must be left standing, not forgotten completely, not dismissed or wiped away, but under erasure, becoming an offense without offense, so to speak. Forgiveness does not revise history so that the sin never occurred, but it steals the power from the *past itself*, releases us, unlocks the gates of the prison of the past so that the weight of the past is lifted. By forgiving, we repair the past by giving it a new meaning and by giving the offender a new beginning.

As a result, the sinner who receives forgiveness, whose past has been repaired, and who has received new life, is open to the possibility of *metanoia* himself, of changing his mind, of receiving a new heart. As forgiven sinners, our pasts are given a new interpretation, one that includes love and reconciliation within its realm. So we see that the past and the event of the sin are not completely forgotten: we still remember, but for a purpose. In remembering the sin, we remember its cleansing through forgiveness so that both the sin and its forgiveness are remembered simultaneously. Just as in great works of art one may detect the artist's errors and subsequent corrections by the faint traces of lines that have been "erased" (interestingly named pentimenti, or "repentances"), forgiveness of the sin "erases" the errors and covers them with new color, giving vibrancy, new life, and hope for a future of reconciled and restored relationships.

Transforming the Future

Forgiveness doesn't just repair the past; it also transforms the future. It prepares our hearts and minds for a better way into the future. Forgiveness redeems the past and makes possible a hopeful future. In his foreword to the book *Exploring Forgiveness*, Desmond Tutu writes that "without forgiveness, there is no future" (xiii). Forgiveness acts as a catalyst for reconciliation and renewal of a relationship with God and others, which generates hope for a new, transformed future. Through forgiveness the Spirit of God seeks to transform sinners into saints and saints into service for the furtherance of the kingdom, so that unconditional love and forgiveness effectively operate outside the vicious economic circles of retributive "justice."

Unconditional forgiveness that freely releases the offender from sin rather than retributive forgiveness that makes the offender pay his just deserts first is what philosopher John Caputo calls a "mad economy" of the kingdom of God. This kingdom economy is really no economy, but instead is good news, the good news of forgiveness without return, with no conditions attached, of reconciliation, renewal, transformation, and loving service in the name of Jesus. Such is the gift of God, the kingdom of God, the mad economy of forgiveness, justice, and love that seek to reconcile all creation to God.

Paul attests to the madness of God's forgiveness when he writes that in Christ "we have redemption, the forgiveness of sins" (Col. 1:14), and "that God was in Christ reconciling the world to Himself, not counting their trespasses against them" (2 Cor. 5:19). How did God reconcile the world to God's self? By not counting our sins against us. In a display of divine reconciling justice, God forgives us— God just up and forgives us as a gift that we only need to open. In *The Lost Message of Jesus*, Chalke and Mann say it well: "When it comes to the God of the Bible, there is only one kind of sin in the world—forgiven sin" (109).

FORGIVENESS AND OUR RESPONSE

"Wait a minute here!" Lisa interjected during another one of our phone conversations. "If God forgives with total abandon, without payback, with no strings attached, then we don't even need a hell. That's just not scriptural!"

When I told Brooke about Lisa's objection to God's no-strings-attached policy on forgiveness, she burst out with "Oh darn! I just knew something would spoil the beauty of forgiveness if we thought very hard about it. Can we have forgiveness and accountability for sin too?"

Eric, glad that those who have never heard of Jesus might stand a chance at heaven after all, wondered if we could somehow hold on to unconditional forgiveness, the kind that we've talked about, and still look for a response from those whom God forgives.

Even though all three of our conversation partners worded their questions differently, they really wanted to explore the same issue: does God desire, require, or hope for a response to God's freely given forgiveness? The answer in short form: yes, but God's forgiveness is not contingent upon our response.

Let's look again at the verse we talked about above, 2 Corinthians 5:19. The repetition helps us to remember. "God was in Christ *reconciling* the world to himself" (emphasis added). Before this we concentrated on the *forgiveness* aspect of this verse. Now let's concentrate on the *reconciling* piece. This important verse tells us that God did not count our trespasses or sins against us. Hence, God forgave us our sins. Why? Well, in order to reconcile us to God! Although God forgave us freely, it seems as though God forgave in hopes of reconciling with us.

"Oh, I see," Lisa added, "there are two steps involved here. One, God forgives. Two, we acknowledge that forgiveness, repent, and reconcile with God."

Right. God forgives everyone's sin through the life, death, and resurrection of Jesus—everyone's. Even those who don't know Jesus and won't on this side of heaven (or hell). The work of Jesus was so complete and so entirely effective that God forgave it all: the sins of every person who ever lived, lives now, and ever will live. *But . . .* in order for true restoration to take place, before we can step into God's kingdom, we must choose to receive that forgiveness and reconcile with God through Jesus (we'll discuss the "through Jesus" part in a later chapter).

"Okay, good. I get it," Lisa said happily. "But let's talk just a bit about reconciliation. What is it, and how does it work? And what is its relationship to justice?"

Great questions. So let's delve just a little into the heart of reconciliation, especially how it serves justice and connects us to God.

FORGIVENESS AND RESTORATIVE JUSTICE

Restorative justice draws upon forgiveness and grows out of the notion that God is reconciling the world to God's self. The very character of the Christian faith is forgiveness, which opens up the possibility of reconciliation leading to restoration. Accordingly, the character of divine justice must also be reconciling and restorative—an idea supported by the biblical witness. For instance, the law seems more concerned with reconciling or restorative issues rather than with retributive justice. Moreover, we understand the meaning of justice in the Old Testament by contemplating God's repeated deliverance of the people from oppression and God's continual attempts to reconcile and restore the covenant relationship. Over and over again, God seeks to reconcile with offenders with undeserved love, forgiveness, and mercy, in spite of their actions. We may even say that the most important ingredient of God's justice is in rescuing, reconciling, and restoring, and that reconciling justice forms the cornerstone of God's hopes and intentions for the world.

The prophet Isaiah speaks of divine reconciling justice and the peace it fosters, proclaiming that "justice will dwell in the wilderness, and righteousness abide in the fruitful field. The effect of righteousness will be peace, and the result of righteousness, quietness and trust forever" (Isa. 32:16–20 NRSV). The prophet Amos reveals God's ultimately redemptive purpose and points out that the people and their nations benefit by living according to God's reconciling justice, because such justice brings peace (5:14–15, 24; 9:14–15).

Reconciling rather than retributive justice is also a major theme in the New Testament (e.g., Luke 1:68–79; 2:29–32). New Testament writers do not focus on retributive justice, but on a justice that redeems. In Western terms, justice is closely tied to the civil arena of lawmaking and penalties for lawbreaking; but New Testament justice goes beyond the legal sphere into the realm of reconciliation. We see a movement away from the pursuit of retributive justice toward the pursuit of reconciliation that leads to restoration.

As we discussed earlier, Jesus implies this movement during his visit to the synagogue in Luke 4:16–20. He reads from Isaiah 61:1–2 saying, "The Spirit of the Lord is upon me, because he has anointed me to bring good news to the poor. He has sent me to proclaim release to the captives, and recovery of sight to the blind, to let the oppressed go free, to proclaim the year of the Lord's favor" (NRSV). And remember, he closed the book without finishing the rest of the Isaiah passage, which continues, "and the day of vengeance of our God." As you know, his omission of vengeance acts as a rejection of retributive justice and an acceptance of his commission to bring about the justice of reconciliation and restoration.

Romans describes reconciling justice by stating, "God proves his love for us in that while we were still sinners Christ died for us. . . . While we were enemies, we were reconciled to God" (5:8, 10 NRSV). God's love triggers God's forgiveness through the sacrificial death of Jesus, which then paves the way for God's reconciliation. In addition, the book of Colossians discloses the spirit of divine justice as well. Beginning in the first chapter, God works through Jesus to deliver people from evil and to reconcile them to God and to each other. The life, death, and resurrection of Jesus result in radical reconciliation between normally estranged or segregated groups of people, first between God and human beings, then between Jews and Gentiles, slaves and free persons, male and female (Col. 3:11). As it appears in Colossians, divine justice reconciles and restores. It delivers us from the domain of darkness (1:13); it forgives us and redeems us from sin (1:14); God's reconciling justice unifies us in the perfect bond of peace (3:14); and it knits "hearts . . . together in love" (2:2)—good news to be sure!

Reconciling justice is also transformational justice. It pierces the darkness of retributive violence with the grace of God and the message of peace through love, forgiveness, and reconciliation. To do justice is to love; to do justice is to forgive; to do justice is to reconcile; this is a chain reaction in which love forgives, forgiveness reconciles, and reconciliation restores—all characteristics of divine justice, God's reconciling justice.

God calls us to serve this form of justice through forgiving others. Without forgiveness, reconciliation would not be possible; and without reconciliation, no one could enter into a restored relationship with God. Reconciliation opens the way and makes possible the redemption of our past and the restoration of our future as we enter forever into the loving presence of God. "To reconcile" means "to make peace between enemies." Romans 5:10 confirms this definition, stating that "while we were still enemies, we were reconciled to God through the death of his Son" (NRSV).

I believe we may safely say that reconciliation is the purpose of God in salvation history. The repetitive appeal in the Gospels for us to repent of our sin and to forgive others their sin emphasizes the importance of reconciliation. We repent in order to reconcile with God, and we forgive in order to reconcile with others.

Our worship of God takes second place to reconciling with a brother or sister. Matthew tells his readers that if they are worshiping at the altar of God and remember that they aren't reconciled with someone, they are to stop worshiping at the altar for the moment, leave the altar, and *first* go and reconcile with that person (Matt. 5:23–24). Paul also talks about the vital importance of reconciliation, declaring that the ministry of Jesus and now our ministry as ambassadors of Christ is to appeal for reconciliation (2 Cor. 5:18–21). It epitomizes the crux of the entire gospel message, the goal of the life, death, and resurrection of Jesus, and the purpose of our participation in the kingdom of God. Through Jesus and now through his body the church, the voice of the Spirit calls all persons to be reconciled to God, to work as ambassadors of Christ, ministers of reconciliation, entreating others to be reconciled to God as well. Reconciliation releases us from death to life, from revenge to restoration.

FORGIVING OTHERS AS GOD HAS FORGIVEN US .

During a telephone conversation, Lisa wondered about what she had always been taught concerning forgiveness. "The idea that we need to repent before God will forgive is so ingrained into my theology," she said. "Where did we get these notions? And how has our tradition been able to make them stick for so many centuries? We torment people with guilt over it! Yet at the same time, we have Bible verses like Matthew 6:14–15, which tells us that if we don't forgive others of their sin, God will not forgive us. Isn't that conditional rather than unconditional forgiveness?"

Although we can't really pinpoint for certain how our theories of forgiveness have developed, we can assume that cultural norms, Scripture, and various church traditions had something to do with it. A number of Bible verses, if interpreted through the lens of a tit-for-tat type of forgiveness (and remember that much of our society is based upon these kind of retributive ideas), lead us to believe that God will not *just* forgive sin without some action on our part. For instance, making amends, forgiving others, repenting, or serving some sort of penance as a prior condition complicates forgiveness and makes it an economic exchange. But there are other ways to look at it. Let's discuss the passages in Matthew 6:14–15 and 18:21–25. The gist of these verses reveals to us that if we don't forgive others, God won't forgive us. Those are serious conditions placed on the promise of forgiveness! How many of us hold unforgiveness in our hearts against someone who has wronged us? Most of us, I'd say! So if we take these passages of Scripture literally, and if we died right now, we'd die outside of God's forgiveness and, therefore, outside the kingdom. In other words, we could possibly end up in hell! Do you believe that? If not, then we need to look for interpretations of those Bible verses consistent with what we know about God and about the work and teachings of Jesus.

In his book *Evil and the Justice of God*, theologian N. T. Wright gives us some help with this passage:

> He is telling us, in effect, that the faculty we have for receiving forgiveness and the faculty we have for granting forgiveness are one and the same thing. If we open the one we shall open the other. God is not being arbitrary. If you are the sort of person who will accuse a neighbor over every small thing and keep him or her under your anger until each item has been dealt with (perhaps by gaining your revenge), then you are also the sort of person who will be incapable of opening your heart to receive God's generous forgiveness. Indeed you will probably not admit that you need it in the first place. (158–59)

Forgiveness not only releases the person being forgiven; it also releases the one doing the forgiving, releases him or her from anger and bitterness and the need for revenge. The clear message here is this: offer genuine forgiveness, and you will be able to receive genuine forgiveness in return.

So we see that forgiveness opens the doors to reconciliation with God and to the restoration of our relationship first with God and then with others. Forgiveness overcomes evil with good. It gets rid of our enemies (and God's) not by destroying them in the eternal fires of hell, but by forgiving them through the eternal love of God found in Jesus Christ. In fact, God's kingdom came to earth through the forgiveness of Jesus: remember his words from the cross, "Father, forgive them." We are to live by that kingdom ethics; the kingdom is made up of those who forgive just as God has forgiven us. After all, if God's will triumphs in the end, forgiveness, reconciliation, and restoration will rule out the need for eternal punishment in hell.

Lisa still hesitated to believe a more liberal (as in liberally or freely given) view of forgiveness. Doubt was obvious in her voice as she said, "Don't get me wrong; I love grace, and without forgiveness I'd be in big trouble. And I don't have any problem with God forgiving people after they have received Jesus as their Savior. But those who die without Jesus, well . . . they die in sin. Period. It's too late, right? The Bible says that 'it is appointed for [people] to die once and after this *comes* judgment'" (Heb. 9:27, emphasis added).

Because of his heart for missions, this idea of reconciling forgiveness sat quite well with Eric. He said, "The Bible does say that people are judged after they die. But can't God forgive sin at the time of judgment? If so, then all those people who haven't heard of Jesus can still be saved!"

THE QUESTION OF FORGIVING SIN AFTER DEATH

Let's look at what the Bible says about God's dealings with sin and go from there. At first glance we see that sin entered the world through human beings. And we see that God immediately sought to liberate us from its grasp. I couldn't find any place in the Bible where God comes down and *destroys* sin with one lightning bolt of divine power. However,

— God *forgives* sin in Exodus 34:7.
— God forgets sin (Jer. 31:34).
— God removes sin (Ps. 103:12).
— God does not deal with us according to our sin (Ps. 103:10).
— God wins the victory over sin by conquering death (1 Cor. 15:54–58).
— God forgives us through Jesus, not counting our sins against us (2 Cor. 5:19–21).
— God takes sin away through Jesus (Matt. 1:21).
— God cleanses us from sin (Ps. 51; 1 John 1:7–9).
— God releases us from sin through Jesus Christ (Rev. 1:5).
— God subjects even enemies to the divine will so that someday every knee will bow and every tongue confess that Jesus Christ is Lord—all to God's glory (1 Cor. 15:24–28; Phil. 2:10–11).

All of these activities of God in the face of sin boil down to the fact that God *destroys* sin, not in one fell swoop with hundreds of thousands of angels perched above with flaming swords, but by *forgiving* sin and opening the door for reconciliation. Think about it; sin came into the world through human beings. We give sin its momentum. Without us, sin would not exist. In order to destroy sin, God must transform the sinner into a saint, into a righteous person. Therefore, God defeats sin only through forgiveness and reconciliation. We can even say that God overcomes evil with good, the good act of forgiveness (Rom. 12:21).

But does the defeat of sin within the person take place only in the temporal realm, within time itself, while we live in this body? Why should it? If we are beings who live on after death, like the Bible seems to say, what makes us think that God limits the bestowing of eternal grace to one time period? Why can't God extend the offer of grace, forgiveness, and reconciliation through Jesus even at judgment—when all will be laid bare, when all persons will see the extent of their sin and the extravagance of God's love? If the effectiveness of Jesus' work on our behalf extends even beyond the grave, that means that no one is ever beyond grace. In part 3, we'll explore this notion further, propose what an alternative view of hell might look like, and discuss what it all means for how we should live our lives today.

PART 3

A New View of Hell

9

The Fire, the Wicked,
and the Redeemed

The ring with the clearest flame
was that which lay least far from the pure spark
because it shares most deeply that point's truth.
My lady . . . said, . . . "Its revolutions are so swift
because of burning love that urges it."

—Dante, *Paradiso*, Canto 28

That at the name of Jesus every knee will bow,
of those who are in heaven
and on earth and under the earth,
and that every tongue will confess
that Jesus Christ is Lord,
to the glory of God the Father.

—Philippians 2:10–11

After studying the nature of God, justice, and forgiveness in Scripture, Eric felt just about ready to give up his traditional ideas of hell. A couple of questions still nagged him, however: "It's just so hard to ditch beliefs we've held for so long, heard preached all of our lives, and that are so different from what all my friends and family believe." Yet he had to admit, "The evidence truly does point to the necessity for an alternative interpretation."

Lisa, although happy at the thought that she possibly need not abandon hope for her grandmother, remained suspicious that this good news seemed a bit too good to be true. "Okay," she said with caution in her voice, "I'm ready for the punch line. . . . I guess. I want to hear it, but I don't want to be swayed by any feel-good doctrines. As much as I hate the old concept and believe it contradicts what the Bible says about God, any new theory of hell has to line up with what the Bible says, too."

At the same time, Brooke, on board and ready to move forward, was anxious to hear the alternative to eternal punishment in the fires of hell.

WHAT WE'VE DISCOVERED SO FAR

In previous chapters, we examined the nature of divine violence, justice, and forgiveness in a new light. The source of that light is Jesus and the teachings of the Bible. We see that God's nature as love manifests itself in the world through peace, reconciling justice, and forgiveness according to God's plan to redeem all creation. We also concluded that our traditional ideas about hell do not harmonize with a God of goodness and love who desires to reconcile with and to restore all people. Now let's think through hell in a new way and in light of what we have learned so far.

Although the image of God as a wrathful, seething, destroying judge, out to put the thumbscrews to all who provoke God's anger, remains prominent in the Christian tradition, we will consider an alternative interpretation of God's judgment. Many theologians connect wrath, and therefore hell, to fire. When Jesus talks about condemnation or punishment in the Bible, he often connects it with fire. Although Jesus is talking in metaphorical or figurative language, which he actually says in John 16, his fiery metaphors point to something real. Any reinterpretation of divine wrath, judgment, and the traditional doctrines of hell, then, should start off by edging closer to the fire, peering over the edge of the flaming abyss, so to speak, to investigate the nature of the fire.

INTO THE FIRE

In the Bible

Let's begin with Scripture. Fire and God are intimately connected in the Bible, as shown in the following texts:

— God is a consuming or devouring fire (Deut. 4:24; Ezek. 1:27; 8:2; Heb. 12:29).
— Fire flows out from God's presence (Dan. 7:10).
— God appears as fire in a burning bush to Moses (Exod. 3:2–3).
— A pillar of fire symbolizes God's presence (Exod. 13:21–22).
— God's tongue, breath, eyes, and mouth are like flames of fire (Isa. 30:27, 33; Rev. 2:18).
— Flames of fire issue from God's nostrils and voice (Deut. 4:36; Isa. 65:5; Jer. 23:29).

— God's glory is a flame of fire (Zech. 2:5).

— Ezekiel sees God as a flashing fire that burns with splendor, like glowing amber (Ezek. 1:4, 13–14).

— Both Daniel and John envision God as sitting on a throne of fire, with a face shining like lightning, with eyes like flaming torches (Dan. 7:9–11; Rev. 1:14–15; 4:5).

— For Malachi, God is the fire that purifies and refines (Mal. 3:2–3; 4:1).

The symbol of fire also expresses God's wrath or judgment, which devours and consumes. In judgment of evil, the fire of God devours and consumes its target. It also reveals and administers God's wrath. To enter into the presence of God and God's wrathful judgment, therefore, in the words of Jesus, is akin to entering into a "fiery furnace." You've heard the old adage, "Where there's smoke, there's fire." Well, we can say, "Where there's God, there's fire!" Fire comes from God, surrounds God, and *is* God.

That said, the fire of God, whether it issues from God or surrounds and envelops God, serves a very significant purpose. Upon further investigation of Scripture, we see that fire burns up whatever is evil, wicked, or sinful. It devours it, consumes it, so that it no longer exists. In Psalms and Isaiah, the fire of God burns and devours wickedness like stubble so that it no longer exists. Fire also cleanses and purifies what remains (Isa. 6:6–7). Numbers 31:23 reveals that everything that can withstand fire shall be passed through fire, and then it shall be clean. When Isaiah came before the throne of God, the seraphim (which, by the way, is the plural form of the Hebrew word for "fire") that continually surround God touched his lips with a live coal so that his sin was blotted out and he was made clean, ready to serve God in ministry (Isa. 6:6). Zechariah prophesies that God will put the wicked "into the fire, and refine them as one refines silver, and test them as gold is tested" (13:9 NRSV). The apostle Peter supports this purifying process in the New Testament when he writes about the testing of our faith through fire (1 Pet. 1:7).

We also see that the fire of God will not burn up whatever is righteous and pure. For instance, Isaiah reminds us in beautiful prose, "When you [righteous people of God] pass through the waters, I will be with you; and through the rivers, they shall not overwhelm you; when you walk through the fire you shall not be burned, and the flame shall not consume you" (43:2 NRSV). Remember that Daniel's friends walked about in a fire that devoured the men who threw them in, but they themselves were unscathed. Why? Because they were righteous before God, and the fire only burns evil, wickedness, and unrighteousness. So they were safe from its destruction: there wasn't anything impure to burn up (Dan. 3:20–27).

Now, we'll turn to the burning bush in Exodus 3:2–3. Moses sees a bush on fire, not an unusual sight in the dry mountainous terrain. Strangely enough, the bush did not burn up. Why wasn't the bush consumed in the fire? Well, because it wasn't evil, wicked, or unrighteous, and therefore the fire did not devour it. You might be wondering why fire burns real bushes and trees and stubble when they have no condition of evil either. Remember, Jesus spoke in figurative language, metaphors, or parables. The pages of the Bible speak of mountains singing, trees clapping their hands, stones shouting out, creation groaning—you get the picture. By using figurative language, these metaphors teach us deep and otherwise complicated truths about God and faith through something familiar to us. So although our metaphors do refer to a reality, we want to use good interpretive skills and not be too literal when speaking figuratively. We will talk more about metaphor in the next chapter.

In a nutshell, we see so far that fire not only surrounds God, but God *is* a consuming fire. Fire symbolizes God's wrath, which we will discuss soon. The fire of God burns up evil and wickedness so that it no longer exists. What remains, if anything, is pure and righteous, like silver, gold, and precious stones (and the blood of Jesus, according to 1 Pet. 1:19). Fire does not consume, devour, or even scorch the pure and the righteous. But what does this have to do with hell?

First Corinthians 3:10–15 provides a clue. This passage reveals that every person builds upon the foundation of Jesus Christ. "Now if any [person] builds on the foundation with gold, silver, precious stones, wood, hay, straw, each [person's] work will become evident; for the day will show it because it is to be revealed with fire; and the fire will test the quality of each [person's] work. If [anyone's] work which he has built upon it remains, he will receive a reward. If any [person's] work is burned up, he will suffer loss; but *he himself will be saved, yet so as through fire*" (emphasis added). Did you catch that? It seems that in the final judgment, *everyone* will go through the fire—through the fire that surrounds God, comes from God, and *is* God. Because fire burns away impurities, any pure works built upon the foundation of Jesus Christ will remain, and the person will receive a reward. The impure works do not survive the fire. The person himself, however, will still be saved, yet only after going through the flames. If God is the devouring fire, then standing in the presence of God is to stand in the fire. Though the passage in 1 Corinthians most likely refers to the judgment of Christians, the Bible talks elsewhere about a similar judgment of unbelievers. We'll talk about the differences between believers and unbelievers in a later chapter. Nevertheless, every person will eventually stand before God, with or without Jesus, to give an account of his or her life (1 Cor. 4:5; 2 Cor. 5:10–11). To stand in God's presence entails standing in the flames. To stand in the flames means burning away chaff, wickedness, and sinfulness.

To give you a clearer picture of what the biblical account of standing in the consuming fire of God's presence at the judgment might look like, I'll sketch a hypothetical illustration based upon what we have seen in Scripture thus far. After all, even C. S. Lewis used fictional imagery to get his theological and biblical points across!

JUDGMENT DAY IN A HYPOTHETICAL HELL

Picture a person who has committed much evil in his life, someone who rejected Jesus while living, someone who may have abused a spouse or child, or a person who perhaps committed terrible acts of terrorism against innocent people. Imagine a person, any person, whom you would like to see get what's coming to him (or her)—and it's judgment day. For the sake of the illustration, let's call him Otto: an international leader who has launched preemptive wars and terrorized nations with his arrogant dominance, leading to the death of thousands upon thousands of men, women, and children. He prepares to go into the presence of God. His attitude smacks of rebellion, anger, and hatred because he knows the time for payback has arrived. He just knows that God is going to judge harshly and throw him in eternal torture as punishment, and he hates God for it.

Otto comes into the throne room of God. Glaring flames of fire, so bright and hot that he cannot see, confront him. His anger and rebellion turn to sheer terror. He moves closer to the flames, and as he does so, he realizes that the blazing fire *is* God. The closer he gets to God, the more deeply he feels, not God's hatred or judgment, but God's love. It is a love of such magnitude that, with its abundance, it acts as wrath, judging him for his deficiency, and with its purity, it serves as a hell, punishing him for his depravity. God's love and mercy, both acting as judgment, are so extravagant, so abundant, so incomprehensible that they completely overwhelm Otto. Then he hears a voice from the fire. He does not hear, "You evil, vile murderer! I am going to get you now. Revenge, punishment, and torture forever and ever!" Instead, he hears God say with sorrow forged from love, "I have loved you with an everlasting love. But look at your life; what have you done?"

Totally undone by God's unorthodox approach, Otto falls to his face, still afraid but with his hatred replaced by remorse. As his life flashes before his eyes, he sees all the victims, mothers crying for lost sons, children begging for the return of their murdered fathers, the eighteen-year-old boy dying alone on the battlefield, crying for his mother. Otto hears their screams, sees their bloody and battered bodies, listens as they cry out for mercy. And he knows he gave none. Yet here he stands in the fire of God, receiving what he never gave. He looks to his right and sees his victims. Still in the fire, God makes him go to each one and lay his hand upon their hearts. As he does so, he feels all of their pain, all of their disappointments, all of their fear, and knows that he has caused it all. Within the crowd of victims, the last one he has left to touch, he sees Jesus.

When he places his hand on Jesus' heart, he not only feels the pain, sorrow, and the disappointment he has caused Jesus; he also feels the unconditional love that Jesus has for him, Otto. All the while the fire of God burns, devouring Otto's wickedness and evil deeds. Lest you think he gets off too easy, this is hell for him. With gnashing teeth and uncontrollable weeping, his heart breaks, and he cries out in utter remorse, in unmitigated repentance, knowing he can never undo the damage he has caused. Seeing his repentance and the unendurable and seemingly unending pain he feels as the fire burns off the chaff of his evil deeds, the victims are vindicated. The one thing victims most often wish for is that their offender feel remorse and know the terrible pain he has caused them. Otto's immense remorse and pain at the knowledge of his sin against them satisfy this need.

George MacDonald, one of my favorite theologians, explains the pain of the fire, which I call "hell," saying that "the fire of God, which is His essential being, His love, His creative power, is a fire unlikely in its earthly symbol in this, that it is only at a distance it burns—that the further from Him, it burns the worse." The farther a person stands from God in that day, the more pain the fire causes as it burns away the impurities. Otto doesn't get away with murder; he doesn't get to take a walk without suffering any consequences. He burns in God's eternal fire. The more he burns, the closer he gets to God, until finally he stands next to God, purified, free from sin, and ready to hear God's words.

Then Otto hears God say, "I forgive you. Will you be reconciled to me and to those you have wronged?" Barely able to answer, Otto nods his head in utter disbelief. Much to his astonishment, God asks Otto's victims to draw near to Otto and to put their hands on his heart. As they touch him, each one feels Otto's pain, his fears, his disappointments; they can hear his cries as a child, know his shame as an adult, and understand who he was as an evil ruler. Themselves forgiven and embraced by the love of God, they extend that same kind of grace to Otto, forgiving him his sins against them. At last Jesus stands before him, touches Otto's heart, and says, "I have loved you with an everlasting love, and I forgive you. Will you enter into my kingdom and be restored to God?" And Otto accepts. He has been judged by the fire of love; he has walked through the fire of God's wrath; he has been purified by the fire of God's mercy. He receives forgiveness, reconciliation, and restoration, and he enters the kingdom of God, tested by fire, forgiven by grace.

The possibility exists, however, that Otto does not accept God's offer of restoration, or that after the testing by fire, nothing remains of him at all. Nothing. In order to preserve human freedom, which God gave to us at creation, we must allow for the possibility that some people will still reject God. The fire does not eliminate the gift of human freedom. Those who say no to God's yes, however, end up in the "lake of fire," which annihilates them—another topic reserved for the next chapter.

"I love the story!" Brooke said when she heard it. "But doesn't he get off too easily in this hypothetical hell? Shouldn't he suffer just a bit to make up for the suffering he caused other people?"

"Well," I asked her, "what if Otto had made a deathbed confession and received Jesus as his Savior a minute before he died, after which he is ushered into God's kingdom. Couldn't the same be said in that scenario? And yet Christians aren't traditionally troubled by that notion."

"Oh, right. I get your point," she said quietly.

"You see how wrapped up we are in the traditional sense of justice as retributive? But when God serves justice, the goal becomes reconciliation and restoration. God's justice doesn't demand retribution in which Otto must suffer a certain amount in order to pay back his victims for the harm he caused, but instead truly seeks to restore relationships in love."

"I like that," Brooke conceded. "We see justice in a whole new way. It's going to take some getting used to!"

FINAL JUDGMENT AS LOVE

This little story, although speaking literally of things metaphorical, gives us a possible picture of God's judgment of sin based on what we have seen in the Bible. God's judgment takes the form of inexplicable, extravagant love, which brings a person to repentance. The judgment of love resulting in repentance reminds me of an incident with my sons when they were young. We were living in Brandon, Florida, a suburb of Tampa, and a tropical storm had just blown through. Because of the storm, I kept the boys home that morning and drove them to school around eleven o'clock. I hugged them good-bye at the door, told them to go straight to their classrooms, whispered a prayer, and drove home. In the meantime, my mother-in-law came to visit for a couple days. She hadn't seen the kids for a while and looked forward to meeting them when they got off the school bus. About the time the bus usually dropped them off, the phone rang. The Tampa police officer on the other end of the phone asked me if I had two sons named Collin and Nicholas. I won't talk about the fear that gripped my heart when I considered all the possible reasons for his call. He must have sensed that because he quickly told me that they were safe and he had them in custody at the police station in Tampa. "What? You have the wrong children," I told him. "I drove my boys to school and saw them walk into the building. The bus just dropped them off; they should be walking in the door any minute. Hang on." At that moment, my third son, Kelly, walked into the house—alone.

Evidently, after arriving at school Collin (eight years old) and Nicholas (six years old) took their younger brother to his kindergarten class and decided to walk home. Along three four-lane highways. With no sidewalks. By themselves. I still shudder to think of it. At any rate, they stopped at Walgreens along the way, spent their lunch money on candy, and made the mistake (not the first one of the day obviously) of running in and out of the automatic doors a few times, which drew the attention of a police officer trying to enter the store. They had their first, and I hoped last, ride in a police cruiser.

I jumped in the car with my mother-in-law, and we went to the police station to pick up my sons. I cried all the way there and all the way home. Not an ugly cry, but silent tears of sadness, fear, relief, and gratitude that God had protected them. In spite of my tears, they feared the worst, especially from their father: spanking (yes, we did spank our boys occasionally; those were the old days, remember), grounding, no TV, no Nintendo, but plenty of anger, wrath, weeping, and gnashing of teeth for what would feel like an eternity possibly awaited them. So they sat in the backseat, silent, afraid, but stubbornly ready to defend their actions, more sorry that they got caught than sorry that they did something so horrendous.

But when we all sat around the table to discuss the consequences of their behavior, their expected "tortures" did not happen. We cried— their dad and I. The consequences could have devastated us, destroyed them, irreparably. Yet through pained conversation, the kind you have with your kids when they do something really wrong, we forgave them. When they saw the extent of our pain and realized the love we had for them, they broke down in tears, apologizing to us, hugging us, and telling us they wouldn't do such a stupid thing again, and they wouldn't complain about the consequences we decided on. Our love, rather than harsh judgment and strict punishment, served as judgment enough and brought them to repentance.

Similarly, our alternative view of hell speaks of God's love as the most grueling judgment—judgment that brings repentance and reconciliation. As when Zacchaeus (Luke 19) came down from his perch in the tree and experienced the unconditional forgiveness of Jesus, genuine forgiveness often leads to repentance. Nonretaliatory forgiveness may have profound consequences for the one released from sin with such sacrificial abandon. In fact, as in the case of our fictional offender Otto, the expenditure of forgiveness often results in a response of repentance that proves just as costly.

When a person is brought face-to-face with his or her sins and experiences the unexpected grace of forgiveness rather than the expected retributive punishment, real repentance may occur. Theologian Gil Bailie says it well: "Jesus seems to have understood that the only real and lasting contrition occurs, not when one is confronted with one's sin, but when one experiences the gust of grace that makes a loving and forgiving God plausible" (*Violence Unveiled*, 208–9). So too, medieval monk Peter Abelard believed that forgiveness wins a person over because of the act of love that motivates it. It stimulates and brings out the good in one who expects (and deserves) retribution but receives redemption instead. As we talked about in chapter 8, forgiveness calls to the offender with love, summoning him or her to take responsibility for the offense, to give up the self-involvement, and to repent. Forgiveness and the love that prompts it is a form of judgment that acknowledges the sin (hence the need to forgive it), but out of love gives up the right for exacting vengeance in favor of the forgiveness that seeks to restore a relationship.

Again I turn to George MacDonald. In beautiful prose he describes the burning love and mercy of God that judges the sin and draws the sinner into the center of God's presence for an eternal intimacy:

> Such is the mercy of God that He will hold His children in the consuming fire of His distance until they pay the uttermost farthing, until they drop the purse of selfishness with all the dross that is in it, and rush home to the Father and the Son and the many brethren— rush inside the center of the life-giving fire whose outer circles burn.

GOD'S FINAL WRATH IN HARMONY WITH LOVE

Lisa resonated with a hell that loved people into repentance and, therefore, into a reconciled relationship with God and others. But she still wondered about God's wrath: "The Bible says so much about God's wrath and vengeance. What about Romans 12:19? It says, 'Leave room for the wrath of God, for it is written, "Vengeance is mine, says the Lord."'"

Her question was good. We often misinterpret this verse. When we read it in context, it takes on a meaning different than the one we get if we just read it by itself (the practice of interpreting Bible verses without taking context into consideration is called "proof-texting"). The context of Romans 12:9–21 talks about Christians' responsibilities toward others in the church and in the community as a whole: it is a call to discipleship. It tells us to love each other, to give preference to one another, to bless even those who persecute us, and to be at peace with everyone. Then comes the verse about God's vengeance. It says: "Never take your own revenge, beloved, but leave room for the wrath of God, for it is written, 'Vengeance is mine, I will repay,' says the Lord" (12:19). We can't interpret this verse without taking the next two verses into consideration: "'But if your enemy is hungry, feed him, and if he is thirsty, give him a drink; for in so doing, you will heap burning coals on his head.' Do not be overcome with evil, but overcome evil with good" (12:20–21).

Let's put this all together so we can get a clear picture of what it means. After exhorting Christians to treat others with love, including our enemies, not returning evil for evil, 12:19 reminds us that retribution or vengeance belongs to God. In other words, we should not return evil for evil, but God may do so. Although Paul may refer here to Deuteronomy 32:35, we may assume that Paul, like Jesus in Luke 4:20, is providing us with a reinterpretation of the Old Testament sense of vengeance. If we keep reading Romans 12 in context, the next verse (12:20) rebuts divine vengeance, indicating that even God does not take revenge but instead feeds, clothes, provides water, and blesses God's enemies. As disciples, we are to imitate God in these actions, just as Jesus, God in the flesh, did.

Would God command us to love enemies, feed the hungry, clothe the naked, and return evil with blessing and then do the opposite? We're told to imitate God, right (Eph. 5:1)? That wouldn't make sense, especially in light of the life of Jesus, who revealed to us the character and behavior of God and exhorted us to imitate him. Rather than striking out in vengeance, God overcomes evil with love and goodness and directs us to do the same. Our enemies keep laying up offenses against us, but we overcome their evil with God's good. So Romans 12:19–21 really contradicts the idea of a vengeful God whose wrath demands retribution. In this case, the retributive action *is* to respond in love. When we "leave room for the wrath of God," we deal with enemies the way God does: we bless them.

Now I know that many other passages in the Bible talk about the wrath of God. Take Romans 1:18–32, for instance. This set of verses lists some of the actions that incur God's wrath. How does God exercise that wrath? By giving the offenders over to their sin, by allowing sin to take its course in their lives. The phrase "God gave them over" to their desires, passions, and depravity is mentioned three times in this one passage. It must be an important point! We can interpret the wrath of God, then, as allowing wrongdoers to suffer the consequences of their sin. Just as God's love allows us the freedom to make our own choices, God's wrath allows us to suffer consequences for our sin. For instance, if we hold up a bank, the wrath of God gives us over to our actions and their consequences, and we spend time in jail. If we gossip about a neighbor and she finds out and will no longer speak to us, God's wrath gives us over to those consequences, and we lose a friend.

In order to connect the idea of God's wrath as nonvengeful and compassionate to our illustration of hell and Otto at the last judgment, we turn to Isaiah's message from God: "I will pour out my wrath on my enemies, and avenge myself on my foes!" (1:24 NRSV). Yet in the very next verse, God talks about a process of purification at the hands of God: "I will smelt away your dross as with lye and remove all your alloy" (1:25 NRSV). Just as the fire of the goldsmith burns off impurities in the precious metal, so the painful treatment that purifying entails burns off the dross in the fiery presence of God at the last judgment. At the same time that we encounter the wrath and judgment of God, we also encounter God's love. Far from being vindictive, divine wrath is part of the reconciling activity of God as the fire of God burns away unrighteousness and leaves only the righteous parts of us behind. Only then can true reconciliation take place between God and those who previously had rejected God. God's liberating work of reconciliation and restoration continues all the way through the final judgment. Although the possibility exists that some may still reject God after walking through the divine fire, God never forsakes or abandons those God loves—ever.

So we have two aspects of divine wrath. In the first aspect, God gives us over to the earthly consequences of our sin (which can be hell on earth for us). The second aspect of wrath occurs at the final judgment of those who have not received Jesus as their Savior. They stand in the fiery presence of God and suffer the purifying flames of God's love. This burning love might feel like burning wrath to the one who experiences it. In fact, one of the words translated as "wrath" in the Bible actually means "to burn." Again, as with justice, we see divine wrath through a different lens, through a God of love, who desires more than anything else to have a restored relationship with all people. The wrath of God, rather than anger, is love that burns away the sin, purifying the sinner so that true reconciliation and restoration can take place.

WHAT ABOUT US?

"Okay," Lisa agreed, "that makes sense. But if God still redeems people even at the final judgment, that means those who rejected Jesus during their lifetime get a second chance at the end. Why is that fair, when all my life I have lived for Jesus, through thick and thin, and these wicked people get into heaven at the last second after a life of horrendous sin?"

Actually, Brooke asked the same question but didn't seem as bothered by the idea of skin-of-the-teeth salvation as Lisa was. Maybe because Lisa has more years in "living for Jesus" than Brooke has. A bit bothered by the same issue, Eric thought it would be fair treatment, at least for those who had never heard of Jesus. But for those who had a chance and didn't take it, he agreed that late entry into heaven (or late escape from hell) just wasn't fair to those who had worked hard all their lives to follow Jesus. Eric also wondered about all of those devout people of faith from other religions or those who have lived generous, loving, good lives. What happens to them? That's a good question and one that requires an answer beyond the scope of this book. I've decided to write one dealing solely with that issue. For now, suffice it to say that they too will stand in the fire of God's purifying presence and will have the same choice that Otto had.

I didn't quite know where to begin with Lisa's question. First of all, wondering why she bothered to live all her life for Jesus if she too could have gotten in at the last second misses the point of salvation. This type of question sees salvation as mere fire insurance, rather than as partners with God in fulfilling the mission of Jesus. But we'll talk more about that in the last chapter. The other aspect of Eric's, Brooke's, and Lisa's questions reminds me of the parable of the wage earners in Matthew 20:1–16. The laborers who worked all day received the same wage as those who worked only an hour. When they complained to the land-owner about the injustice, he reproved them: "Friend, I am doing you no wrong; did you not agree with me for the usual daily wage? Take what belongs to you and go; I choose to give to this last the same as I give to you. Am I not allowed to do what I choose with what belongs to me? Or are you envious because I am generous? So the last will be first, and the first will be last" (NRSV). If God desires to continue the work of reconciliation up to the last second, how can we protest? A sermon I heard as a new Christian put forth one of my favorite images of God as a God of second chances, a God who never gives up on us, who pursues us like a hound of heaven, always offering opportunities for repentance and reconciliation. Why wouldn't God offer that same invitation on that final day? Why would God's work of salvation end just because someone's body dies? The work of Jesus must still be effective after the end of time or even after time runs out.

Jesus' work of conquering sin did not end with the resurrection. God, through Jesus, continues conquering sin until the end and after, until sin and evil finally meet their death. When we see Jesus at the final judg-ment, therefore, the extravagant depth and breadth of his "It is finished" will finally come to light. Although Jesus opened the way for salvation once and for all, it is truly finished, completely consummated, when all people, even all God's enemies, stand in the fiery presence of the God of second chances (and third and fourth and fifth, if you know what I mean), and experience the purifying power of God's burning love. This is the fulfillment of all Jesus' promises: "In [Christ], every one of God's promises is a 'Yes' . . . [and] 'Amen'" (2 Cor. 1:20 NRSV). That was Brooke's reaction too: "Yes! Finally a hell I can live with!"

FINAL QUESTIONS TO CONSIDER

I leave us with these questions: Which vision of hell most coheres with the God revealed in Jesus—the view of hell in which persons suffer for all eternity with no hope for reconciliation with God, or the view of hell in which persons understand the depth of their sins, take full responsibility for them, and reconcile not only with God, but also with their victims? Which view offers a more compassionate eschatology? Which view takes more seriously the extensive significance of the life, death, and resurrection of Jesus? Which view most adequately and permanently exterminates evil? Can hell coexist with God's kingdom of love?

First Corinthians 13 tells us that love endures forever, that after all is said and done, only faith, hope, and love remain (in contrast to fear, hopelessness, and hatred), but the greatest of all is love. If all else is done away with, burned up, perished, gone when time comes to an end, and only faith, hope, and love abide eternally, we may legitimately say that hell is not eternal, only love is. Nothing but the burning love of God can rid the world of sin. Although Jonathan Edwards says that God's wrath toward you burns like fire, I say that God's love toward you burns like fire. May none of us abandon hope.

10

Outer Darkness, Gnashing of Teeth, and the Lake of Fire

I did not bear it long, but not so briefly
As not to see it sparkling round about,
Like molten iron emerging from the fire;
And suddenly it seemed that day had been
Added to day, as if the One who can
Had graced the heavens with a second sun.

—Dante, *Paradiso*, Canto 1

These things I have spoken to you
in figurative language;
an hour is coming when I
will speak no more to you
in figurative language, but
will tell you plainly of the Father.

—Jesus, in John 16:25

Lisa called this morning. After discussing our young adult children for a bit, we moved on to the new view of hell—not a random topic transition when living with teenagers! About the view of hell in the last chapter, Lisa exclaimed, "I love it! This view of hell does give us a more consistent picture of God. And it accomplishes God's goal to redeem the world. The picture of justice and forgiveness it gives us truly seems more biblical. But how do you reconcile this view with the sayings of Jesus on hell in the Bible? For instance, Jesus tells his disciples that at the end of the age "the angels shall come forth and take out the wicked from among the righteous, and will cast them into the furnace of fire; . . . there will be weeping and gnashing of teeth" (Matt. 13:49–50). We can't forget those verses or just brush them away as if they didn't exist, you know."

She's right.

Later I caught Eric in the hallway. I had let him read a draft of the last chapter, and he seemed extremely pleased with the new view. He too was concerned about the hell verses in the Bible and mentioned that he had heard various interpretations of Jesus' sayings on hell. "Bible scholars interpret those sayings in different ways," he added. "In my Bible class I learned that the people who heard Jesus talk about hell knew what he was saying and what he referred to. But because so many years have lapsed between our time and the time of Jesus, we can't really know for sure what Jesus meant. . . ."

He's right.

Although Brooke had already accepted the alternate view of hell expressed in the last chapter, she too admitted that we have to deal with the sayings of Jesus on hell in the Gospels. And she's right, too. Any reinterpretation of a traditional doctrine must take into consideration what the Bible says. So let's take a look at the Bible, along with its historical background, and see what we can glean from the teachings of Jesus on hell. But first, a word on context.

CONTEXT—CULTURE AND HISTORY

My old Sunday school teacher "Bob" drilled into our heads a very important point. And I still find this element indispensible for interpreting the Bible, one that I learned over and over while gaining a formal education in theological and biblical studies. Bob would stand in front of the class every Sunday and say, "Always remember, context is king!" Context *is* king; or context is *king*; or *context* is king. Whatever emphasis you put on each word, the point is clear: *context is king!* So before we explore the sayings of Jesus, we need to talk about the context, Jesus' context, the culture that Jesus lived in and its history. To find the meaning of the text, we have to take into consideration Jesus' community of discourse (context), what *they* would have heard Jesus say, and how *they* would interpret it.

Think about the word "context." Literally, it means "con" (with) and "text" (what is written), or "with the text." The context, then, is what goes with or alongside what is written: the history, the language, the culture, the metaphors of those times, and the ways of speaking and thinking. Nothing is written in a vacuum, without influences from culture, community, and history. Not even the Bible. God used human beings, persons within a certain context, to write the Bible. To understand what they wrote, we need to understand the context in which they wrote.

For example, I composed and sent an e-mail to a friend today, asking him to go over the details of a contract for me. He wrote back and said, "Sure, send it over." In Jesus' context, "Send it over" would mean something entirely different than it did to me in my context. "Send it over" might mean that Jesus would have to find a courier to run the contract over to the attorney. It might take a couple days or longer. "Send it over" in my context means that I need to hit the reply button, attach the file containing the contract to an e-mail, and push the "send" button. As I sit here at my computer, trying to think of good examples of metaphors we use in our context that only those from our own culture or decade would understand and that someone from Jesus' day couldn't possibly understand, I cannot think of a single one. Why? Because we are so deeply and completely situated in our own contexts that we are not even aware of them. We remain oblivious to our own metaphors and methods of communicating meaning to each other. But even if we can't separate and identify our own situatedness, when we talk to one another or read books and stories from within our own context, we understand each other.

Mike Cosby, a Bible professor and author, tells a joke in order to illustrate the importance of knowing the cultural context when interpreting the Bible:

> Did you hear about the chap who walks into a pub in northern Ireland carrying a alligator under his arm that is painted bright green? He asks in a loud voice, "Do you serve Protestants here?"
>
> "We do," replies the publican.
>
> "Well then," says the customer, "I'll have a Guinness for meself and a Protestant for me alligator."

Mike told this joke to his wife at the dinner table in the presence of his two small sons. His wife, Lynne, laughed, but his sons asked, "What's so funny, Dad?" In telling this story to me, Mike said: "So I needed to explain about the Irish and Kelly green, as well as the long conflict between Protestants and Catholics in Northern Ireland. Then I had to explain that a pub is a bar, a publican is a bartender, and Guinness is a brand of beer. And after explaining enough details so that my sons could understand the point of the joke, it was no longer funny." Surely most adults in Western culture know Irish beer brands and the significance of the color green. We are familiar with the Irish culture and have knowledge of the conflicts between Protestants and Catholics. We have an immediacy with the joke that Mike's children do not, so we understand its humor. We know what Mike is talking about when he tells the story.

In the same way, Jesus' first audience understood what Jesus meant when he talked about Gehenna; but because we did not live in that context, we have more trouble identifying Jesus' meaning. We can interpret what Jesus said more accurately if we understand the context out of which he spoke, if we understand the metaphors and ways of communicating of Jesus' culture. We want to hear and understand what the people heard and understood when they heard Jesus tell a story. So let's move on to hell, or as Jesus said it in Aramaic, "Gehenna."

GEHENNA IN THE TIME OF JESUS

Historically, we appeal to Jesus' sayings on Gehenna, eternal torment, and gnashing of teeth to build a doctrine of hell as a fiery place of eternal punishment. But should we? What lies behind the words of Jesus? The idea of a place of fiery judgment developed late in Jewish thought. The Old Testament refers to "Sheol," a shadowy type of underworld where the dead dwell (Job 3:17–19; Ps. 6:4–5; 88:3–6; Isa. 5:14; 14:9). Sheol does not divide the good from the bad or the wicked from the righteous (Eccles. 9:2–6, 10). No judgment of character or deeds takes place at all. This was usually true of the place of the dead in Greek thought, called "Hades" (eleven times in the New Testament). So we can't use the Old Testament by itself to construct a doctrine of hell.

If we move ahead a few centuries, outside of Judaism and into the surrounding cultures, we find some idea of a place for the dead and a final judgment, in which the wicked suffer in a river of lava. During that time, the later books of the Old Testament were still being written and, therefore, they spoke a bit more about a place of judgment and punishment, but only vaguely. Theories of a final judgment and eternal punishment in flames came from Persian religions like Zoroastrianism. This theory of hell as a place of eternal punishment and fiery torture seeped little by little from Persia into the Jewish culture and belief systems. So by the time we reach the period between the Old and New Testaments, hell had grown in popularity and had developed into something that more closely resembles our traditional views today. Jesus would have known these popular ideas and spoken of them because they were familiar to the people at the time. But what did Jesus mean when he talked about "hell"?

When Jesus spoke of "hell," he used the word "Gehenna." We translate it "hell" in our English versions of the Bible. But "hell" might not accurately describe the "Gehenna" Jesus talked about. The word *gehenna*, used twelve times in the New Testament, comes from the

Aramaic/Hebrew word *ge-hinnom*. It means "valley of [the son of] Hinnom" (Josh. 15:8), an actual valley located southwest of the city of Jerusalem, which served as the boundary line between the inheritance of the tribes of Benjamin and Judah. The Hinnom Valley has a quite interesting history, familiar to Jews of the first century.

That valley saw much bloodshed, beginning (as far as we know) with the Canaanite worship of the gods Molech and Baal. These gods demanded the sacrifice of children by passing them through the fire and into the hands of the gods. The practice of child sacrifice by fire continued in the valley for centuries, even throughout the rule of the Hebrew Kings Ahaz and Manasseh (2 Kgs. 23:10). The prophet Jeremiah believed that these kings even sacrificed their own children in the fires honoring Molech and Baal (7:29–34; 19:1–15). The prophecies of Isaiah and Jeremiah speak of the fires in the valley as devouring flames that burn forever, that are never quenched (Isa. 30:33). During times of war, soldiers piled dead bodies in the valley, where they burned seemingly forever. And for centuries, the community dumped the dead bodies of criminals into Gehenna. Many centuries later, after the siege of Jerusalem in the year 70, the Romans heaped up and burned dead bodies of Jews in Gehenna. Because of all this, the people referred to Gehenna as the abyss or the accursed valley. Only the guilty and the accursed ended up there, where their bodies would seem to burn forever, where they forever dwelt in darkness, at the outer limits of civilization.

Well before the time of Jesus, the valley was also used as a refuse heap. The people in the surrounding areas dumped their trash in Gehenna, where it burned day and night. The fire never went out. It smoldered there beneath the surface, incinerating the rotting, smelly garbage. New garbage was piled on top of the old decaying garbage: rotting fish, slimy vegetation, decaying human refuse of every imaginable sort. And as you know from experience, a dump without flies is a dump without garbage. The flies laid eggs on the surface of the dump. So just imagine the hundreds of thousands of squirmy, wormy maggots living there, eating the rotting refuse. All the while, under the surface, the fire still burned, devouring the putrid garbage from days and weeks past.

It was a fire that burned forever, where the worm did not die and where people went to throw their trash, grimacing from the stench, gritting their teeth in revulsion, never venturing too close for fear of falling into the abhorrent abyss. In times of war, decaying human flesh mingled with the rotting garbage—imagine the vile vision. When Jesus spoke of Gehenna, his hearers would think of the valley of rotting, worm-infested garbage, where the fire always burned, smoke always lingered, and if the wind blew just right, a smell that sickened the senses wafted in the air. The word "Gehenna" called to mind total horror and disgust.

"Yuck, you're grossing me out!" That from an indignant Brooke.

"What's that got to do with what Jesus says about hell in the Bible?" Lisa wanted to know—as usual, back to the Bible! Maybe I am stereotyping males here, but I think Eric wanted to hear more about rotting bodies. So let's stop the trash talk and move on to what the New Testament tells us about hell in general. Then we'll see how it connects to Gehenna.

THE BIBLE ON HELL

The Bible does give us some information about what we interpret as hell (including verses that refer to the outer darkness). To avoid confusion, I will list the main points. Where I use the word "hell," most often the New Testament uses the words "Gehenna" or "Hades" (in the Greek) or refers to it indirectly in the passage. So think of the garbage pit always aflame with worms that never die. That's what the people who heard Jesus would be thinking. Here we go. The following list describes the New Testament's take on Gehenna:

— Hell is the ever-burning garbage dump just southwest of Jerusalem (Matt. 5:22; 18:9; Mark 9:47).
— In hell both body and soul are destroyed (Matt. 10:28).
— Bodies of humans are thrown into hell by Jesus (Matt. 3:12), by an unknown entity (Matt. 7:19–23; 8:11–12; 18:6–9; Mark 9:42–48), by the angel reapers (Matt. 13:30, 40, 49–50), by the servants of the king in the parable of the Marriage Feast (Matt. 22:13–14), by the slave master in the parable of the Two Servants and in the parable of the Talents (Matt. 24:50–51; 25:30), by the wicked themselves (Matt. 25:46).
— In hell, there is unquenchable fire (Matt. 3:12; Mark 9:42–48).
— In hell, worms don't die (Mark 9:42–48).
— Those who cause a child to stumble are thrown into "hell," says Jesus to his disciples, to those already within the kingdom of God. We may take it as a saying to the church (Matt. 18:6, 9; Mark 9:42–48).

—Those who don't cut off a hand or a foot or poke out an eye if it causes them to sin are in danger of hell (Matt. 5:22–30; 18:8; Mark 9:43–48).

—Those who don't "hate" their mother, father, sisters, and brothers (Luke 14:26; John 12:25), we usually assume, go to "hell" (Matt. 19:27–30; Mark 10:28–31; Luke 14:25–26).

—A man dressed in the wrong clothes is thrown into "hell" (Matt. 22:13).

—Angels will live in hell, where sinful angels are chained until the judgment day (1 Pet. 3:19; 2 Pet. 2:4).

—Entire towns will be in hell; Capernaum will be brought there (Matt. 11:23).

—The gates of hell cannot prevail against Jesus and his followers (Matt. 16:18).

—People in hell see those not in hell and vice versa; a certain rich man looks at Lazarus in Abraham's bosom (Luke 16:23).

—Jesus as the risen Lord has the keys to hell (Rev. 1:18).

—Hell follows a green horse and kills with the sword, famine, and horrible diseases (Rev. 6:8).

—Hell is to give up the dead that are in it (Rev. 20:13).

—Hell is to be thrown into the lake of fire (Rev. 20:14).

As we see, most of the passages that mention or allude to hell are in figurative language or parable form. Like the centuries of rabbis ("rabbi" means "[my] teacher") before him, Jesus uses parables as a teaching tool to make one or (at most) two main points. Details of hell that we can glean from these passages differ so drastically that we cannot take them literally. Hell cannot be all these things at the same time. And we certainly can't literally say all those things simply about the garbage dump outside Jerusalem. How many bad angels or rich men or entire towns do we see burning in the valley of Gehenna? Yet what the Bible says about hell (Gehenna) does point to something. Gehenna symbolizes *some reality*. The question is What reality?

I strongly believe that this "reality" should harmonize with the character of God that we see revealed through Jesus and through the major themes of the Bible, such as God's mercy, love, faithfulness, and desire to reconcile with all creation. Through his life, death, and resurrection, Jesus modeled these characteristics for us to see. So our doctrine of hell must harmonize with these things too—if we want to be theologically consistent. And we do! Let's move on next to figuring out what Jesus might have meant when he talked about Gehenna.

JESUS ON HELL

Metaphorical Language

Many Bible scholars believe that what Jesus said about hell had a purpose different from the one we have traditionally believed. His interest lies not in hell but in salvation into the kingdom of God. He does not ever go into detail about damnation or the torments of those who find themselves damned. In tune with the methods of his time, Jesus' words on hell function as a teaching device, as warnings to those in danger of rejecting God's kingdom and the promise of liberation from the sin of their oppressive rulers, and liberation from their own sin.

After one of the passages in which Jesus talks about Gehenna (Matt. 18:6–10), he says to his disciples *not* that he comes to cast the lost into hell, but that he comes "to seek and to save that which was lost" (v. 11). His point is not to teach the disciples about the exact nature of hell, who goes there, and how long they suffer. He instead tries to tell them about their salvation and his role in it. Remember, context is king. In the context of Jesus' teachings, he focuses on salvation, on liberation from sin, on healing and transformation of souls. The eternal fire, gnashing of teeth, darkness, and fiery furnace that Jesus speaks about are all metaphors meant to warn the people into straightening out their lives, to keep them from missing out on the good news of God's kingdom ushered in by Jesus. Jesus wanted the people to take God and God's proclamation of the kingdom seriously—or suffer lasting consequences. Some of our old church fathers, such as Gregory of Nyssa, interpreted the fire metaphorically as God's wrath. Yet if we take these sayings of Jesus and try to build entire doctrines of a literal hell full of fire and damnation around them, that surely is not what Jesus had in mind!

But let's look at a few other metaphors that Jesus used to teach the people how to follow God. We almost have to interpret the verses on Gehenna as metaphorical when taken in context with other things Jesus said. For instance, he exhorts his followers to leave their families, their mothers, fathers, and children so that they can have eternal life (Matt. 19:27, 29; Mark 10:28–31; Luke 14:25–26). In Luke 14:26,

Jesus actually says to "hate" our family members or we cannot gain eternal life. (Our English meaning/sense of "hate" doesn't apply here. Jesus asks that we give our highest regard to him rather than to family members.) If we cannot gain eternal life, according to our tradition, the only other option remaining to us is to burn in hell, or Gehenna, as Jesus would say.

Do we take literally the sayings of Jesus about hating our families and leaving them? Of course not. Pastors have juggled these verses for an eternity, trying all kinds of mental gyrations to make them say something different. They don't have to try so hard! Jesus, in keeping with the ancient and contemporary Jewish teaching tradition, spoke metaphorically in order to make his main point: love God and God's kingdom *first*, then love your family. In fact, Matthew supports Jesus' point by telling us to seek God's kingdom first, and everything else will fall into place (Matt. 6:33).

If we have no problem in taking the sayings of Jesus on family metaphorically, even though they speak about how to receive eternal life after death, why do we take the Gehenna sayings literally? We need to concentrate on the main point that Jesus intends to make when he uses metaphorical language. If we interpret the Gehenna passages as literal images of unbelievers burning in eternal torment in a place called "hell," then we miss the point.

If we take Jesus literally in everything he says, we can easily come to the wrong conclusion. We'll compare two passages in the Gospels as an example. In the first passage, Jesus tells his audience that he has come to cast fire upon the earth, to bring not peace but a sword. He says that this sword will divide households, fathers against sons, mothers against daughters, and in-laws against in-laws (Luke 12:49–53). If we take this literally, we will think that Jesus comes to bring war on earth, between nations and between families. So we might even act in obedience and start swinging our swords around! Oh, wait! We've already done that! Remember the Crusades and Inquisition? Taking metaphorical teachings literally can cause hell on earth!

Now compare these verses to Matthew 5. "Blessed are the merciful, for they shall receive mercy" (v. 7). "Blessed are the peacemakers, for they shall be called sons [and daughters] of God" (v. 9). Then Jesus goes on to say that if we call our brother a fool, we are guilty enough to be thrown into the fires of Gehenna (v. 22). Just because we called our brother a fool? Why? If I take this passage literally, I can probably get away with calling my brother a "jerk," but not a "fool," right?

Wrong! By using these metaphorical examples, Jesus tries to point out that calling our brother or sister a fool usually indicates a lack of love for him, and Jesus asks us to love God and others. If we read on in Matthew, we see that Jesus asks us to love even our enemies! If we compare this passage to the one in which Jesus tells his listeners to hate their brothers, we have a blatant contradiction. In one passage Jesus asks us to hate, and in another he asks us to love. Taking all of these passages literally leaves us with major inconsistencies in how Jesus tells us to treat others. Jesus uses stories, metaphors, and overstatements in order to get his listeners to pay attention to his main point—the cost of discipleship, to love others, and to make peace—and his hearers understand this.

Hyperbole

In addition to metaphorical language, Jesus often used another teaching tool meant to grab the attention of his listeners. He spoke in what we call hyperbole, overstatement, or exaggeration in order to make an important point.

We do this all the time. When I first moved from Texas to Pennsylvania, I was terribly cold in the winter and would often wrap my arms around my body and exclaim, "I'm freezing!" Was I really freezing? No, but I uttered a hyperbolic statement to get across the point that I wasn't used to the Northeast's winter frigidity and was cold, darn cold! I often hear colleagues at school express their exasperation with a lazy student by saying, "He's driving me crazy!" Now, I know that my colleague is not really going crazy, even though his students might disagree, but he is using hyperbolic language.

In our example on family (above), Jesus uses hyperbolic language in much the same way and makes extreme statements about hating father, mother, wife, children, and even our own lives. He completely surprises his listeners with such a ridiculous demand. Admit it: these sayings of Jesus in the Gospels shock us too. And we don't have the same cultural attitude toward family that those in Mediterranean cultures did in the time of Jesus. They had a quite high degree of respect for parents, and their lives centered around their responsibilities to their families. When Jesus told them to "hate" their families, he had their attention! They knew he must have been making a very important point by using hyperbolic language or overstatement. He uses the same linguistic strategy with the sayings about Gehenna and shocks his hearers into realizing that he has come to liberate them from their sin through loving God and others.

How to Discern

"Hold on!" Lisa says during another phone conversation on this topic. "How do we know when to take something Jesus says literally or hyperbolically or metaphorically?" I knew she, like most of us, feared the slippery slope again.

"That's not as difficult as you think," I told her. And it isn't. In the first place, the ancient people hearing Jesus were familiar enough with their language and culture to know the difference between literal and figurative language. We know that difference in our culture and language too. If I begin a sentence with, "Once upon a time . . ." am I going to tell you a literal or figurative/fictional story?

"Duh," Brooke said, rolling her eyes. "Everyone knows that's how fairy tales begin!" Exactly. The problem begins when we, from our culture and language, have to interpret a story from an ancient culture and language. We don't know what the people hearing Jesus understood. We are not familiar with all of their cultural metaphors. But we can tell when Jesus obviously uses hyperbolic language. And if the literal interpretation gives us very unusual results, we can figure that Jesus is using hyperbole or metaphor.

For instance, Jesus makes a number of comments about prayer, trying to get across to his hearers that God does answer prayer if they pray faithfully. God doesn't abandon them to fend for themselves, but informs them that they have a Father in heaven who cares for them, loves them, and wants to shower good things on them. He tells them in Mark 11:22–24 that if they tell a mountain to be cast into the sea, it will happen. How many times have you seen a mountain cast into the sea because someone prayed for it to happen? So taken in its context, we know that Jesus uses metaphorical and hyperbolic language here.

The same holds true for his teachings in Matthew (7:1–5) about taking the log out of our own eye before we try to take the splinter out of our brother's eye. We know that Jesus has to be using hyperbolic and metaphorical language here. See? It is not so difficult to tell the difference.

Middle Eastern cultures commonly used figurative language, the most explicitly vivid metaphorical language they could find, to make an important point—one that the people would remember. Most of the time, when Jesus was teaching a lesson, he used figurative language too, in order to make an important point. The same holds true for the language about Gehenna or, as we translate it, "hell." He referred to the horrible, smelly, eternally flaming, wormy, rotting garbage heap in the valley of Hinnom just southwest of Jerusalem, a place to which no one wanted to go. He used that terrible imagery as hyperbole to grab the attention of his listeners, to communicate to them the seriousness of a life without faith in God, a life without living according to God's ways. And they got it! Well, many of them did.

THE ETERNALITY OF "ETERNAL"

The Meaning of "Eternal"

Lisa still needed more evidence supporting the metaphorical character of Jesus' sayings on Gehenna. She asked, "What about Matthew 25:46? Jesus says that all those who don't feed the hungry and clothe the poor will 'go away into eternal punishment, but the righteous into eternal life.' Eternal means eternal, forever, doesn't it? And punishment means to inflict suffering for a wrong done, right?"

Important questions. Let's take a look at what the word meant in the ancient context in which it was used. The Hebrew and Greek languages do not have a word that expresses the idea of a timeless, never-ending eternity. In fact, such a concept never crossed the ancient thinkers' minds.

Aiōn in the New Testament and *'olam* in the Old Testament, in most cases, just mean a period of time, an age, whether long or short. No specific duration attaches itself to the word at all. For instance, Jonah cries out to God from the belly of the huge fish, "The earth with its bars was around me forever" (2:6). He refers to his captivity in the fish for three days and three nights, but the word he uses to speak of the three days and three nights is *'olam,* the Hebrew word we translate and interpret as "forever" or "eternity." Jonah's bout in the fish lasted three days and three nights—a very short eternity. When I told Brooke about the "eternity of Jonah," she said, "Gosh, if I was swallowed by a big fish and had to sit there in its gross digestive juices for any length of time, it sure would feel like an eternity! It must have to Jonah too!"

In addition, the word appears in the Old Testament many times, but unless it's applied to God, it never means an eternity, as in an unending period of "time" outside of time. God told the Hebrews that they must keep the Passover for *'olam,* which our Bibles translate as "forever." But as Christians we believe that the Passover ended with the cross. God commanded the priests to offer incense for *'olam,* but in our tradition the Hebrew priesthood ended with Jesus. It did not last an eternity in our sense of the word. Even for Jewish people, those events don't last forever.

As we turn to the New Testament, we see that the meaning of the word *aiōn* doesn't refer to an unending eternity either. *Aiōn* means an age, a specific period of time, a short period of time in comparison to all "eternity." We are inconsistent with our translation of this Greek word. In many instances we translate the word as "eternity," and in other passages we translate it as "age." For example, Paul tells Philemon that he now had his slave Onesimus back with him for *aiōn,* "forever" (Phlm. 15–16). We can't say that Onesimus would be Philemon's slave forever, for all eternity, can we? In Romans 12:2, Paul tells us not to be conformed to "this world [*aiōn*]." If we interpret this the way we traditionally interpret the word when applied to Jesus' Gehenna sayings, we would be saying, "Don't be conformed to this eternity." It doesn't make sense.

Let's look at John 9:32: "Since the beginning of time [*aiōn*] it has never been heard that anyone opened the eyes of a person born blind." Since the beginning of "eternity"? Eternity, as we conceive of it, has no beginning and no end. John refers here to a specific period of time that has a beginning and an end, so we know that he references a time period other than "forever and ever."

One more, although I could give many examples from the New Testament: a short sentence in the conclusion of the Second Letter to Timothy (4:10) states that Demas, a friend of Paul's, "loved this present *aiōn*" and deserted Paul. Demas did not love this *present eternity*! He loved the world's ways more than God's ways. He loved the world that he lived in right at that moment, in this time period—of relatively short duration.

"I can buy that," Eric said when we talked about it one day. "How should we interpret the words *'olam* and *aiōn,* then?" Well, the words can be interpreted in a variety of ways. One of the ways we have already discussed above: "eternal" refers to a period of time. Another way to view the concept of "eternal" in the sayings of Jesus takes us to a verse in Jude that describes the "eternal fire." It says, "Just as Sodom and Gomorrah and the cities around them, since they in the same way as these indulged in gross immorality and went after strange flesh, are exhibited as an example, in undergoing the punishment of *eternal fire*" (v. 7, emphasis added). Yet the fire that burned these cities does not still burn and will not burn for all eternity, in our traditional sense of the term.

But still, the word "eternal" does refer to some sort of reality. To get an idea of that "eternal" reality, we'll look at John 17:3, which says: "This is eternal life, that they may know You [God]." If eternal life *is* knowing God, we can infer that eternal life *is* the life of God, the life that God gives and sustains. Eternal life corresponds to the quality of our relationship to God. So the question of eternality as never ending only truly applies to God. Only God is eternal, as in having no beginning and no end. The eternal fire, from this perspective, therefore, refers to the fire that surrounds God. Because God *is* a consuming fire, as we saw in chapter 9, the fire is eternal too.

This theory lines up perfectly with our little story about Otto (in chap. 9). Otto burns in the eternal fire—the eternal fire of God, the eternal fire that surrounds the eternal God, and the eternal fire that *is* the eternal God. The eternal fire purifies, convicts of sin, and brings repentance, reconciliation, and restoration. Eternal, then, means "without end" only when it applies to God, the only eternal one.

The Meaning of Eternal "Punishment"

Brooke and I had a very long (seemed like an eternity) conversation about the concept of "eternal." As I finished explaining it all, she slowly nodded. "But the verse also talks about eternal punishment. How would you interpret that?" Again, most of the uses of the word *aiōn* in the New Testament and the word '*olam* in the Old Testament, unless speaking of something intimately connected to God, refer to a specific period of time, one with a beginning and an end, one that sometimes lasts mere days or many, many years. Yet when Jesus says some will suffer eternal punishment, we interpret his words to mean a never-ending torment in the flames of an eternal hell. To steal a line from the robot in *Lost in Space*, "It does not compute—literally!"

So what does this mean when we construct a view of hell? Actually, we can interpret punishment in the same light, as punishment that comes from God in the age to come. We've already seen what that punishment might entail in our story about Otto. After all, "weeping may last for the night, but a shout of joy comes in the morning" (Ps. 30:5). We can rest in hope since God will not abandon our souls, or anyone's, in Sheol forever (Ps. 16:9–10).

But we can also interpret "eternal punishment" in another way. Remember that the verse talks about eternal punishment, not eternal torture. The word for "punishment" in the Greek means an agony, a toiling, being tossed with the waves. The word actually presents a great word picture of putting something to the test by rubbing it on a stone, to test a metal to see if it's genuine or fake. We think here of the testing by fire that we see in 1 Corinthians 3, which we talked about in chapter 9. The testing, as we've mentioned before, tests the person through fire so that sin dwells within them no more. The eternal punishment, then, involves Otto standing in the eternal fire of God as that fire tests (punishes) him, burns away the chaff, and makes him pure—not forever and ever, amen, but for a short duration, the time it takes to burn away the chaff, instantly.

OTTO, THE GNASHING OF TEETH, OUTER DARKNESS, AND ETERNAL WORMS

"Okay," Brooke responds during one of our conversations about it, "if punishment is a testing and purifying that comes from the eternal fire of God, and if Jesus did not refer to a literal place of fire where literal worms never die a literal death, where literal flames consume wicked people, where literal teeth gnash and literal eyes weep forever and ever and ever and ever, amen—then what reality did he refer to?"

As with all metaphors, Jesus did refer to something real. But what is that "something"?

Many Bible teachers willingly forget what Jesus says about the fiery furnace, gnashing of teeth, and worms that seem never to die. After all, the main point has nothing to do with those incidentals. In their minds, Jesus uses that imagery merely to make the story more poignant. At the same time, metaphorical and hyperbolical or not, Jesus' sayings on Gehenna refer to some sort of reality even if the main point is to warn his listeners about the consequences of not living a life of faith, of not loving God and others. But what does Gehenna point to?

Some believe that Jesus warns us of consequences in *this* lifetime. In that sense, Gehenna applies to life now and to life in the future, right here on earth. We can see how this is possible in Romans 1:24–32, where God gives wrongdoers over to the consequences of their sin. These people suffer trials that may seem like a fiery furnace. They may experience the anguish indicated by "gnashing of teeth" and may feel like they are living in some sort of "outer darkness." Although the experience of suffering consequences for sin can seem like pure hell for many of us, I think Jesus refers to something more, something beyond that, when he uses the Gehenna imagery as a metaphor. Again, in order to illustrate an important and serious point, let's use Jesus' metaphorical tactics and turn once more to the fictional Otto.

The moment Otto comes before God, hating God and afraid for his life, he experiences the intensity of God's fire. The horror of the heat and threat of annihilation cause him severe anxiety and pain. When Otto realizes that the flames of God consume him with love rather than anger and retribution, as they begin the process of burning off his wickedness, his anxiety turns to extreme remorse for his sin. His experience of the purifying process in the fiery furnace of God is no picnic in the park. He seems to be in unending agony; his teeth gnash together as his sin and the damage he has caused others confronts him face-to-face and heart to heart. The severity of his grief serves as a sort of punishment for sure! Albeit a punishment that tests, purifies, and transforms. He wonders if he will ever find relief from the flames and the pain they cause him, pain from knowing the hurt he has caused, pain from experiencing the extravagant love of God in spite of the horrific gravity of his own wrongdoing. God's incomprehensible love faces off with Otto's incomprehensible sin. The love, in the sheer extravagance of its force, acts as judgment against the total excessiveness of Otto's sin. He is not let off the hook. Instead, his confrontation with God's love forces him to face the gravity of his own sin. He sees his sin as God sees it and feels the pain of his testing and purification by fire. Although his experience is brief, relatively speaking, he goes through hell.

In the realm of God's timetable, the whole process might happen in an instant, in the twinkling of an eye, although it may seem much longer to those standing in the flames of God's presence. The difference between this view and the traditional view of hell is the end result. Rather than God's wreaking vengeance and retribution through eternal punishment, God bestows reconciliation and restoration through loving forgiveness so that eternity, rather than a period of unending time, is life in God, the only eternal one.

FREEDOM TO CHOOSE: RESTORATION OR ANNIHILATION?

On a rainy morning in November, I sat in my office, grading papers, when Brooke rushed in all out of breath. "Do you have a minute?" she gasped.

"Sure. What's up?" *Hell*, I guessed.

"I tried your Otto story out on the professor in theology class today, and he said it sounds like universalism! What's universalism, and why did he say it like it tasted bad or something?"

Yes, hell again. "Well," I responded, "universalism comes in many shapes, but basically it is the belief that at the end, after the judgment, all people from all faiths or no faith are reconciled to God."

"That sounds great! Why would anyone object to that?" Brooke asked.

"Some people think universalism takes away our freedom to say 'no' to God, to choose not to reconcile with God. They hold freedom in very high regard because to love God authentically, we must be able to choose God personally. If God makes the choice for us, then the possibility exists that God forces us to reconcile against our will. Those who believe in freedom say that God respects our choices, even when we choose not to have a relationship with God."

"So are you a universalist?" Darn, I knew she would ask me that.

"No. I believe that God respects the freedom given to us to choose for ourselves whether or not we want a relationship with God. We either choose God during our lifetime on earth, or we can choose God at the time of judgment, after going through the fire that burns away impurities, as we saw in Otto's case."

"Okay," Brooke agreed, "what happens then if Otto stands in God's fiery presence, receives forgiveness, and then decides he doesn't want it? He turns God down flat. Does God say, 'Too bad, Otto, you don't have a choice; you are going to reconcile with me whether you like it or not'? Or does he go to the place we call hell? Or to the lake of fire mentioned in the book of Revelation?"

Where to start? Since I promised earlier that we'd talk about human freedom, the freedom to choose reconciliation with God (or not) at the time of judgment, let's do that right now. We'll go back to our illustration of Otto and his time of judgment in God's presence. As Brooke said, Otto stands before God and turns down the offer of a restored relationship. If God truly respects Otto's freedom to say no, God will not force reconciliation. After all, forced reconciliation does not bode well for the success of a relationship. We can argue that the nature of reconciliation requires the mutual desire for relationship. Forcing or coercing a person to reconcile defeats the purpose. That said, let's look at Revelation 20:14–15 to see what might happen next, depending on how literally we take the passage. We see that "Death and Hades," along with those who reject God, are thrown into "the lake of fire" (NRSV). To understand what may actually happen to Otto, we need to explore the lake of fire.

Lake of Fire

Unfortunately, diverse interpretations of "the lake of fire" make it more difficult for us to propose its precise meaning. We can't know for certain what it is or what reality it metaphorically refers to. Based upon the historical and cultural context, however, we can speculate. Revelation 20:10 refers to it as a "lake of fire and brimstone." Another translation from the Greek for the word "brimstone" is the word "sulfur" (NRSV). From historical studies we know that, in those days, the sulfur fire burned hotter than any other fire, so hot that it completely disintegrated any substance that came close to it.

We see an example of the fierce hotness of this fire in the story about Daniel's friends Shadrach, Meshach, and Abed-nego and their jaunt into Nebuchadnezzar's fiery furnace. Daniel 3:23 tells us that the furnace fire was so hot that it completely incinerated the men who threw them in. Nothing was left of them. A sulfur fire burns so hot that it leaves nothing behind, no remains, no body, nothing! It completely annihilates its victims.

When theologians talk about hell as annihilation, they mean that those thrown into the lake's sulfur fire suffer complete destruction or annihilation. They do not suffer eternal torment in hell but cease to exist completely. So the lake-of-fire imagery suggests a fire that completely consumes whatever is thrown into it rather than eternal torment. We see the same type of imagery in Psalm 37:38, which tells us that the wicked will be utterly destroyed. Malachi 4:1 tells us basically the same thing: "The day is coming, burning like a furnace; and all the arrogant and every evildoer will be chaff; and the day that is coming will set them ablaze, . . . so that it will leave them neither root nor branch." The arrogant and evil will be as chaff. God will burn them so that there is nothing left. These verses speak of complete destruction or annihilation.

New Testament verses also support an annihilation view. In Matthew 3:10, 12, John the Baptist tells the religious leaders that every tree that doesn't "bear good fruit" will be "thrown into the fire." In the same way, God "will burn up the chaff with unquenchable fire." Matthew 10:28 talks about God destroying both soul and body in Gehenna. Chaff does not burn for all eternity; neither do human bodies and souls. The burning and destruction in these verses completely annihilate the chaff, the branches, and the bodies and souls. The fire may burn for all eternity, especially if that fire *is* God or surrounds God, as we talked about in chapter 9. Second Thessalonians 1:9 gives us an additional image of what happens to those who reject God's forgiveness and offer of restoration. It says that the wicked "will pay the penalty of eternal destruction." That means they will be destroyed or annihilated. This verse and many others like it do not in any way support the idea of eternal punishment in hell.

That's just one way to interpret the meaning of the lake of fire. I'll give you one more that makes a lot of sense when we also consider the loving character of God and God's desire to reconcile with all people. Some believe that the lake of fire refers to the same reality as Gehenna. In our case, then, the lake of fire actually is the fire of God, the fire that *is* the presence of God. As the fire burns away the chaff—a metaphor for evil—it leaves only the pure behind. Remember that "Death and Hades" are thrown into the fire and destroyed (Rev. 20:14–15 NRSV). The lake of fire, in this perspective, puts death and evil to death and leaves *life*. Think about it: If death is destroyed, what's left? Life—eternally, in God—the only eternal one. As such, the lake of fire annihilates death and evil, restoring life as it burns away the wickedness and purifies the soul.

Interestingly, we can also interpret the word "brimstone" (Rev. 19:20; 20:10; 21:8 [NRSV: sulfur]) as fire from heaven. The Greek noun for it, *theion,* is spelled the same as the adjective "divine." Brimstone not only burns as the hottest fire; it also comes from heaven or from God. The fire in the lake actually comes from God, the fire that surrounds God, the fire that *is* God's very presence. The metaphor of the lake of fire mentions "brimstone," a sulfur fire that burns hotter than other fires.

Interestingly, people use sulfur as a purifier, a cleanser, and a preservative. The ancient Greeks used it in order to purify and dedicate the temple or the people to the gods. They used it in their incense as a purifying scent. They also believed that the purity of the fire came from God, just as brimstone is a fire from heaven. So the people reading about the lake of fire would interpret it as a lake of divine purification, a lake of cleansing so that the purified object (in our case, a person) can be dedicated and restored to God. It seems, then, that we can interpret the lake of fire as standing in the fiery presence of God, as Otto did. The fire burns off the chaff (evil as a result of sin), purifies him, destroys death in him, and gives him the eternal life of God.

The Choice

"Okay, great!" Eric said when he heard this explanation. "Tell me how this interpretation of the lake of fire works with human free will. If the fire burns away all of a person's impurities, wickedness, and unrighteousness, can that person still reject God's offer of forgiveness and restoration?"

Excellent question. Let's go back to Otto standing in the fire of God's presence. We saw in our illustration that Otto said yes to God. But depending on our view of the lake of fire, we can imagine a couple of different endings. Suppose Otto stands in God's fiery presence, goes through the purification process, meets his victims and Jesus. After the fire has burned off the wickedness, there might not be much of Otto left. What does remain of him, however, still rejects God. If we hold to the first theory we talked about, a lake of fire separate from God, then Otto would be thrown into it and completely destroyed or annihilated. If the second theory makes more sense to us, that the lake of fire is the same as God's fiery presence at judgment, then the lake of fire tests, purifies, and puts death and evil to death. So Otto stands in the fire. It burns away impurities. But what if Otto has no good at all in him? The fire would burn all of him. It would completely destroy him. There would be nothing left of him, which means that he would be annihilated. If something good still remains, however, that remaining part, being good, would never reject God's offer of forgiveness and restoration.

We still have a choice. But because, by standing in the fire of God's presence, we have been freed from our slavery to evil and sin, we are also free to choose the good. Since we are no longer slaves to sin, we no longer desire to choose evil or sin (Rom. 6:22). Only something impure could reject God. A purified, righteous Otto would naturally choose life with God. Because the fire destroyed death in Otto, only life, God's life, would remain. "He himself will be saved, yet so as through fire" (1 Cor. 3:15). This view of the lake of fire and of judgment respects human freedom, yet at the same time it sees God's will to save all people fulfilled (1 Tim. 2:4; 2 Pet. 3:9). With the writer of Philippians, we could actually say that every knee will choose to bow and every tongue will choose to confess that Jesus Christ is Lord.

We've now seen two variations of the lake of fire. The first view, in which the lake of fire is a separate "place," finds Otto rejecting God and suffering annihilation after he lands in the lake of fire. The second view, in which the lake of fire is the same as God's eternal fire, finds Otto in one of two conditions: totally annihilated because after testing and purification nothing good and righteous remains (the second death—the death of death), or the completely good and righteous Otto standing before God, tested and purified. Under these conditions, Otto surely chooses life with God. The choice is yours!

Which view seems most biblical? Which view conforms most closely to the character of a loving God who desires nothing more than the reconciliation of all creation? After all is said and done, our understanding of hell should harmonize with a loving, just, reconciling God; a God who doesn't close the door on grace after closing the door on time, whose entire purpose centers around rescuing and redeeming a sin-enslaved world, whose absolute will focuses on reconciliation and restoration. Actually, our restorative view of hell, in which no one ever finds oneself beyond God's grace, solves all the troubles we talked about in the first chapter.

RESOLVING THE TROUBLES

Justifying God

A view of hell that conquers evil with love, that wins the battle with sin by winning over the heart of the sinner, solves the problem of evil and suffering in the face of a loving, powerful God. Remember our argument from chapter 1? If God is all-powerful, why wouldn't God exercise that power to keep people out of the flames of hell? If God is all good, why would God choose to send people into eternal punishment? Our alternative view of hell does not compromise God's power and goodness. No one suffers in eternal flames. No one spends eternity in hell. They stand in the fiery presence of God and find themselves forgiven, tested, purified, reconciled, restored, and transformed by divine power and love. God's goodness desires all to be saved, and God's power works to make it happen.

Eternal Hopelessness

If you recall, we talked about traditional views of hell cutting off grace after temporal life comes to an end, leaving the unredeemed with eternal hopelessness in hell. From a number of New Testament verses, we've already seen that God wants to redeem the world and through Jesus has worked to do so. Let's move to the Old Testament and look again at Isaiah 30:18: "The LORD longs to be gracious to you, and therefore He waits on high to have compassion on you. For the LORD is a God of justice; how blessed are all those who long for Him." In the Hebrew language, this verse paints a beautiful word picture of God sitting on high, longing with unquenchable thirst, with a desire so strong that it consumes every thought, longing to shower us with grace. And this longing is somehow related to justice (which we talked about in other chapters). The fact that God so strongly desires to gift us with divine grace makes it very hard to believe that the death of the body would put anyone beyond grace, beyond God's eternal grace, out of God's reach forever. If God exists outside of time, as we traditionally believe, why would grace exist only within time? Does a dead body necessarily mean that hope for God's grace dies too? The writer of Hebrews reveals to us that Jesus is forever a priest, forever interceding, forever praying for us (4:14–16; 7:17–25), and that "Jesus Christ is the same yesterday and today and forever" (13:8). These verses speak of a hope that extends beyond bodily death, an eternal hope based upon the love, justice, and grace of an eternally loving God. If God gives even people like Otto a chance to repent, receive forgiveness, and reconciliation, no one needs to abandon hope for any other person. None finds themselves beyond God's extravagant grace—even after death, even at the time of judgment.

Eternal Evil

Obviously, if hell as a place of eternal punishment does not exist eternally, then the wicked cannot dwell there eternally either. Those who still reject God, who choose to refuse God's grace even after standing in God's fiery presence, would suffer annihilation in the lake of fire, as we talked about earlier.

Justice in Opposition to Love

As we covered in our chapter (3) on justice, justice and love in our new view of hell no longer live in tension with one another but in perfect harmony. God's restorative justice fulfills the law of love. To love *is* to serve justice by forgiving, reconciling, and restoring "whosoever will" to God and to others.

Eternal Divine Violence

As we discussed in another chapter (5), if eternal torture in hell exists, then peace does not—at least not in hell. After all, there's nothing peaceful about the violence of continual torment. Our alternative view of hell, however, takes care of the problem of never-ending violence coexisting with God's kingdom of eternal love and peace. Our view also harmonizes with the character of God as nonviolent, not only as a God who exhorts us to make and keep peace, but also as a God whose central message and purpose for all creation is peace and restoration. Violence has no part in the peaceful kingdom in the new heavens and earth to come.

Retributive Justice and the Bible

Chapter 7 clearly discusses the harmony between God's justice and love. *Because* God loves us, God serves justice, not by making us pay for all of our shortcomings and sins, as in retributive justice, but by forgiving us with an eye and a heart toward reconciliation and restoration of our relationship to God and to all others. The alternative view of hell not only allows for God and sinners to reconcile; it also allows for reconciliation between victims and their victimizers. Total peace that accompanies reconciliation and restoration rules in God's realm.

Eternal Punishment for Temporal Sin

Obviously, the punishment in our new view of hell is not eternal. It fits the crime. Otto suffers the pain and anguish for his sins done during his lifetime. But then his victims get to see his remorse, witness his repentance, and take part in his reconciliation and restoration. They enter into a new relationship with Otto, having repaired the past rather than perpetuating it by preserving the pain and punishment for all eternity.

MAXIMIZING THE POWER OF THE CROSS

I remember many sermons in which the preacher thumped his fist on the pulpit and with a loud, firm voice asserted with confidence: "Only a remnant will enter the kingdom of heaven. The way is narrow that leads to life, and only a small number of people will find themselves on that road. Everyone else will walk the wide road that leads to destruction!" From there on out until the end of the sermon, we'd hear about the horrors of hell that most of the human race will suffer for all "eternity," in the "forever" sense of the term. He based part of his argument on the notion that sending the unrepentant to hell glorifies God because it serves divine justice. Think about it. Is eternal punishment for temporal sins just? If so, then the God of traditional theories of hell commits worse destruction than Hitler, worse than Osama bin Laden. In his death camps, Hitler tortured and killed six million Jews plus five million others. Their torture lasted for much less than an eternity (although it may have seemed an eternity to them). We cast Hitler as *the* villain in history, the archetype of a horribly evil person. But our traditional views of hell cast God as worse, as one who tortures and puts billions and billions of people through a second death, not for a few days, months, or years, but for *all* eternity, forever and ever and ever! Their only offense? Not confessing Jesus as Savior. They are no worse than we are: all sin and fall short of God's glory. But for a temporal error, shall they endure endless torture and torment? We call this God's justice?

In addition, traditional views of hell diminish God's power to redeem all humanity. If billions of people suffer eternal damnation and separation from God, the effectiveness of sin, evil, and Adam's condemnation is greater than the effectiveness of God's grace through Jesus' life, death, and resurrection. If hell as eternal torment is true, then God's mission of reconciliation through Jesus loses the full force of its effectiveness. If our traditional hell is real, God's power has not prevailed against evil, and God's power has not overcome our sin—for the most part.

In fact, if my old preacher is right, only one-third or less of the human population throughout all history will receive eternal life with God. Let's speak figuratively for the sake of an illustration that will help make our point. If we think about the number of people entering heaven (God's team) and the number of people entering hell (the devil's team) in terms of a football game and post the numbers on a scoreboard, it would look something like this: Devil 666 billion; God 333 billion (please forgive me for using the number 666—I just couldn't resist). God's team loses big time to hell! What does such a heavy loss say about God's power? About Jesus' work on the cross? In fact, traditional views of hell do not bring God glory; they usurp God's glory by diminishing God's power!

With our alternative view of hell, we maximize the powerful effectiveness of the cross. Jesus wins the final and absolute victory over evil and death. He breaks the power of sin. He fully, completely, absolutely accomplishes God's mission to reconcile the world to himself. Glory to God—truly!

"I like it," Lisa interjected during one of our conversations. "But if God's fire burns off the chaff and purifies us so that we choose to reconcile with God, what purpose does the cross serve? I mean, where does Jesus fit into this picture?" A very important question—so important, actually, that we will devote the entire next chapter to it.

11

The Savior

From matter's largest sphere,
we now have reached the heaven of pure light,
light of the intellect, light filled with love,
love of true good, love filled with happiness,
a happiness surpassing every sweetness.

—Dante, *Paradiso*, Canto 30

Do not be afraid; . . .
I have the keys of Death and of Hades.

—Jesus, in Revelation 1:18 (NRSV)

Eleven at night, and the phone rings. The caller ID shows Lisa on the other end. "Hello?"

"Hi, it's Lisa. I just finished reading the chapter on a new view of hell. It makes sense if we want to keep consistent with a God of love who desires reconciliation with all people. But if everyone stands before God, engulfed in the flames of divine consuming love, what difference does the life, death, and resurrection of Jesus make? Why did God bother with the cross at all?"

These questions from Lisa beg answers, good biblical answers. Throughout history the Christian community has mined the riches of the Bible in search of ways to talk about what exactly happened when Jesus died on the cross and rose from the dead. Let's review these views briefly.

The early persecuted church, longing for victory over their oppressive, enslaving governments, spoke about the cross in terms of *Christus Victor*, of Christ as Victor over the powers of slavery to sin and death. Later, after Christianity victoriously ruled the realm, theologians described the cross as an event in which Jesus satisfied God's offended honor so that God would forgive sin. Others conceived of the cross as a grand display of God's love, which set an example for all of us to follow as we live out our own lives. In the sixteenth century, the reformers Martin Luther and John Calvin thought of Jesus' death on the cross as divine punishment for sin so that God could forgive it. Many believed that God punished Jesus for our sin instead of punishing us. Theologians from the Anabaptist tradition articulated the cross event a bit differently, focusing on the life and teachings of Jesus as well as on the death and resurrection.

No matter which theory we support, no matter how we view the life and death of Jesus, something momentous happened. God worked through Jesus to reconcile us to God and to others. The profundity and significance of the topic of Jesus' life, death, and resurrection have produced libraries full of shelves and shelves of books on the topic—and I am in the process of writing another one!

CASTING THE CROSS IN LANGUAGE

"I'm writing a paper on Jesus for one of my classes. I'd like to talk about the cross, but the Bible talks about it in so many different ways. I don't know where to start. Why can't our Scriptures just make it simple? Can you help?" Another text message from Brooke.

"Let's talk this weekend. Sushi on Saturday around two?"

"Whoo hoo! See you then—sushi and the Son. Can't wait!"

I know that in Germany they don't do theology without a cold beer in front of them, but Brooke and I don't do theology without a scrumptious platter of sushi on the table. Brain food. At any rate, she's right. The Bible casts the cross in multiple metaphors for very good reasons. So before we tackle Lisa's questions about the *reason* for Jesus' life, death, and resurrection, let's first discuss the *ways* we talk about it.

One of the predominant ways is through metaphor. John of Damascus, a seventh- and eighth-century monk, believed that God gave us metaphor and figurative language as gifts. He writes that "in his ineffable goodness he sees fit to be named from things that are on the level of our nature, that we may not be entirely bereft of knowledge of him but may have at least some dim understanding."

We discussed Jesus' use of metaphor and hyperbolic language in chapter 10, but those who composed the Old and New Testaments also used metaphorical language in order to teach a truth otherwise difficult to understand. We must remember, however, that just because the Bible uses metaphors and stories to communicate deep truths, it doesn't diminish the reality of what the metaphors try to describe to us. Metaphors illustrate God as a rock, as an eagle, as a compassionate mother, as a strong tower, a shepherd, a king, a servant, and many others. We certainly know that God is not a piece of calcium carbonate or a bird with huge wings covered in feathers, yet the rock metaphor tells us something true about God.

Taking familiar elements from our everyday lives, metaphors tell the truth about God in word pictures that we can easily understand. The tales of creation, Jonah in the belly of the big fish, the flood, Job—all reveal important truths through stories. As the most popular storyteller ever, Jesus taught profound truth through parables: storytelling using metaphorical language that helps the community of readers comprehend the mind, heart, and actions of an incomprehensible God.

The language used to explain the redemption of the human race through Jesus Christ is also metaphorical language. Paul and the other writers of the New Testament books interpret the saving life, death, and resurrection of Christ in ways that their own communities could understand and grasp through the use of figurative or metaphorical language, borrowing well-known images from the social structure. These metaphors, taken from life's common daily circumstances, enabled the Christian community to explain an otherwise unexplainable event: the saving qualities of Jesus' life, death, and resurrection.

Biblical language describing Christ's work of redemption served specific communities of faith. The New Testament used the language of sacrifice, ransom, and expulsion to explain the work of Christ, language and metaphors that the people of that culture, in that time period, could understand. The New Testament explains Christ's life, death, and resurrection as economic, substitutionary, militaristic, sacrificial, and priestly. These motifs function as metaphors, language used to create word pictures for the sole purpose of helping God's community to understand the extent of divine love and the extravagance of divine forgiveness through Jesus—all in ways familiar to them, in ways they could understand.

The Christian community has traditionally reinterpreted the metaphors in order to make the good news understandable and relevant to their changing cultures. For instance, throughout Christian history we see faithful theologians reinterpreting the salvific work of Jesus according to their contemporary situation. Irenaeus, one of the earliest advocates of the *Christus Victor* theory, lived in conflict with the social and political structure of his day. Christianity was illegal, and Caesar was lord. He related the earthly conflicts between Caesar and Christianity to a cosmic battle between celestial powers. Centuries later, medieval theologian Anselm of Canterbury interpreted the atonement according to the feudal system prevalent in his age, giving us the still-popular satisfaction theory of atonement. Around the same time, Abelard interpreted the atonement according to the notions of "courtly love" and the new humanist culture just becoming popular in his society. With the assimilation of Aristotle, Aquinas interpreted the atonement according to and in harmony with the philosophical categories and ethical principles of his day. With the growth of the nation-state in the thirteenth and fourteenth centuries, judicial power was transferred from the community to the state, which brought about a focus on alternative methods for dealing with criminals and the popularity of penitentiaries. In a culture obsessed with sin and guilt along with the institution of newer civil laws, the Reformers interpreted the atonement through the lens of punishment and justification. The liberal social theologians reinterpreted atonement according to the Enlightenment's positive humanistic attitudes and the new scientific discoveries that appeared to undermine faith in an invisible, nonverifiable God. After the devastation of two world wars, theologians like Karl Barth reinterpreted atonement for a world reeling from profound suffering and disenchantment with humankind. The liberation theologians, concerned with making the gospel of Christ relevant for the millions of innocent people oppressed, abused, and murdered by empires, wars, and crooked governments, reinterpreted the atonement for their suffering communities.

The layers of reinterpretation in both the biblical texts and in the history of Christian doctrine lead to the realization that the tradition *is* to *reinterpret* the tradition. We reinterpret continually, repeatedly, with a repetition of reinterpretation that preserves the relevance of the living and active Word of God. The responsibility to reinterpret the character and heart of God—from that of a violent and vengeful deity eager to throw sinners into the eternal fire, to that of a loving and compassionate Savior yearning for restored relationships with the beloved creation— looms before us as we work toward a theology of peace, reconciliation, and restoration through Christ. Our contemporary Christian community has the responsibility to continue the tradition through reinterpreting these divine truths, to make them relevant for the world in which we all live. That has been the pursuit of this book on hell.

Unlike some contemporary theologians, I do not want to discard the tradition. Our Christian tradition richly expresses the community's efforts to understand the mind of God and hands down to us valuable insights that we can continue to treasure and remember. At the same time, we need to reevaluate, continually putting tradition to the test of time, preserving what enriches and serves the community and reinterpreting those portions of the tradition that no longer speak relevantly to the contemporary situation.

Unfortunately, tradition does not always come to us in the form of a rich heritage. The New Testament word commonly translated "tradition" (*paradosis*) means "handed down" or "handed over"; its cognate verb is translated as "hand over" in the story of Judas, who betrayed Jesus to the authorities, handing him over to be crucified. According to this double meaning, therefore, our own construction of our tradition either enriches us or betrays us with the wisdom of the past. Brooke, Eric, and Lisa have decided that they truly want to expose the areas of their theology where our construction of the tradition has betrayed them. They want to wisely and carefully rethink their beliefs in order to identify the points of betrayal, especially when it comes to knowing the heart and mind of God on issues of salvation and eternal destiny.

HAS TRADITION BETRAYED US?

Before addressing Lisa's questions about Jesus at the beginning of this chapter, we must answer the question "Has our tradition betrayed us with its interpretations of the cross?" I think that it has. If, that is, we want to think consistently with the image of God as love, who desires a restored relationship with every person created in the image of God. Unfortunately, most traditional ways of thinking about the cross present God in a quite different light.

When it comes to the cross, many of us see only one side of the coin. We see the extravagance of divine love toward *us*—toward those of *us* who benefit from the death and resurrection of Jesus. We fail to take into consideration the fact that God required the horrific, unjust death of an innocent man, a man we say is God's own Son. We don't notice the fact that God will forgive sin *only* if this atrociously painful death occurs, *only* if someone innocent takes the hit for sin. So we are left with an image of God that contradicts the meaning of genuine forgiveness and true justice. Our traditional interpretations of the cross have betrayed us by constructing an image of God opposite from the one revealed in Jesus. And for centuries we have bowed down and worshiped this distorted image.

The image of God as punishing, who demands a rightful pound of flesh in order to balance the scales of justice, who requires satisfaction to restore offended honor, retribution in order to reconcile—all this bleeds into the structures of the world's governments, courts of law, and familial relations. The image of a God who must rule and domi- nate at all costs, using our violence as a tool and in the name of Christ, promotes violence as positive, as redemptive, as constitutive of God's mercy and justice in a divine (and thus human) system of domination.

We've talked about the difficulties that lie in this image, the least of which is that it simulates an artificial tension between divine mercy and divine justice, divine love and divine wrath, divine domination and divine servitude. Would not an image of God as love, as reconciling, and as peace loving harmonize more effectively with the image of God as love by focusing on the restoration of a broken relationship rather than on forms of retribution? As we saw in chapter 7, wouldn't God's goal of saving the world more likely be successful by taking restorative rather than retributive measures?

For example, in the protest against racial segregation seen in the Amer- ican South during the 1960s, violent act upon violent act was inflicted on black American communities nationwide. One response was to retaliate with retributive violence in the name of justice, matching hatred with hatred and violence with violence. These actions fed the escalating cycle of violence, fostering riots and killing. Some black American leaders, however, responded differently to the violence. In the hopes of recon- ciliation and the restoration of black-white relationships, they sat peace- ably at lunch counters while others shouted insults at them and inflicted bodily harm. They moved silently and peacefully to the front of buses, responding to hatred with love. They loved their enemies and prayed for them, and they interrupted the cycle of violence with that love.

In the same way, by taking restorative measures, God in Christ interrupted the cycle of violence with divine love that sought and acted to reconcile and restore rather than punish and retaliate. God in Christ worked to tear down structures of violence and to redeem the world with love and forgiveness. The life, death, and resurrection of Christ reveal to us that God does not prefer violent means to gain what God desires. Jesus reveals to us that God's justice is mercy in the form of restoration, reconciliation, and redemption from the strong powers of the world. Where reconciliation is the focus, violence is cut short. Where restoration of relationship is foremost in theories of atonement, violence is precluded from the divine character. Where violence is seen as a human act free from any connection with God's way of acting or redeeming humanity, "legitimate" use of coercive power no longer holds sway over society, governments, or families.

This alone is one of the most important reasons for thinking differently about the image of God and the work of God through Jesus Christ, the work of atonement.

AT-ONE-MENT

No matter which metaphors we use to describe it, suffice it to say that God, through Jesus, provided not only for our salvation, but also for the redemption of the entire creation (Rom. 8:19–22). Although the Bible uses diverse metaphors to communicate to us how God takes care of the sin problem, reconciles with us, and draws us back into the fold as a lover does his beloved or a mother hen her chicks, something of cosmic significance happened through Jesus. We call it "atonement" or in other words, *at-one-ment*. God, through Jesus, reconciles the world to God, unites us, makes us *at one* with God and others. In fact Jesus prays for our at-one-ment in John 17:21–23. He beseeches God on our behalf:

> I do not ask in behalf of these alone, but for those also who believe in Me through their word, that they may all be one; even as You, Father, are in Me, and I in You, that they also may be in Us, so that the world may believe that You sent Me. The glory which You have given Me I have given to them, that they may be one, just as We are one; I in them and You in Me, that they may be perfected in unity, so that the world may know that You sent Me, and loved them, even as You have loved Me.

In the Eastern Orthodox tradition, the early church fathers spoke of at-one-ment as union with God, or as *theōsis*. They believed (and still do) that Jesus was made human so that humans could be made divine. The Orthodox Church doesn't mean to say that humanity will be God or equal to God, but that we will be so like Jesus, so united with God, that we will be one relationally. So the word "at-one-ment" describes the union of our whole person with God in the divine kingdom. Through our unity with Christ, our human nature is remade into its original beauty, reborn to new life. Through the perfect unity of the divine and human in Jesus, God participates in the life of humanity. Through that perfect union in Jesus, we also participate in the life of God.

The metaphor of participation, God participating in our humanness and we participating in God's divinity, illustrates the beauty of reconciliation and the restoration of our relationship with God. We actually participate in God's nature, and God participates in ours. As 2 Peter 1:4 tells us, we become partakers of the divine nature, liberated from our corrupt nature through the work of Jesus. Jesus, then, acts as the true mediator between God and humans (and all creation, actually!) by uniting the human and divine into one, so that we are "at one," thus supplying the meaning of "at-one-ment."

The at-one-ment of God's nature and ours through Jesus means that God's heart becomes ours; God's desires, God's purposes, and God's kingdom vision are ours as well. To be at one with God also means to be at one with Christ, so at one that Jesus actually lives his life through us. For us, then, at-one-ment means that, for us, "living is Christ" (Phil. 1:21 NRSV). No longer do we live, but Christ lives within us (Gal. 2:20). This is the nature of at-one-ment. What's more, nothing can separate us from our at-one-ment with God, not "tribulation, or distress, or persecution, or famine, or nakedness, or peril, or sword . . . For . . . neither death, nor life, nor angels, nor principalities, nor things present, nor things to come, nor powers, nor height, nor depth, nor any other created thing, will be able to separate us from the love of God, which is in Christ Jesus our Lord" (Rom. 8:35–39). Our at-one-ment through Jesus endures forever and is offered to all those created in the image of God.

"Wow! That's so cool!" Brooke again. This time our conversation took place during a parallel parking lesson. I caught the little glimmer of mischief in her eyes and the hint of a smile on her face as she looked at me sideways, threw the car into reverse, and put way too much pressure on the gas pedal. As the car bolted backward, the look of shock on my face (her purpose for the pressure on the pedal) matched the tone in my voice.

"We'll end up being at one with that tree if you don't slow down!"

Completely delighted with herself, she asked, "How exactly did Jesus accomplish this at-one-ment? I know he died on the cross and rose again; but what's the connection between that and at-one-ment?" Good. I wanted to talk about that next.

IT'S ALL ABOUT PURIFICATION

Sixteenth-century Protestant reformer William Tyndale used the word "atonement" in a theological sense and understood it literally as "at-one-ment," describing the double act of God's cleansing our sin and reconciling us into union with God. We see the word "atonement" quite often in our English translations of the Old Testament book of Leviticus and its instructions for animal sacrifice. When the priest sprinkles the blood of the lamb or goat on the altar, he atones for sin. In fact, whenever we see the word "atonement" or "atone" in the Old Testament, it most often comes from the Hebrew word *kippur,* which carries with it a deeply significant meaning that gets lost in translation.

Kippur means "to wipe away," "to cleanse," or "to purify." The blood of the sacrificial animal, then, cleanses the people from sin, wipes it away, expiates it, and in so doing, purifies the people. When Moses or the priests sprinkled the blood on the people or on the altar, they were cleansed and purified (Exod. 24:8; 29:20–21; Lev. 16:15). Interestingly, the two Hebrew verbs translated "sprinkle" in these passages illustrate the purifying process bound up with God's forgiveness. In fact, the Hebrew word for forgiveness can also carry the meaning of "sprinkling in order to purify." The symbolism is profound. As the priests in these various incidents sprinkle themselves, the people, and the altar with blood, they are cleansed and purified. Or we could say, they are forgiven, that God's forgiveness cleanses and purifies them. Old Testament scholars make it clear that the shedding of the animal's blood to atone for sin is in no way punitive. The priest kills the animal only for its blood. It has nothing to do with punishing the animal in place of punishing the people. It has everything to do with blood as the life force that cleanses and purifies the people.

In fact, Leviticus 17:11 provides us with the meaning of blood as the life force. It tells us that "the life of the flesh is in the blood": flesh lives only because the blood gives it life. No blood, no life. For the Hebrew people, then, blood was a symbol for life or the giving of life represented in the Old Testament sacrificial system. So when the priests sprinkled the blood on the altar, it symbolized the people giving their own lives up to God as living and holy sacrifices. The blood served as an outward symbol of an inward reality: the life of the worshiper given to God, set apart (the meaning of "holy") for God's purposes.

SACRIFICE MISINTERPRETED

Unfortunately, the people focused only on the external ritual and forgot its profound internal symbolism. They began to trust only in their sacrifices to gain favor with God. The ritual became the end in itself rather than what it symbolized. They sacrificed the blood of animals and then set their lives apart for their own purposes rather than for God's. The Old Testament prophets admonished the people because their sacrifices had no meaning; they were empty, symbolizing nothing at all. In fact, the prophet Amos basically told them that God would be more pleased with them if they didn't perform these empty sacrifices. After all, they had lived righteously in God's eyes before God instituted ritual sacrifices (Amos 5:21–24). Through the mouth of Amos, God says, "I *hate*, I *reject* your festivals. . . . Even though you offer up to Me burnt offerings and your grain offerings, I will not accept them; and I will not even look at the peace offerings of your fatlings" (emphasis added). Here God rejects meaningless sacrifices. God actually hates the blood sacrifices. The blood of goats and bulls *in itself*, without the inward giving of life to God, voids the sacrifice in God's eyes. The important thing for God, the only sacrifice God accepts, is the life of the sacrifice symbolized in the blood.

But their hearts were not in it, and therefore the sacrifices meant nothing to God. Jeremiah, too, gets on the Israelites' case for their heartless, lifeless sacrifices. He says that God never told them to offer merely external sacrifices. The kind of sacrifice that God desired, symbolized in the blood of the animal only, was obedience, their lives given to God as a sacrifice, lives lived according to God's ways for God's purposes (Jer. 7:20–23). In fact, the prophets have so much to say about the blood sacrifices empty of any meaning that I'll quote a few for you just to make the point clear:

First Samuel 15:22. In response to Saul's disobedience, indicative of a life not given to God, Samuel speaks the words of God saying, "Has the LORD as much delight in burnt offerings and sacrifices as in obeying the voice of the LORD? Behold, to obey is better than sacrifice, and to heed [God] than the fat of rams." The sacrifice that God wanted from Saul wasn't found in the external ritual of slaying an animal and sprinkling its blood about. God desired the internal heart condition of giving his life to God made manifest with acts of obedience to God's will.

Psalm 40:6–8. The psalmist expresses his desire to give his entire life to God and says, "Sacrifice and meal offering You have not desired; My ears you have opened [He listened to the true message of sacrifice]; burnt offering and sin offering You have not required. Then I said, 'Behold, I come; in the scroll of the book it is written of me; I delight to do Your will, O my God; Your Law is within my heart.'" Notice that the psalmist realizes the law, which established the sacrificial system, is fulfilled only when it is written on the heart rather than performed as an outward ritual only. The true sacrifice, symbolized in the blood, is the life given to God in order to do God's will. This is also the genuine meaning of being holy: setting your *life* apart for God's use.

Isaiah 1:10–15. "'What are your multiplied sacrifices to Me?' says the LORD. 'I have had enough of burnt offerings of rams and the fat of fed cattle. And I take no pleasure in the blood of bulls, lambs or goats. . . . Bring your worthless offerings no longer" (vv. 11–13). Now why does God respond this way to their sacrifices? Because they offer them as an external exercise only, without giving their lives to God. In fact, the next phrase tells us what they have done that makes God hate their empty sacrifices: "I will hide My eyes from you; yes, even though you multiply prayers, I will not listen. *Your hands are covered with blood*" (v. 15, emphasis added). God rejects their sacrifices because they live lives for their own purpose and resort to violence. Isaiah 29:13 explains it better than I can. God rejects their blood sacrifices because "This people draw near with their words and honor Me with their lip service, but they remove their hearts [read 'lives' here] far from Me, and their reverence for Me consists of tradition learned by rote [read 'external ritual sacrifices' here]."

Jeremiah 6:20. Jeremiah can't state this more simply! He repeats God's words in a nutshell: "Your burnt offerings are not acceptable, and your sacrifices are not pleasing to Me."

Okay, that's enough for now. I hope I've made the point clear. We needed to see the message of the prophets, proclaiming that God rejected blood sacrifices, the formalism of worship without the heart to go with it, and the shedding of blood without the investment of a life given to God to back it up. I'll reiterate for the sake of emphasis: God never intended for Israel to kill animals and pour their blood out on the altar as an exercise in itself. God hoped the people would catch on to the true meaning of the blood poured out and perform their external sacrifices as a symbol for the true internal sacrifice of their very lives set apart to God and for God.

Now, if God didn't want these blood sacrifices without the internal giving of life that they symbolized, what, in God's eyes, do we suppose the set-apart life looked like in the Old Testament? To simplify, I'll quote a few of the verses again:

Proverbs 21:3. "To do righteousness and justice is desired by the LORD rather than sacrifice." As we discussed in previous chapters, those who do justice and righteousness act as ambassadors for God; they have given their whole life to God.

Isaiah 1:16–17. These verses follow the ones I quoted above and are in the context of offering external sacrifices, which God rejects. Here we see a beautiful picture of what it looks like to live a life for God. "Wash yourselves [remember the meaning of *kippur,* 'to wash or cleanse'], make yourselves clean; remove the evil of your deeds from My sight. Cease to do evil, learn to do good; seek justice, reprove the ruthless; defend the orphan, plead for the widow."

Isaiah 58:6–7. These verses fall in the context of God reproving the people for empty worship, worship without the heart to accompany it. After admonishing them for their counterfeit worship, Isaiah reminds them of what true, sacrificial actions look like—which is true worship. God wants them to "loosen the bonds of wickedness, to undo the bands of the yoke, and to let the oppressed go free and break every yoke, . . . to divide [their] bread with the hungry, and bring the homeless poor into the house." He goes on to tell them to give clothes to the naked and be generous to others—all actions of those whose lives belong to God.

Hosea 6:6. God says to them, "For I delight in loyalty rather than sacrifice, and in the knowledge of God rather than burnt offerings." An alternate translation goes like this: "It is love that I want, not sacrifices." Again, these are traits of a life sacrificed to God. (Remember, the life is represented by the blood of the sacrifices.)

Amos 5:21–24. Remember these verses from above. God rejects the people's blood sacrifices and tells them the nature of a true sacrifice, the sacrifice of their lives to God. So hear God say, "I don't want your empty sacrifices. They're worthless." Now for the big *but instead.* "But let justice roll down like waters and righteousness like an ever-flowing stream" (v. 24).

Micah 6:8. This is a favorite. After reprimanding the people for offering meaningless sacrifices of blood, Micah tells them the kind of sacrifice God wants, as symbolized in the external ritual: "He has told you, O [people], what is good; and what the does the LORD require of you but to do justice, to love kindness, and to walk humbly with your God?"

From these verses we see that God desires and demands an internal, life-giving commitment, one symbolized by the life-giving blood sacrifices of the Israelites, and one that they ignored for the most part. If blood symbolizes life, how can we apply those sacrifices to our walk with God today?

OUR SACRIFICE TODAY

In order to figure out how we apply the symbolism of the blood sacrifice to our walk with God today, we'll turn to Romans 12:1: "I urge you, therefore, [brothers and sisters], by the mercies of God, to present your bodies a living and holy sacrifice, acceptable to God, which is your spiritual service of worship." You don't see us lying around on altars and shedding our own blood in worship to God. Instead, Paul gets right to the point of the true meaning of sacrifice. We give our lives to God. We present our entire body, mind, and soul to God and submit our lives to God's service. So you see, the symbolism of the blood, revealed to the ancient Hebrew people through the familiar symbolic rite of sacrificing animals, finds its fulfillment as we give our own lives to God. And God calls it "worship"! In giving our lives as a living and holy sacrifice, we worship God.

In addition, we see in Hebrews 10:22 that the image of sprinkling blood (the giving of our lives) is spiritualized in the hearts and minds of believers and cleanses and purifies us at the same time: "Let us draw near with a sincere heart in full assurance of faith, having our hearts sprinkled clean from an evil conscience and our bodies washed with pure water." As newly created people, we are made one by a purification that cleanses body, hearts, and conscience and ushers them into the presence of God, ready for a life of service (which, as we saw, is also a form of worship, according to Rom. 12:1). We take to heart the forgiveness we have already received from God and live a life of forgiving others, a sacrifice in itself.

Speaking of forgiveness, we also read in Hebrews 9:22 that "without shedding of blood there is no forgiveness." Remember, the Hebrew words we translate as "sprinkle" can also mean "forgive." In the verse I quoted above, we who give our lives to God as a sacrifice have our hearts and consciences *sprinkled* and therefore washed and purified. We could say, we have our hearts and minds *forgiven* and therefore washed and purified. Without giving our lives to God as a living sacrifice, we wouldn't be aware of the washing and purifying power of God's forgiveness. The washing and purification enable us to realize God's forgiveness. With that in mind, Hebrews 9:22 could instead read, "Without the giving of your life as a living sacrifice, as symbolized in the Old Testament by the shedding of lifeblood, you will not know the blessings of God's purifying forgiveness." We now live our lives in that forgiveness and are at one with God through Jesus.

Now that we've sacrificed our lives upon God's altar, what does our life look like? How do we *do* that sacrificial life-giving, practically speaking? Romans 12:2 and Hebrews 10:23–24 tell us. "Do not be conformed to this world, but be transformed by the renewing of your mind, so that you may prove what the will of God is, that which is good, acceptable, and perfect"; and "Let us hold fast the confession of our hope without wavering, for He who promised is faithful; and let us consider how to stimulate one another to love and good deeds." That wraps it up rather well, doesn't it? Basically, we no longer live, but Christ lives within us. We think with the mind of God. We love God and others and work to spread that love around the world. In this way, we give our lives as living and holy (set-apart) sacrifices to God.

THE JESUS CONNECTION

Okay, now back to Brooke's question about how, through the sacrifice of his life, Jesus brought about our at-one-ment. Since this is a topic for an entire book, we'll go over it quickly and move on to the role of Jesus at judgment time. I'll sum up what we have discussed thus far. Remember our word meanings: *Kippur* means "to atone." "To sprinkle" in Hebrew also includes the concept of forgiveness. The blood symbolizes life. If we look in Hebrews 10 we see that Jesus lives without blemish, without sin, as our perfect high priest. In the Old Testament the high priest would sprinkle the blood on the altar. Now Jesus acts as the high priest for our salvation. Only he didn't come to the altar of God with the blood (life) of bulls or goats. He came offering his own blood (life), sprinkling it on the altar for the forgiveness of sin. With all this in mind, then, we can say the following in the context of Jesus, our perfect high priest: The blood (life) of Jesus given to us cleanses and purifies us from all sin as he sprinkles (forgives) it on the mercy seat (*kapporet*) before God. In other words, Jesus, who had no sin, atones (cleanses) for our sin by giving his life for us and by saying from the cross, "Father, forgive them [the whole human race]; they don't know what they are doing." And God did.

God's forgiveness through Jesus washes us clean, purifies us from our sin so that we in turn can give our lives to God as living and holy sacrifices. When we receive Jesus as Savior, we are at one with him. It is as if we die with him. We are baptized (immersed) into his life-giving sacrifice and raised with him to walk as he walked, cleansed and purified, in a whole new life. One with Jesus and indwelled by the Holy Spirit, we are at one with God. So Jesus accomplished our at-one-ment.

In doing so, Jesus reversed the law of retribution and instituted the law of forgiveness, which is coin of the realm in God's kingdom. We see from 2 Corinthians 5:19 that "God was in Christ reconciling the world to Himself." Exactly how did God do that? God did it by "not counting our sins against us": in Christ we attain our at-one-ment through forgiveness. When we apprehend our forgiveness, forgiveness already offered through the life-giving Jesus, we are reconciled with God. We have been reconciled and restored, and at judgment time we face God with Jesus at our side, love burning away the rest of the chaff (1 Cor. 3:10–15). With that in mind, let's go back to Lisa's questions at the beginning of this chapter and their relationship to our new view of hell. She asked what difference Jesus makes in the fire of God's presence for those who chose to follow him during their lifetime.

JESUS AND "HELL"

My mother is concerned about the same thing as Lisa. I had a conversation with her yesterday after she had read the first few chapters of this book. She expressed her uncertainty about this more hospitable view of hell. She worries that it might lessen the validity of Jesus' death on the cross. I told her that a more hospitable hell in no way compromises or diminishes the reconciling work of the cross of Christ. In fact, it enhances it! It makes the life, death, and resurrection of Jesus vastly more effective and completely unlimited. All those we normally deem suitable for the fires of hell have a chance in the fire of God's presence to receive the forgiveness already there for them and to reconcile with God—through the atonement that Jesus made possible. I think what Lisa and my mother worry about, however, is whether or not believers will have to stand in that same fire and suffer the hellish agonies of having their impurities burned away. So I'll tell you a fictional story about a woman named Anne who received the forgiveness of God through Jesus and lived a full life of serving him.

Anne loved Jesus with all of her heart. She spent her life serving God, first as a Youth for Christ leader in high school, then as a student chaplain in college, and finally as a missionary in Uganda, Africa. She taught Bible study classes and worked in hospitals with sick and diseased children. On judgment day she came into the presence of God with joy and with a bit of trepidation (some would call it the fear of God). The blinding light of God's presence dazzled her, its burning heat encompassed her; and its boundless love embraced her. At first she feared that the fire would totally consume her. But as she experienced and then understood its inexpressible and excessive love, she hoped it would. She had never known such love, mercy, and compassion. And as she stood there, she turned her head and saw Jesus standing there *with her* in the flames. (Could he be the same one who walked with Daniel's friends in the fiery furnace?) He spoke. "Come, faithful servant, into the fellowship of God's community. You are now perfected in unity with God. Come and be one with me as I am one with the Father, my beloved child" (cf. John 17:22–23). As the fire of God's love continued to burn, she knew that the purification that began for her during her lifetime was finally finished. But rather than the pain and the hellish work of repentance that unbelievers face in the fire, Anne experienced the intense joy of divine love. She walked, with Jesus next to her, into the center of the fire, into her at-one-ment with God.

Again I turn to George MacDonald, who certainly has a way with words:

> He will shake heaven and earth, that only the unshakable may remain: he is a consuming fire, that only that which cannot be consumed may stand forth eternal. It is the nature of God, so terribly pure that it destroys all that is not pure as fire, which demands like purity in our worship. He will have purity. It is not that the fire will burn us if we do not worship thus; yea, [it] will go on burning within us after all that is foreign to it has yielded its force, no longer with pain and consuming, but as the highest consciousness of life, the presence of God. (2)

You see, we will all appear before the judgment seat of Christ. We will all experience the intense burning love of God that rids us, once and for all, of our remaining impurities. We will all be saved through the fire; but notice that in the Greek "saved" also means "healed." The fire of God purifies and heals so that finally, in the end, God's will prevails. Every knee will bow, every tongue will sing praise to God, and all will confess that Jesus Christ is Lord (Rom. 14:10–11; 2 Cor. 5:10; 1 Cor. 3:13–15). The unbelieving will experience the fire of God's presence as the fiery wrath of love. In that fire they will be judged with the burning intensity of the unconditional love of God. The fire will encompass them, love will convict them, and the flames will burn away their impurities. Unlike believers, they will stand in the fire alone and bear the hell of facing their sin in light of the incomprehensible extravagance of divine love. For them, the judgment of love burns, heals, and finally redeems so that, cleansed and purified, these persons can finally receive the forgiveness that was always there for them through Jesus and be reconciled to God if they so choose. So when all is said and done, we all will dwell in the eternal fiery presence of God and be consumed by God's love. At one, at last.

12

How Then Shall We Live?

Here force failed my high fantasy; but my
desire and will were moved already—like
a wheel revolving uniformly—by
the Love that moves the sun and the other stars.
                          —Dante, *Paradiso*, Canto 33

Beloved, if God so loved us,
we also ought to love one another.

                          —1 John 4.11

SHEEP AND GOATS

"What about the sheep and the goats in Matthew 25? You haven't talked about them yet, but Jesus did. We can't have our view of hell without dealing with these verses." Another telephone conversation. And true to form, Lisa holds our feet to the flames when it comes to staying faithful to the biblical texts. I am continually thankful to her for that! Eric brought up the same topic: the sheep and the goats. But as a ministry student called to missions, his concern was less for the Bible than for the goats, the ones who, Jesus says, "will go away into eternal punishment" (Matt. 25:46).

We find the parable of the sheep and the goats in Matthew 25:32–46. Remember that Jesus told parables in order to get a main point across to his listeners. We can't build an entire doctrine around a parable, but we can identify the message that Jesus wanted us to hear. In this story, the nations come before "the Son of Man" for judgment. So we can assume that Jesus is talking metaphorically about the last judgment. As the king, he separates the sheep from the goats, herding the sheep off to the right so that they may enter God's kingdom. He corrals the goats off to his left for judgment and "eternal punishment." So what's the main message here?

If you read the entire parable, you see that Jesus rewards the sheep with immediate entry into God's kingdom. Why? Because they took care of the poor. The goats did not. Jesus considered taking care of the poor so important that he spoke in extreme hyperbole in order to get his message across!

We talked about the use of parables in another chapter. This parable in Matthew says nothing about faith in Christ. It says nothing about receiving Jesus as Savior or off to hell you go. It says nothing at all about repenting of sin, nothing at all about walking down the aisle in your church to be saved, nothing at all about getting baptized. Now, I'm not saying those things aren't important: they are. But this specific parable, one that we use to threaten others with hell, separates the sheep from the goats based upon their care for the hungry, the naked, and the thirsty—those who can't afford clothes, food, or drink.

We have to think about the context, the society and culture during the time when Jesus lived. Poverty was epidemic in Jesus' day. The Roman leaders bled the people dry with high taxes. The violence of Jewish rebels often left lands burned and husbands and sons dead, with no way for their women and children to earn a living. Jesus commanded his followers to love God, but he also commanded them to love others. Loving others means you take care of them if they are in need.

Remember what the first Christian communities did—how they lived? Acts 2:42–47 tells us that they shared "all things in common." They took care of each other. One of my professors at Southern Methodist University, where I worked on my PhD, said that "if the church took care of the poor as Jesus commanded it to, that would eliminate poverty completely." I think Jesus tried to tell us just that in hyperbolic form in Matthew 25. If that's the case, then the parable actually tells us that if we don't take care of the poor, we're goats, and Jesus will shuffle us off into eternal punishment. Fortunately, Jesus uses hyperbolic language here to motivate his followers to live kingdom lives by loving and caring for others.

But let's just say that Jesus' main message in this parable really is about who goes to heaven and who goes to hell. The sheep go to heaven and the goats go to hell, like some of our traditions have taught us. Poised in the context of our alternative view of hell, in which "eternal" can mean any length of time, and the grief of coming face-to-face with the gravity of your personal sin (and your victims) serves as punishment, we can explain the separation of the sheep and goats. This fits perfectly with our stories about Otto (in this case, the goat) and Anne (the sheep). On the one hand, Anne, already a believer, has already acknowledged and received the forgiveness of God through Christ; thus she stands before God with Jesus by her side, not for judgment for sin but to complete her at-one-ment with God. She experiences the fire of God's presence as a burning love that completes her purification and makes her one with God and the community of those washed (sprinkled/forgiven), cleansed, and purified by Jesus. She goes off at once into the kingdom that God has prepared for her.

On the other hand, Otto stands alone before God and experiences the fire of God's presence as a burning love that judges his sin, burns off the impurities, and brings him to repentance. He then chooses whether or not to receive the forgiveness of God through Jesus. So the love of God through the work of Jesus saves even goats! Good news or what? So in light of this parable, how should we live, we who already know God's love, compassion, mercy, justice, and forgiveness? The next chapter offers some suggestions. We already know one way because Matthew told us: take care of the poor. But there's more to kingdom life. Let's discuss what that might look like for us.

LIFE IN THE KINGDOM—NOW

"The kingdom of God is at hand" (Mark 1:15). Jesus spoke these words, and I believe he means that the kingdom of God isn't only for some future hereafter but for our time. Jesus taught the people to pray for the kingdom to "come . . . on earth as it is in heaven" (Matt. 6:10). Come, kingdom, now, on earth. Bring the heavenly rule of God here, right here on earth. Just as God rules in heaven, let God rule here on earth. God answers prayer.

When the Jews heard Jesus pronounce the good news of the kingdom of God, they knew that he wasn't talking about some otherworldly rule that they would enter upon death, but a kingdom for this world, the rule of God on earth, right then, a present reality. In fact, in the first three centuries of the early church, the ancient artwork depicts paradise itself, not as a place to live in constant joy in the afterlife, but as the kingdom of God on earth, in this life.

I believe that those early Christians put their focus in the right place at the right time—earthly time—and, as active participants in God's kingdom, worked to bring about paradise on earth. As part of his ministry, Jesus set up God's kingdom on earth and left us here with the help of God's Holy Spirit to see to its growth and success, to show the rest of the world what it means to live as active members of the kingdom, living lives that follow in the footsteps of Jesus.

The scope of Christ's love and the boundlessness of his forgiveness provide not only reconciliation to God; they also serve as an example to others who desire to live their lives following in his steps. Christ enables us to live a new kind of life, loving the unlovable and forgiving the unforgivable, promoting peace and justice rather than violence and abuse, standing in solidarity with those less fortunate, with the lepers of today's society, with those suffering from AIDS, with gays, lesbians, blacks, Jews, Arabs—in short, all those abused by "the powers that be" (Rom. 13:1 KJV). The kingdom of God is made up of such as these; through Christ's words and actions, he called forth the kingdom and set it in motion on earth. By announcing that the kingdom of God is at hand, Jesus proclaimed that the kingdom is here, now, right at this minute, a kingdom made up of all those who hear God's call to justice, to love, and to peace. The kingdom of God takes place as an event of extravagant hospitality shown to the stranger, of love offered freely and without expectation of return, of justice shown even to those who do not deserve it in the eyes of society, of the transformation and changed lives that experience the healing touch of God.

So if God's kingdom is here, then what does it look like? How should we, as citizens of the heavenly realm of God on earth, think, act, and live (Phil. 3:20)? From my search through Scripture, I came up with the following characteristics of God's kingdom. Although not exhaustive, these characteristics also prescribe how we, as kingdom participants, ought to govern our lives. The Bible describes the kingdom of God as the following:

A Kingdom of Peace

As we've already seen throughout this book, God desires and promotes peace. Isaiah 9:6–7 represents God's kingdom as one of unending peace, calling its ruler the "Prince of Peace." As the Prince of Peace, Jesus came to bring us peace with God and to establish God's peace on earth among all people (Isa. 52:7; Luke 2:14; Rom. 5:1; Eph. 2:13–17; Col. 1:20). All of the prophets preached the good news about the peace that would bless every nation with the inauguration of God's kingdom.

Even the name of the ancient city of God, "Jerusalem," actually means "city of peace" and thus symbolizes for us the true nature of God's kingdom rule and the activity of God's kingdom people. The peace of God that prevails in the heavenly kingdom should characterize our own lives. Read the beginnings of each of the letters in the New Testament. Out of twenty-two letters, eighteen of them explicitly exhort the readers to lives of peace in the greeting. Peace must be an extremely significant characteristic of the people of God's kingdom. Paul tells us to live in peace with one another (2 Cor. 13:11). The Second Letter to Timothy expresses its significance for kingdom living by exhorting us to pursue peace (2:22). God has granted us the peace of the Lord and has called us to live in peace (1 Cor. 7:15; 2 Thess. 3:16). Jesus tells us that he gives us his peace and leaves it with us, for us to practice it in our lives as we further the kingdom of God with our peaceful living (John 14:27). One of the fruits of the Spirit is peace (Gal. 5:22). And we certainly can't forget Matthew 5:9 (NRSV), "Blessed are the peacemakers, for they will be called children of God." Peacemaking is the distinguishing mark of those who bear the name of God as God's sons and daughters! One of the ways we promote peace, the way that Jesus enables us to make peace with God, is through forgiveness and forgivingness, also a kingdom characteristic.

A Kingdom of Forgiveness

Since we've devoted an entire chapter (4) to forgiveness, I won't expound on it here. Suffice it to say that, as people of God's kingdom, we are also a forgiving people. Just as God in Christ has forgiven us, so we must forgive others. This sounds easy, doesn't it? But we see that two opposite realities confront one another in the radical call of the kingdom of God: the law of retribution, which demands its ounce of flesh; and the law of grace, which loves the enemy and forgives without measure. God calls us to reverse the law of retaliation, which seeks satisfaction through violence, with the law of love, which desires restoration through forgiveness.

God's kingdom forgiveness acts as a catalyst for reconciliation and renewal of a relationship with God and others. Through forgiveness, God seeks to transform sinners into saints and saints into service for the furtherance of the kingdom, in which unconditional love and forgiveness effectively operate outside the vicious economic circles of retributive "justice" and quid pro quo. Forgiveness, which brings peace and enables the forgiven to be peacemakers, truly defines God's justice—another characteristic of the kingdom.

A Kingdom of Justice

Again, we have already read two chapters (3 and 7) on divine justice. By now you know its significance for God's kingdom and for our behavior. You have seen that typical human justice opposes God's justice: one is violent and retributive; the other is peaceful and restorative. Sadly, however, by bowing down to the image of God as violent and punishing, we have advocated, promoted, and participated in centuries of bloodshed in the name of our God. The radical call of the kingdom, however, turns the tables on retributive ways of thinking and acting, exhorting us to do justice through peaceful means, through loving others, taking care of the poor, and seeking to reconcile others to God through our example. Such justice is hospitable justice—and yes, hospitality also characterizes the kingdom of God!

A Kingdom of Hospitality

Those who follow Christ in the kingdom of God open up themselves to others in hospitality. Unlike the world's form of hospitality, which carefully calculates its conditions and extends itself only to those who are on the list of invited guests—those who can be counted on to reciprocate—kingdom hospitality lets the outsiders in. It pushes against the limits of worldly hospitality, practicing instead the unconditional hospitality that marks the kingdom of God, the love that reaches out to all with the desire to forgive and reconcile.

Romans 12:13 describes how we are to behave toward others, exhorting us to practice hospitality. Being hospitable includes blessing those who persecute us, rejoicing with those who rejoice, weeping with those who weep, acting with humility, associating with others outside our social group, and returning good for evil. Titus 1:8 and 1 Peter 4:9 tell us that as God's stewards we are to show hospitality to others by keeping our tempers in control, loving others, and serving them without complaint. In other words, as servants of God, as active citizens of

God's kingdom, and as stewards of God's good gifts to all humankind, we are to open our homes, our arms, and our hearts to all those whom God loves—for God so loved the world.

Everyone is invited to the wedding feast in the kingdom of God, accepted without discrimination like the Prodigal Son, whose father welcomes him with open arms, or the one lost sheep, who counts as much as the ninety-nine who did not stray (Luke 15). Hospitality so rules in the kingdom of God that, as philosopher John Caputo says, "*doing* hospitality *constitutes* membership in the Kingdom." Consequently, in God's kingdom, hospitality generates community as it flourishes as a city without walls, a nation without borders, and a people without prejudice. In this community, love is the powerless power that draws and binds all persons toward God and toward each other in gracious hospitality.

A Kingdom of Weakness

Although at first we may balk at the thought of a "weak" God, the weakness of God as love and forgiveness merely seems like weakness to a world bent on the world's view of "strong" power as coercion and force that pushes its agenda with guns in hand and the threat of bombs from the air. In truth, the weak power of God is a strong power for reconciliation and restoration, for peace and justice that does away with the need for the world's "strong" power through the gentle power of divine love.

So we see that the call of God's kingdom disturbs the status quo, demanding that we behave differently from the rest of the world. This radical call reverses our definitions of power from that of strength and might, which coerces and forces obedience, to that of weakness and humility, which gently persuades and lovingly lures. Whereas the world turns strangers away, the kingdom welcomes the strangers, offering them invitations to the feast. In the kingdom, where weakness is power, God rolls out the red carpet for the disenfranchised, the weak, the poor, and the oppressed, giving them the royal treatment, a welcome worthy of kings.

The good news of the kingdom proclaims the noncoercive power of God to melt hardened hearts, to forgive the unforgivable, to love the unlovable, to breathe new life into the dead, to revive the spirits of the dispirited, and to offer peace in a world at war. Unlike the power of the kingdoms of the world, the power of God revealed in the kingdom of God turns death into life and mourning into joy; it boasts in its weakness and in its power to shame the wise and the strong with the foolishness of the cross and weakness of God (1 Cor. 1:18–31). Powerlessness reigns with the weak force of love, with a refusal to retaliate, with forgiveness, and with the giving of life in peace and compassion.

Be warned, however. We must not underestimate the weak reign of God because it is a weak force. It is still capable of shocking us, of shaking our foundations as it exerts its "force" like a "whisper" that moves mountains and topples empires, confounding and displacing the powers of the world among us. As such, the weak force of God interrupts and shocks the high and mighty powers that be, not with aggression and war, but with offers of love and peace as Jesus did. In God's kingdom, instead of hands holding swords for violence, God disrupts the scene with hands held out to help and to heal with the power of love. I love the way the liberation theologian Leonardo Boff put it in his book *Jesus Christ the Liberator*. He says that God is "weak in power but strong in love" (27).

A Kingdom of Love

I believe that peace, forgiveness, justice, and hospitality are all accomplished with love, a noncoercive power that the "world" deems as weakness. Just as the kingdom of God is always at hand, the love of God is always at hand, forgiving, bringing justice through reconciliation, inviting all to come to the feast, healing and changing hearts, loving those who make love difficult, those impossible to love. Similar to God's forgiveness, justice, and hospitality, God loves without any expectation of return, without counting the cost, with a passion that seems impossible to those used to the world's way of loving. The kingdom of God, therefore, hinges on love, the love of God, which objectively is God's love for all creation and subjectively is all creation's love for God. God loves unconditionally, without measure, and no one is excluded. God's love is hospitable and just.

Since God's love opens itself to the other, so must our love open itself to the other, always offered, always responding to the call of the kingdom. Just as love flows in excess from God, as we see in the life, death, and resurrection of Christ, we are responsible to see that love flows in excess from us. We can never love too much, and we can never love enough. Love is not an economy that keeps track of what is rendered and what is returned. Love loves without concern for gain and without expectation of return.

We love because we are loved by God. In the Spirit of truth, God's Spirit, we love those who are unlovable, those who do not love us, and we love our enemies, an impossible love that transforms us and those we love. Religion, as practiced in the kingdom of God, is for lovers. Considered by many in the kingdoms of this world as a weakness, I argue that the weak power of kingdom love heals, transforms, and restores. Love in the kingdom of God seems weak but is actually strong with the power of reconciliation and restoration of all people to God. If kingdom love truly holds sway, if those called by love respond to love, then we can say with Augustine, "Love and do what you will" (*Sermons on 1 John*, 7th sermon), since love (and God *is* love) always wills love.

So, if God's kingdom characteristics include peace, forgiveness, justice, hospitality, and the weak force of love, how can we ever believe that the kingdom exists coeternally with a place so opposite to it—eternal hell? How can we believe that a place like hell exists as part of God's will? Such a view of God and God's kingdom should drive us to think differently about the end of all things, to think in harmony with a God who desires nothing other than reconciliation, restoration, and eternal peace for all creation. This is what the good news is all about, isn't it?

WHY BE GOOD, WHY WITNESS?

When I present this alternative view of hell to my students, one of them always asks, "Why be good if we don't have to worry about eternal punishment in hell? If no place of eternal punishment exists, what motivation do we have to live as Jesus says?" As a ministry major with a heart for evangelism, the question of missions became very significant for Eric. He caught me in the hallway one day and asked, "If eternal hell doesn't exist, why should we bother to witness to others? What reason will anyone have for receiving Jesus as Savior or for living their lives in imitation of him?" In other words, if he decided to change his view of hell, Eric also needed to change his approach to witnessing. He needed new evangelistic content and rationale! Threats of hell would no longer work! Good! Or should I say, "Good news!"

Isn't it sad that we even think to ask these types of questions? They reveal that we are more interested in obtaining fire insurance for ourselves than we are in seeing the world transformed by the power of Jesus Christ lived out in each of our lives. They reveal that we view salvation as otherworldly rather than this-worldly. I'm not saying that eternal life in God isn't a cause for rejoicing. But I am saying that our afterlife shouldn't be the focus of our salvation, our evangelism, or our earthly existence.

As a new Christian, I attended an Evangelism Explosion course at my Baptist church. I still remember the main question we were taught to ask people in order to lead them to Jesus. It goes something like this: "If you were to die tonight, would you go to heaven? Why or why not?" This was a totally otherworldly focused marketing strategy for obtaining fire insurance. It wasn't until many years later that I realized the reason for my salvation was not to keep me out of hell but for me to work with God and others to bring about the good news, the kingdom of God right here on earth, by transforming lives with the gospel. If the kingdom of God is now, then salvation is now too—not merely for some eternal existence, but for this existence (Luke 19:9).

So why do we live according to the example of Jesus? Why should we try to do good? Why do we witness? We do these things so that the world can be transformed by the power of God. So that violence can cease through the message of love, even love for enemies. So that all can know the joy of the Lord, the love of God, and bring glory to God through lives lived according to the law of love.

I have often told my students that even if eternal life didn't exist, even if faith in Jesus benefited us nothing after this lifetime, it would still be worth it all. Why? Because Jesus enables us to commune with God. Life with Jesus gives us life united with God. Living as Jesus lived makes us God's partners in the work of transforming the world into a better place for all to live. How do we do that?

Jesus makes this clear to us in John 13:35. He says that all people will know we are his disciples . . . how? By preaching hellfire and brimstone? By throwing around threats of eternal punishment for those who reject Jesus? No! All people will know we are the disciples of Jesus by the *love* we have for one another. Through our *love* for others! The very nature of our reconciliation with God through Jesus makes us God's agents, God's ministers of reconciliation—not so that we can work to keep people out of hell, but so we can transform the world through reconciliation. The only way to get rid of enemies is not to throw them into an eternal hell, but to preach divine forgiveness and guide them to a life reconciled with God and others.

The reason for our at-one-ment is so that we live differently: to live is Christ. The saying in Galatians 2:20, "It is no longer I who live, but Christ lives in me," has radical implications for how we live on earth. It is not about fire insurance. It is about transformed life, kingdom-of-God growth, binding up the brokenhearted, proclaiming liberty to the captives and freedom to prisoners. It's about proclaiming the favorable year of the Lord, comforting those who mourn, and giving a garland instead of ashes. Out of hospitality we give the oil of gladness instead of mourning, the mantle of praise instead of a spirit of fainting, so that God may be glorified (Isa. 61:1–3). And I do believe that eternal life in unity with God is definitely an added joy!

WHO'S IN

After discussing God's goal for saving the world and our participation in seeing God's goal fulfilled, Eric felt that not only would he truly be preaching good news, but that he would also be fulfilling his true calling as a minister of the gospel. He would change his approach from one of stagnating doom and gloom in the fires of hell, to one of transforming faith and hope and love in the kingdom of God. Again, because of its profound significance, I'll repeat the main message here: Rather than the mere possession of a get-out-of-hell-free card, the goal of salvation is to transform the world by seeing it reconciled to God through Jesus Christ. Only a transformed world can stanch the flow of evil, stop the vicious cycles of violence, and propagate peace on earth through goodwill toward all people. This is good news, is it not?

And yes, the entire world is included in God's task for peace. Isaiah tells us that in the end, the light of divine glory will draw all nations to God: "Arise, shine, for your light has come, and the glory of the LORD has risen upon you. For behold, darkness will cover the earth, and deep darkness the peoples; but the LORD will rise upon you, and His glory will appear upon you. Nations will come to your light, and kings to the brightness of your rising" (Isa. 60:1–3). In another important passage, Isaiah speaks for God, saying that all the nations, to the ends of the earth, will bow before God: "There is no other god besides me, a righteous God and a Savior; there is no one besides me. Turn to me and be saved, all the ends of the earth! For I am God, and there is no other. By myself I have sworn, from my mouth has gone forth in righteousness a word that shall not return: 'To me *every* knee shall bow, *every* tongue shall swear.' Only in the LORD, it shall be said of me, are righteousness and strength; all who were incensed against him shall come to him and be ashamed. In the LORD all the offspring of Israel shall triumph and glory" (45:21–25 NRSV, emphasis added; Phil. 2:9–11).

I know that Bible scholars don't agree on how we apply Old Testament verses to Christian doctrines surrounding salvation through Jesus, but if we couple these verses in Isaiah with Romans 3:23–24, we see a more complete picture: "For all have sinned and fall short of the glory of God; they are now justified by grace as a gift, through the redemption that is in Christ Jesus" (NRSV). Notice that *all* have sinned and that those same *all* have been justified as a gift of grace: salvation is a gift to *all.* So we can say with faith that every knee will (willingly) bow and every tongue praise God. But how will that happen?

According to Isaiah, all the nations will come before God terrified and ashamed (remember Otto), standing in God's fiery presence (hell for them). Like Otto, they will tremble in terror before God. Isaiah 45:24 tells us what will happen to them after they come before God in fear and trembling, inconsolably shamed because of their sins. The psalmist gives us a brief glimpse into the reason for their shame. He prays that the nations will be filled with shame *so that they may seek God.* In other words, God's people desire their enemies to feel tremendous shame in the presence of God, not in order to condemn or to destroy them, but in hopes that their shame will humble them enough to reconcile them to God. So in the fiery and purifying presence of God, their evil (and shame) will be burned away, leaving only the pure behind (1 Cor. 3:15). Standing purified before God, they will know the forgiveness that is theirs through Christ and be reconciled to God.

Many verses in the Bible talk about the salvation of all the nations. For example, Psalm 22:27–28 says, "All the ends of the earth will remember and turn to the LORD, and all the families of the nations will worship before [God]. For the kingdom is the LORD's, and he rules over the nations." The prophet Micah lends his voice to the same refrain: "Many nations will come and say, 'Come and let us go up to the mountain of the LORD and to the house of the God of Jacob, that He may teach us about His ways and that we may walk in His paths" (4:2). This passage continues with beautiful prose, painting a picture of the nations beating their swords into plowshares, sitting under their vines in peace, praising and serving God with joy (4:3–4; cf. Ps. 107:1–3; Jer. 31:33–34). Isaiah aptly expresses the joyous time: "For as the earth brings forth its sprouts, and as a garden causes the things sown in it to spring up, so the

Lord GOD will cause righteousness and praise to spring up before all the nations" (61:11). All the nations will see and believe.

Again I turn to Isaiah, who gives us insight into the multitudes of peoples and nations who will receive their salvation. He says to the people, "Seek the LORD; . . . call upon Him. . . . Let the wicked forsake his way and the unrighteous man his thoughts; and let him return to the LORD. . . . [God] will have compassion on him. . . . So will My word be which goes forth from My mouth; it will not return to Me empty, without accomplishing what I desire, and without succeeding in the matter for which I sent it" (55:6–13). In context, the wicked shall return to God, and in the fires of God's compassion and love, the wicked will be reconciled with God. God will accomplish the redemption that God sought for humanity since the time we committed the first sin.

After all is said and done, we see these same nations coming into the holy city of Jerusalem, cleansed and redeemed by the blood (life) of Christ in Revelation 5:13: "Then I heard every creature in heaven and on earth and under the earth and in the sea, and all that is in them, singing: 'To the one seated on the throne and to the Lamb be blessing and honor and glory and might forever and ever!'" This sounds like *every* tongue to me! More good news!

I believe that these verses and others support our alternative view of hell. Those people and those nations of people who rejected Jesus during their lifetime on earth stand before God, cleansed and purified by the fire of God's love and made aware of the forgiveness of their sin through Jesus; they repent, reconcile with God, and live forevermore in perfect, restored relationship with God and others.

CONCLUSION

Lisa called me tonight. Her grandmother just died. And she never received Jesus Christ as her Savior. Now more than ever, Lisa wants to believe in our alternative view of hell. Through her tears she said, "I just can't believe anymore what I've always been taught about God's wrath and judgment. I finally understand the extent of God's love for all people, including for my grandma. I have to believe that a God we define as love would never send my grandma to eternal hell. God will reconcile with her and I'll see her again someday. She's with God—she has to be."

I hope so too. But I admit that I don't know with absolute certainty what will happen at the end of time. I don't know for sure how God will see that justice prevails or that every knee will bow or every tongue confess Jesus as Lord. But I do know that as we go about our business, the world seems to become more and more violent. Innocent multitudes of people suffer injustice and violence every second of every day.

Often the perpetrators of such violence and injustice rationalize their acts or condone the violence of others in the name of God. Because they believe that God is capable of and willing to do violence, including the eternal violence of hell, they believe they too can commit all manner of atrocities in the name of their violent God.

To stem the tide of religious violence in the world, we must offer believers an alternative image of God, one that more closely resembles the teachings and life of Jesus. The God whom Jesus revealed to us is the God of love, who calls us to come and live as active participants in transforming the world from one where violence dominates to one where peace prevails.

I argue that if we do not hear the call of the kingdom; if the call of the other falls on deaf ears and hardened hearts; if we forget the meaning of Jesus' life, death, and resurrection, which reversed the powers of the world with the weak power of love—then we will continue to live as if Jesus never died. We will continue to solve the problem of violence violently, including our buying into the violence of hell. Consequently, we will propagate the image of a violent God and condone the violence that results. Then the anguished cries of our children and their children after them will be drowned by heavy artillery, by the dominant voices of the world's powerful, by the demand for retribution, and by a violent religious intoxication that hinges upon theories of a violent God who liberally throws the majority of all humanity into the eternal fires of hell.

The only way to gain liberation from the structures of violence is to give up the idea of retribution. To do this we must give up the violent forms of justice, peacemaking, government, and behavior that retribution has led us to create in the belief that they were legitimate, necessary, or divine. As Jesus gave up his right for self-defense and reprisals in the name of true justice (restorative and reconciling justice, which loves and forgives), we too, in the power of Christ's forgiveness and love and through lives transformed by that love, can give up our right for reprisal, retribution, and remuneration, including our views of eternal punishment that so oppose the reign of God. We too can spread the good news of restoration and reconciliation through our actions and beliefs.

Concern for the victims of violence, even the victims that we would otherwise consign to hell, is our kingdom responsibility (which can also be thought of as response-ability). To heed the cries of those abandoned to injustice, to forgive the persecutors, and to trust in the God of peace—these are all characteristics of hearing and doing the truth in love. These are the characteristics that enable us to hear the other cry out, "I am thirsty, parched, in a desert bereft of the healing waters of justice"; or "I am sick, infected with the world's and religion's structures of violence"; or "I am in prison, in the world's prison, where violence rules"; or "I am tortured by the fear of eternal punishment instilled in me by the community of Christ, where love rather than judgment should reign."

Our alternative view of hell allows our theology to remain consistent with a God of love and forgiveness. It answers the questions about eternal damnation and unending torture that haunt our dreams and break our hearts. And maybe an alternative view of hell will disarm those who lift guns and drop bombs and destroy souls so that instead they live according to the disarming love of God through Jesus Christ. Perhaps, just perhaps, the world will then know Jesus because of the love that we—all of us who claim to follow the Prince of Peace—have for one another, even for our enemies. So rather than scaring people into God's kingdom with horror stories, let's win them over with the greatest love story ever told, the best piece of good news they'll ever hear.

Now, one more thought on a more personal note, just for us who have read and struggled and reflected on this new view of hell. Isn't it wonderful to understand more clearly the extent of God's love and the extravagance of God's grace, which desires nothing more than a relationship with you and with all those you love? And God will settle for nothing less than a redeemed, restored, intimate relationship that lasts, truly, for eternity, no matter what it costs—and it costs a lot. Let's transform our theology, then, into a theology ruled by love. As Dorothy Sayers puts it in her radio dramatization of the Gospels *The Man Born to Be King*, "This is holiness—to love, and be ruled by love; for love can do nothing wrong. . . . Wherever there is love, there is the Kingdom of God."

Appendixes

On the More Academic Side of Hell

References and Commentary

Because this treatise on hell is written for readers without a formal theological education rather than for scholars in the discipline, it didn't seem appropriate to clutter the text with footnotes or endnotes. So although you won't find specific references within the text to the scholarship I consulted in order to write this book, be assured it's there on every page. For those of you with a more academic bent, I have included this additional section where you'll find the sources I used and additional brief commentary for each chapter.

Introduction

Throughout the book I carry on a discussion with three main people. They are not imaginary friends! For over twenty years Lisa and I have wrangled over major theological issues. We raised our small children together; she homeschooled her boy and girl, and I sent my four boys to public school. We sang in the choir together, did Bible study, and served in various women's events at Bell Shoals Baptist Church in Brandon, Florida. So not only did we watch our children grow up together, we ourselves grew up in the Lord together as we learned how to imitate Jesus as wives, mothers, daughters, and friends. I moved off to Texas. Lisa moved off to Georgia. Yet we remained close even though our lives took very different paths: mine to graduate school, a PhD, and a faculty position teaching theology and religion at Messiah College in Grantham, Pennsylvania, and hers as beauty consultant and as a mother of yet another child, an adopted African American boy through a ministry to pregnant women in prison. He's the joy of her life, and she continues to be a constant source of support, encouragement, and accountability to me.

Eric is one of my former students at Messiah College and graduated in May 2009. Although he is a Christian Ministries major, he's one of the smartest theology students I've ever had the pleasure to teach. He struggles constantly over the fate of unreached people groups and over the horrors of hell. Right now he serves as a pastor of a small congregation in central Pennsylvania, preaching the good news every Sunday.

Brooke is a very mature and intelligent senior in high school who attends a private Christian school. She calls me her spiritual mentor, but at times I wonder if it isn't the other way around. We really do have most of our theological discussions over sushi and driving practice. Although our parallel parking adventures are over (she passed her driver's license test yesterday! Whew!), Brooke asks difficult questions and won't accept simple, boiler-plate answers. Her nonviolent image of God and her interest in and respect for other religions causes her to question the legitimacy of hell.

I do have other conversation partners whose questions and conversations appear in some form or another in the book. Many students, my mother, younger brother, sons, aunts, and other friends all contributed to the thought processes involved in writing the text.

As I noted in the introduction, a 2008 Pew Forum on Religion and Public Life survey showed that 59 percent of Americans believe in hell as a place of eternal punishment for all those who did not repent of their sin. (You can read the article online at http://pewforum.org/news/display.php?NewsID=16260.) Although this number has decreased from 71 to 59 percent over the last decade, these survey results show just how entrenched the traditional views of hell still are. Although that's not a problem for some, it is for me, mainly because of my concern for God's reputation and secondarily because of my concern about violence committed in the name of God. If Christians can build a strong biblical case that reveals the God of love as also a lover of peace and as a lover of enemies who seeks above all else to redeem and restore a lost world, then the world may be a better place in which to live. Those who, like my aunt, reject Christianity largely because of the "mean and violent" God it proclaims, may learn to love and trust a God who lives and teaches the way Jesus did: loving enemies, promoting peace, seeking and saving those who are lost. I hope this reinterpretation of hell is a step in that direction.

Chapter 1: The Landscape

In this chapter I wanted to lay the groundwork for the horrific nature of hell. We don't often read various quotes from across the centuries grouped together in one place. Lisa read this chapter shortly after I finished it and couldn't believe the enormity of the violence that we think God takes part in and delights over. She began the process of wondering how she could keep on believing what she had always been taught while knowing what those beliefs communicated about God.

I used Dante's *Divine Comedy* throughout the book, especially in this chapter. Dante's work, written between 1301 and 1321, contributed powerfully to the traditional notions of hell. Dorothy Sayers wrote one of the best translations and commentary in three parts between 1949 and her death in 1957. One of her biographers, Barbara Reynolds, finished the last volume on the *Paradiso* in 1962.

The many quotes on hell came from many different sources, from theological encyclopedias, texts on Christian history, primary sources such as theological treatises, and sermons. They are all easily found online as well. A good source for early descriptions of hell is in Jean Delumeau's work, *Sin and Fear: The Emergence of a Western Guilt Culture 13th–18th Centuries*, trans. Eric Nicholson (New York: Saint Martin's Press, 1990), 373–400. In Augustine of Hippo's *City of God*, books 13, 19, 21, and 37 describe hell in explicit terms as well.

Early church fathers and medieval theologians wrote and preached extensively, trying to provide solutions to the problem of eternal punishment for temporal sin. They justified it in various ways. I'll include one somewhat lengthy quote from M. G. Girard, an eighteenth-century French pastor who drew his support from Gregory of Nyssa. He speaks of two incontestable principles:

> The first is that sin must be punished as it deserves. The second is that sin must be punished according to its degree. . . . For it is incontestable that deadly sin encloses infinite malice. Now, the damned being but creatures, limited and finite beings, they cannot be capable of suffering an infinite penalty of infinite majesty; consequently, their sin must be punished by the most fitting penalty; thus it must be infinite according to its duration: hence eternity.
>
> Sin must be punished insofar as it exists. . . . God . . . must punish sin according to its degree: so it is that sin will remain forever in those who died in this deplorable state, and so it is that it will exist forever.
> (Delumeau, *Sin and Fear*, 376)

Not only did early theologians support infinite punishment for finite sin; they also constructed doctrines that kept sin and evil in existence for all eternity—one of the troubles we talked about in this chapter.

Various works cited in this chapter:

Donald K. McKim, *Westminster Dictionary of Theological Terms* (Louisville, KY: Westminster John Knox Press, 1996), s.v. "Hell."

Dante Alighieri, *The Divine Comedy of Dante Alighieri*. Dante Alighieri, *The Divine Comedy: Hell,* trans. Dorothy L. Sayers (Baltimore: Penguin Books, 1971). Dante Alighieri, *The Divine Comedy,* trans. Allen Mandelbaum (New York: Everyman's Library, 1995).

Jonathan Edwards, "Sinners in the Hands of an Angry God," sermon at Enfield, Connecticut, July 8, 1741, http://www.ccel.org/ccel/edwards/works2.ii .iii.html.

Jonathan Edwards, "Sinners in Zion Tenderly Warned," discourse, 1740, http://www.ccel.org/ccel/edwards/works2.vi.viii.ii.html.

Fray Luis de Granada, *Sermons* 1.72, trans. Orby Shipley, http://www .tentmaker.org/Quotes/hell-fire.htm.

John Wesley, Sermon 15, "The Great Assize," March 10, 1758, http://thrice holy.net/Texts/Assize.html.

Contemplations of the State of Man in This Life, and in That Which Is to Come (London: J. Kidgell, 1684), attributed to Jeremy Taylor but actually selections from Sir Vivian Mullineaux's 1672 translation of Juan Eusebio Nieremberg's *De la diferencia entre lo temporal y eterno* (Zarayera: Ped. Verges, 1657).

Edwards, "Sinners in the Hands of an Angry God."

Jonathan Edwards, in *Discourses on Various Important Subjects* (Boston: S. Kneeland and T. Green, 1738), http://youall.com/HELL/torture.htm.

Richard Baxter, *The Practical Works of Richard Baxter* (London: George Virtue, 1838), 3:146.

Peter Newcome, in *A Catechetical Course of Sermons for the Whole Year,* 2 vols. (London: John Wyat, 1700; 3rd ed., 1712).

Peter Lombard (ca. 1100–1160), *Sentences* 4.50ff.

Andrew Welwood, *Meditations, Representing a Glimpse of Glory; or, A Gospel-Discovery of Emmanuel's Land* (Edinburgh: John Gray and Gavin Alstron, 1763), 186.

Samuel Hopkins, *The Works of Samuel Hopkins,* vol. 1 (Boston: Doctrinal Tract and Book Society, 1852), 202.

Thomas Aquinas (ca. 1224–74), *Summa theologica,* Supplement, Question 94, "The Relation of the Saints to the Damned," art. 1, "Whether the Blessed in Heaven Will See the Suffering of the Damned?" http://www.newadvent.org/ summa/5094.htm.

Anselm of Canterbury's theological method is described as *fides quaerens intellectum,* "faith seeking understanding" of itself.

Chapter 2: The Image of God

One of my main concerns about traditional doctrines of hell stems from the desire to portray God in a way that fits with what Jesus revealed about God as a God of love, compassion, mercy, and justice—justice that seeks to reconcile and restore. If our thinking on the image, character, and nature of God focuses on these aspects rather than on divine violence, I believe our world will be a less-violent place in which to live. I wrote this chapter so that we could see how we have traditionally viewed God and the excuses we make for God when we can't make sense of what we perceive to be God's behavior.

I found Eric Seibert's *Disturbing Divine Behavior: Troubling Old Testament Images of God* (Minneapolis: Fortress Press, 2009) extremely helpful. In this book, Seibert describes the violence of God in the Old Testament, reveals our hermeneutical rationalizations for the violence, and points us in another interpretative direction, which refutes images of a violent God. A couple of the headings I used to describe some of God's behaviors in the Old Testament come from Seibert's book ("Divine Immunity," for example).

Chapter 3: The Justice of God

I primarily wanted to discuss how our traditional doctrines of God, justice, and redemption are based upon retributive notions of justice. Again, my concern for the image of God comes into play here. If we continue to view God as mainly retributive, our own actions will follow suit—as they have in our current civil justice systems and personal lives. If we can learn to rethink God as reconciling and restorative, our actions may change accordingly as well.

I found the work of John Dominic Crossan very helpful regarding the justice of God. In his book *God and Empire*, Crossan details the history of violence in Christian tradition. He explains its roots and delves into the nonviolent character of the early Christians. See John Dominic Crossan, *God and Empire: Jesus against Rome, Then and Now* (San Francisco: HarperOne, 2008).

Raymund Schwager, *Jesus in the Drama of Salvation: Toward a Biblical Doctrine of Redemption* (New York: Crossroad Publishing Co., 1999), also informed my work. Like Seibert, Schwager deals with the violence of God in the Old Testament and offers us alternative interpretations based on the story of Jesus. See also his work titled *Must There Be Scapegoats?* (San Francisco: Harper & Row, Publishers, 1987).

Another important source is a book by Bruce C. Birch, *Let Justice Roll Down: The Old Testament, Ethics, and Christian Life* (Louisville, KY: Westminster John Knox Press, 1991). Birch searches through the Hebrew Scriptures from beginning to end and offers nonviolent interpretations that reveal to us a God of love, peace, and restorative justice.

Chapter 4: The Forgiveness of God

Again, I wanted to discuss how our traditional views of forgiveness found in our doctrines of God and salvation truly compromise authentic forgiveness and perpetuate notions of retributive justice. My constant concern is for the image of God we portray through retributive types of forgiveness. Rather than a loving God who forgives without measure and without payback of any sort, our traditional doctrines present God's forgiveness as something we must earn in one way or another. This is not what Jesus taught about forgiveness.

I am indebted to Crossan for his work in *God and Empire* and to Schwager's two books mentioned in the last chapter. N. T. Wright's work entitled *Evil and the Justice of God* (Downers Grove, IL: IVP Books, 2006) provided rich resources for my work in the areas of forgiveness and justice.

For a current example of a community's forgivingness, see Donald B. Kraybill, Steven M. Nolt, and David L. Weaver-Zercher, *Amish Grace: How Forgiveness Transcended Tragedy* (San Francisco: Jossey Bass, 2007).

For an excellent treatment of atonement and Paul, see Stephen Finlan, *Problems with Atonement* (Collegeville, MN: Liturgical Press, 2005); Finlan, *The Background and Content of Paul's Cultic Atonement Metaphors* (Atlanta: Society for Biblical Literature, 2004).

Chapter 5: Rethinking the Violence of God

The quotes you see in this chapter have page numbers included in the text in parentheses. I highly recommend a new book by Richard Hughes, *Christian America and the Kingdom of God* (Chicago: University of Illinois Press, 2009); the parenthetical page numbers refer to this work.

The quotes from Merrill Unger and Charles Jones come from a book by Paul Boyer, *When Time Shall Be No More: Prophecy Belief in Modern America* (Cambridge, MA: President and Fellows of Harvard College, 1992), 135, 150.

I mention the CNN interview with Jesse Jackson and Jerry Falwell. You can find the interview online at http://www.cnnstudentnews.cnn .com/TRANSCRIPTS/0410/24/le.01.html. Here is the portion I used in this chapter:

JACKSON: I submit to you today that our going to Iraq was a misadventure. It has put America in isolation. We are losing lives, money, and losing our character in that war. We deserve better leadership. And we need . . .

FALWELL: I'd rather be killing them over there than fighting them over here, Jesse. And I think you would . . .

JACKSON: Let's stop the killing and choose peace. Let's choose negotiation over confrontation.

FALWELL: Well, I'm for that too. But you've got to kill the terrorists before the killing stops. And I'm for the president to chase them all over the world. If it takes ten years, blow them all away in the name of the Lord.

JACKSON: That does not sound biblical to me. And that sounds ridiculous.

Many different voices went into the writing of this chapter, and I list them here for you:

Timothy Gorringe, *God's Just Vengeance: Crime, Violence, and the Rhetoric of Salvation* (New York: Cambridge University Press, 1996), 82. Gorringe writes extensively about the influence that Christian theology has had on our justice system and social ideologies.

Raymund Schwager, *Jesus in the Drama of Salvation*, mentioned above, along with his book *Must There Be Scapegoats?* proved to be very helpful in interpreting Old Testament passages in a new light.

Rita Nakashima Brock and Rebecca Ann Parker have written a wonderfully informative book on Christian views of paradise throughout history, starting with the early church. *Saving Paradise: How Christianity Traded Love of This World for Crucifixion and Empire* (Boston: Beacon Press, 2009). For this chapter I incorporated some of their ideas from chapter 10, "Peace by the Blood of the Cross," 254–75. It basically explains that church people needed to explain their involvement in war and violence against rebels, so it took to the Old Testament passages about God as warrior and cloaked Christ in the clothing of a vicious warrior. Even monks took up arms to fight for God. In fact, only taking up arms for the church was acceptable. Any other kind of warfare would incur the wrath of God and eternity in hell. This mentality found its way into contemporary doctrine.

The work of René Girard is taken from the following texts:

I See Satan Fall Like Lightning, trans. James G. Williams (Maryknoll, NY: Orbis Books, 2002).

The Scapegoat, trans. Yvonne Freccero (Baltimore: Johns Hopkins University Press, 1986).

Other sources used for this chapter include these:

Paul Boyer, *When Time Shall Be No More: Prophecy Belief in Modern American Culture* (Cambridge, MA: Harvard University Press, 1992).

Steve Chalke and Alan Mann, *The Lost Message of Jesus* (Grand Rapids: Zondervan Press, 2003).

John Dominic Crossan's *God and Empire* (cited above).

Although I cited a number of biblical texts to support the idea that God desires to redeem humanity despite our sin, I list a few more verses here: Pss. 3:8; 4; Isa. 57:17–19; 61. These verses reveal that God's salvation extends to the whole world: Isa. 2:1–4; 49:6b; Mic. 4:1–4.

Chapter 6: Rethinking the Image of God

I can't stress enough the importance of rethinking the image of God through the lens of Jesus, his teachings, and his life in submission to God's will. I found resources for this chapter mostly from the biblical texts but also from Raymund Schwager and from a little book by Perry Yoder, *Shalom: The Bible's Word for Salvation, Justice, and Peace* (Nappanee, IN: Evangel Publishing House, 1998). In this book Yoder interprets the Bible through the lens of *shalom* and its full depth of meaning. If we understand God as a God of *shalom*, it changes the image of God's justice and the depth of God's desire to redeem the world. Richard Kearney also stresses the importance of our perception in his book *Anatheism: Returning to God after God* (New York: Columbia University Press, 2009). See especially pp. 133–51.

R. Laird Harris, Gleason L. Archer Jr., and Bruce K. Waltke, eds., *The Theological Wordbook of the Old Testament* (Chicago: Moody Press, 1980), s.v. "Shalom."

For the 1963 Baptist Faith and Message, see http://www.baptiststart.com/print/1963_baptist_faith_message.html.

Chapter 7: Rethinking the Justice of God

I am aware that the entire Bible is filled with notions of both retributive justice and restorative justice. The focus, however, has long been on the retributive aspects of justice as is obvious from our criminal justice system, atonement theories, and constructions of an eternal hell. Much of the violence inflicted upon innocent people throughout our history may be due in large part to our concepts of divine justice as retributive. I submit that it is time to focus on divine justice as restorative and reconciling so that our behavior toward others may be based upon love instead of violence and hatred.

The sources I find helpful in the area of justice are the following:

Howard Zehr, *Changing Lenses: A New Focus for Crime and Justice* (Scottdale, PA: Herald Press, 1990).

Robert L. Browning and Roy A. Reed, *Forgiveness, Reconciliation, and Moral Courage: Motives and Designs for Ministry in a Troubled World* (Grand Rapids: Wm. B. Eerdmans Publishing Co., 2004).

Gordon Brubacher, "Just War and the New Community: The Witness of the Old Testament for Christians Today," *Princeton Theological Review* 10, no. 2 (Fall 2006): 19–29.

Raymund Schwager, *Must There Be Scapegoats?* (cited above).

Perry Yoder, *Shalom* (cited above).

N. T. Wright, *What Saint Paul Really Said: Was Paul of Tarsus the Real Founder of Christianity?* (Grand Rapids: Wm. B. Eerdmans Publishing Co., 1997).

Christopher D. Marshall, *Beyond Retribution: A New Testament Vision for Justice, Crime, and Punishment* (Grand Rapids: Wm. B. Eerdmans Publishing Co., 2001).

Arthur P. Boers, *Justice That Heals: A Biblical Vision for Victims and Offenders* (Newton, KS: Faith & Life Press, 1992).

John Dominic Crossan, *God and Empire* (cited above), 190.

Peter Abelard, *Epistle to the Romans*, in *A Scholastic Miscellany: Anselm to Ockham*, ed. Eugene R. Fairweather (Philadelphia: Westminster Press, 1954), 275–77, comments on Rom. 3:23–24. In this work, Abelard equates divine justice with divine love. Divine love forgives human sin.

Timothy Gorringe, *God's Just Vengeance: Crime, Violence, and the Rhetoric of Salvation* (New York: Cambridge University Press, 1996).

C. F. D. Moule, in *Forgiveness and Reconciliation* (London: SPCK, 1998), 44–46, states the notion of divine justice well:

The life of Jesus and his death—the inevitable consequence of total dedication to the way of God—and his total aliveness through and beyond (not in spite of) death, all point in this direction, and exhibit the justice of God at its deepest level: "God in Christ was reconciling the world to himself" (2 Cor. 5:19). No hangover of retributive systems still showing itself in the New Testament can negate this.

Jack Nelson-Pallmeyer, *Jesus against Christianity: Reclaiming the Missing Jesus* (Harrisburg, PA: Trinity Press International, 2001).

Robert K. Massie, *Peter the Great: His Life and Work* (New York: Ballantine Books, 1981).

John D. Caputo provides us with another very helpful resource with his most recent work on God: *The Weakness of God: A Theology of the Event* (Bloomington: Indiana University Press, 2006). Readers interested in Caputo's theories on justice should also read *The Prayers and Tear of Jacques Derrida: Religion without Religion* (Bloomington: Indiana University Press, 1997). Along with Derrida, Caputo likens deconstruction to justice. Deconstruction is not out to level the law or destroy meaning. It is out to open up the law for reinterpretation, difference, to take frozen interpretations and loosen them up so that other voices can be heard, other previously hidden and squelched (valid) interpretations can come to the fore. It brings texts (and institutions such as the church) into question, knocks them off their idolatrous pedestals so that they are level with all the other voices trapped inside. If, for example, historical texts (which are someone's interpretation of what occurred), or even scriptural interpretations, are not revisable, amendable, open to deconstruction, then they are in danger of fostering hatred, abuse, and violence. In this manner, deconstruction is justice.

Along with my own personal knowledge of Hebrew, I referred to the following for the various word studies in the chapter:

John J. Scullion, "Righteousness," in *Anchor Bible Dictionary*, ed. Noel Freedman (New York: Doubleday, 1992): 5:731. The Hebrew word '*asah* in the phrase "righteousness and justice" indicates the doing together of what the two words call for. See Pss. 10:17–18; 33:5; 82:1–8; 99:4; Isa. 1:15–17; 30:18–19; 32:1–2; 42:1–4; 61:1–8; Jer. 9:24; 22:3; Ezek. 34:11–16; Hos. 2:19. When the word *mishpat* is translated in the English Old Testament, it is done so in a manner that indicates the "justice" served in a courtroom. Not so in the Hebrew. The word instead implies continuous, repeated actions, doing justice rather than exacting justice.

Greifswald J. Zobel, "*ḥesed*," in *Theological Dictionary of the Old Testament*, ed. G. Johannes Botterweck and Helmer Ringgren, trans. David E. Green, vol. 5 (Grand Rapids: Wm. B. Eerdmans Publishing Co., 1986), 49. See also Isa. 30:18 (NRSV): "[God] will rise up to show mercy to you. For the Lord is a God of justice." Mercy is often equated with love in Hebrew.

For further study in the Old Testament Hebrew meanings and examples of justice, see Isa. 1:15–17, in which God tells the people to stop shedding blood and do justice; and Job 19:7, in which Job seeks justice and finds only violence. Again, justice is absent in the presence of violence: cf. Isa. 32:16–18; Jer. 22:15–17; Mic. 3:1–3; 7:2–3; Hab. 1:3–4. Also Prov. 2:8–9 speaks of justice as a "good path" (NRSV). In Isa. 59:8–9 justice is absent from the people's path. See also Pss. 1:3; 65:9–13; Isa. 33:5–6; 51:4–5.

See Isa. 42:1–4, which includes "justice" in a list of what pleases or satisfies God, things in which God's soul delights. Verse 4 is particularly interesting and indicates that Jesus, in fulfilling this prophecy, will not be crushed until he has established justice. Can we conclude from this that justice was established or revealed through his ushering in the kingdom of God while he was still alive? See Isa. 59:15. The Hebrew words I am equating with divine satisfaction are *bahar*, in Prov. 21:3, which means to choose based upon the best, the most desired or desirable choice; *ratsah*, in Isa. 42:1, which means to delight it, to take pleasure in, which expresses satisfaction; and *hapets*, in Jer. 9:24, which means that God (in this case) finds great pleasure in doing something. God is pleased or satisfied with doing something. It is not an arbitrary pleasure, but one based upon the best, most serviceable act. All these words can lead to the interpretation that God is satisfied with God's choice of the Servant, that God is satisfied by the Servant's work, and that God is satisfied with the results.

Chapter 8: Rethinking the Forgiveness of God

In this chapter I wanted to provide readers with a new paradigm for thinking about forgiveness, one that doesn't require any sort of punishment or payback before the offended party grants forgiveness. Untold numbers of books have been written on forgiveness. I read so extensively and used so many sources for this chapter that I will merely list the ones I found most significant for my own work. I have included full bibliographic information for some of these sources above in the listings in previous chapters.

Hannah Arendt, *The Human Condition* (Chicago: University of Chicago Press, 1958).

Gil Bailie, *Violence Unveiled: Humanity at the Crossroads* (New York: Crossroad, 1995).

Anthony Bartlett, *Cross Purposes: The Violent Grammar of Christian Atonement* (Harrisburg, PA: Trinity Press International, 2001). Bartlett compares repeated forgiveness to the spirit of nonretaliation carried to term in the death of Christ, a spirit we now imitate in the forgiving of sins. We now take part in the repetition of human forgiveness: "Father, forgive us as we forgive others" (244–45). In addition, Bartlett describes the absolute gift of the cross as a gift that breaks apart the chronology of time. In other words, forgiveness (first realized in the cross) reaches back across chronological time and changes/heals the past. In forgiveness we surrender to loss, transforming the past moment as contingent in a free act of unbounded forgiving. In so doing, we imitate Christ in forgiving again and again in a manner completely undetermined by chronological time (251–54).

Lee C. Camp, *Mere Discipleship: Radical Christianity in a Rebellious World* (Grand Rapids: Brazos Press, 2003).

John D. Caputo, *More Radical Hermeneutics: On Not Knowing Who We Are* (Bloomington: Indiana University Press, 2000).

John D. Caputo, *Weakness of God* (cited above), esp. chap. 10. Caputo clearly believes that the old adage "Forgive the sinner, but not the sin" takes away from forgiveness. He asserts that "if I forgive the doer but not the deed, the offender but not the offense, then I am inserting an important condition into my forgiveness." In a conditional forgiveness of this sort, we imply: "I do not forgive you in those moments of your life where you were or are still sinning or are planning to sin some more. So once again, I am not forgiving sinning, which needs forgiveness, but non-sinning, which does not" (213).

John D. Caputo, *On Religion* (New York: Routledge, 2001).

John D. Caputo, *The Prayers and Tear of Jacques Derrida: Religion without Religion* (cited above).

John D. Caputo, *Against Ethics: Contributions to a Poetics of Obligation with Constant Reference to Deconstruction* (Bloomington: Indiana University Press, 1993).

Steve Chalke and Alan Mann, *The Lost Message of Jesus* (cited above).

James Carroll, *Constantine's Sword: The Church and the Jews, a History* (Boston: Houghton Mifflin Publishers, 2002).

Bruce Chilton, *Rabbi Jesus: An Intimate Biography* (New York: Random House, Doubleday, 2001).

Casiano Floristan and Christian Duquoc, *Forgiveness* (Minneapolis: Fortress Press, 1986).

Ted Grimsrud and Loren J. Johns, *Peace and Justice Shall Embrace: Essays in Honor of Millard Lind* (Telford, PA: Pandora Press; Scottdale, PA: Herald Press, 1999). Grimsrud connects redemption with divine justice (73).

Richard Holloway, *Doubts and Loves: What Is Left of Christianity* (Edinburgh: Canongate Books, 2005).

Emmanuel Lévinas, *Totality and Infinity: An Essay on Exteriority*, trans. Alphonso Lingis (Pittsburgh: Duquesne University Press, 1969). Lévinas claims that pardon, or forgiveness, is retroactive and represents the reversibility of time. Pardon acts upon the past by repeating the event and purifying it. Pardon "conserves the past pardoned in the purified present" (283). It does not make the pardoned person innocent, but allows for a happiness of reconciliation. See also the concept of being made a "new creature" in Christ in 2 Cor. 5:17 (cf. NRSV: "There is a new creation").

Jean-Luc Marion, *Prolegomena to Charity*, trans. Stephen Lewis (New York: Fordham University Press, 2002).

Geiko Muller-Fahrenholz, *The Art of Forgiveness: Theological Reflections on Healing and Reconciliation* (Geneva: World Council of Churches, 1997).

Desmond Tutu, "Introduction," in *Exploring Forgiveness*, ed. Robert D. Enright and Joanna North (Madison: University of Wisconsin Press, 1998).

Miroslav Volf, *Free of Charge: Giving and Forgiving in a Culture Stripped of Grace* (Grand Rapids: Zondervan, 2005).

John H. Yoder, *The Politics of Jesus: Vicit Agnus Noster*, 2nd ed. (Grand Rapids: Wm. B. Eerdmans Publishing Co., 1994). Yoder believes that Jesus' omission of "the year of the Lord's vengeance" would have struck his listeners as a significant statement. Jesus was, in effect, revealing a kingdom of nonviolence (34–35).

More from the Bible:

— The pages of the Bible are filled with Old Testament people asking forgiveness or singing praises because of forgiveness: Pss. 103; 130; Isa. 43:25; 55:7; Jer. 18:23; 31:34; Hos. 14:4; Mic. 7:18. Also Exod. 32:32; 34:6–9; 1 Kgs. 8:27–30, 46–50; Neh. 9:17; Pss. 51:1–2; 86:5.

— There are many examples of Jesus forgiving sinners unconditionally: Luke 5:20; 19:1–10; John 4:1–26; 8:11.

— Jesus came to offer unconditional forgiveness (even while we were still enemies): Luke 1:68–79; 2:29–32; Rom. 5:10.

I make a significant distinction between reconciliation and restoration. While love motivates forgiveness, forgiveness leads to reconciliation so that restoration can then take place. In other words, we are not restored to a full relationship unless we first acknowledge and receive forgiveness and reconcile with God. Restoration is a result of reconciliation. For example, Joseph forgave his brothers their betrayal, but his forgiveness did not bear the fruit of restoration until he spoke words of forgiveness, and both he and his brothers kissed and made up, or reconciled (Gen. 47–50).

Chapter 9: The Fire, the Wicked, and the Redeemed

Much of chapter 9 resulted from my biblical study of fire and hell. As always, Bible dictionaries are a useful tool. My favorites are *The Anchor Bible Dictionary* (cited above) as well as *The International Standard Bible Encyclopedia* (Grand Rapids: Wm. B. Eerdmans Publishing Co., 1988; cf. 1915 edition at http://www.bible-history.com/isbe/).

Another extremely helpful source that hasn't attracted its fair share of readership attention is Gerry Beauchemin's *Hope beyond Hell: The Righteous Purpose of God's Judgment* (Olmito, TX: Malista Press, 2007).

George MacDonald is a longtime favorite writer for me. I used his anthology compiled by C. S. Lewis: Lewis, *George MacDonald: An Anthology* (New York: Touchstone, 1947), 63, 91. The quotes are from "The Fear of God" and "Justice," essays in *Creation in Christ: Unspoken Sermons.* Cf. http://www.readprint.com/author-197/George-MacDonald-books.

Extra thanks goes to David Downing. After talking about this book on hell one evening, he dreamed about the part of the scene in which I describe Otto standing before God and putting his hand on the hearts of all his victims. He gave me permission to include those parts of his dream in this chapter.

Additional Information. Four words in Greek and Hebrew all translated into English as "hell." These words are not interchangeable in the original language, yet we treat them in English as if they were, lumping and dumping them all into "hell." The words are *Sheol*, a subterranean retreat for all the dead, also translated as "grave" or "pit"; *Gehennah*, expounded upon at length in the chapter; *Hades*, also translated "grave" in 1 Cor. 15:55; and *Tartaros*, an underworld prison in Greek mythology.

Chapter 10: Outer Darkness, Gnashing of Teeth, and the Lake of Fire

As in the previous chapters, I used Bible dictionaries (cited above) for additional comments on word studies. Beauchamin's *Hope beyond Hell* continued to inform my work.

For the sections on metaphor and parables, my colleague Michael Cosby's book and conversations proved extremely helpful. Cosby has written a number of books on interpreting the New Testament. I used Michael R. Cosby: *Portraits of Jesus* (Louisville, KY: Westminster John Knox Press, 1999); *Interpreting Biblical Literature: An Introduction to*

Biblical Studies (Grantham, PA: Stony Run Publishing, 2009). See also his *Apostle on the Edge: An Inductive Approach to Paul* (Louisville, KY: Westminster John Knox Press, 2009).

Chapter 11: The Savior

There's so much more to say about at-one-ment than what we read in this chapter. For that reason, I am writing a book on the topic with the same goal in mind: to examine Scripture and tradition in order to interpret God's work to redeem the world in a manner consistent with a God of love.

The quote by George MacDonald comes from the anthology by C. S. Lewis, 2. The full citation is in the source notes for chapter 9.

Again, I will list a few of the sources most significant to the content of this chapter:

Daniel Stökl Ben Ezra, *The Impact of Yom Kippur on Early Christianity: The Day of Atonement from Second Temple Judaism to the Fifth Century* (Tübingen: J. C. B. Mohr / Paul Siebeck, 2003).

Daniel B. Clendenin, ed., *Eastern Orthodox Theology: A Contemporary Reader* (Grand Rapids: Paternoster Press, 2003).

Tom Finger, "Christus Victor as Nonviolent Atonement," in *Atonement and Violence: A Theological Conversation,* ed. John Sanders (Nashville: Abingdon Press, 2006).

Stephen Finlan, *The Problems with Atonement* (Collegeville, MN: Liturgical Press, 2005).

Roy E. Gane, *Cult and Character: Purification Offerings, Day of Atonement, and Theodicy* (Winona Lake, IN: Eisenbrauns, 2005), 62.

John of Damascus, "Orthodox Faith," in *Nicene and Post-Nicene Second Fathers,* Series 2, vol. 9, ed. Philip Schaff (London: T&T Clark, 1980).

Baruch A. Levine, *The JPS Torah Commentary: Leviticus* (Philadelphia: Jewish Publication Society, 1989). The well-known medieval Jewish rabbi Rashi commented on Lev. 17:11 in light of the Jewish tradition reaching back centuries. He said that the blood represents life and that the sacrificial blood was instrumental because it was the symbol of life.

Dennis J. McCarthy, SJ, "The Symbolism of Blood and Sacrifice," in *Journal of Biblical Literature* 88, no. 2 (1969): 166–76.

Roland de Vaux, OP, *Ancient Israel: Its Life and Institutions,* trans. John McHugh (New York: McGraw-Hill Book Co., 1961), 428.

J. Denny Weaver, "Narrative Christus Victor: The Answer to Anselmian Atonement Violence," in *Atonement and Violence: A Theological Conversation* (Nashville: Abingdon Press, 2006).

Additional Information: The meaning of the words "by blood of Christ" (e.g., Rom. 5:9; Eph. 1:7; Heb. 9:14; 1 Pet. 1:19; 1 John 1:7) may possibly be synonymous with cleansing away sin. The word *kippur,* often translated as "to atone," literally means "to cover" or "to cleanse." When the blood of Christ is mentioned in the New Testament, it is also connected with *kippur,* indicating that the blood of Christ cleanses us from sin. In both Testaments there is no connection between *kippur* or "cleansing" and penal or satisfaction theories of atonement. There is a connection, however, between cleansing and forgiveness, so we may be able to say that "cleanse" means "forgive." We can see this connection in Heb. 9:22: "All things are cleansed with blood, and without shedding of blood there is no forgiveness." This topic is an entire chapter of a book project in which shedding blood may be symbolic for sacrificial obedience as in Rom. 12:1 and in John 15:13.

Chapter 12: How Then Shall We Live?

Theology should always result in theological living. Because I have argued throughout the book that our image of God affects our behavior and, therefore, we should interpret God through Jesus, it seemed important to include a chapter on what it would look like to live our lives in accord with our Jesus lens. I used many of the sources cited above, especially those works written by John D. Caputo (*Weakness of God* and *On Religion*) and Raymund Schwager (*Jesus in the Drama of Salvation*).

Caputo's work contributes significantly to the notions of the strength of God's weakness to change the world. Caputo lobbies for the weak force of God in the kingdom event of forgiveness and justice; likewise hospitality also is a weak force that functions in the kingdom as great power without power. In describing God as weak, Caputo is contrasting power and weakness with the world's conception of what constitutes power and weakness, which, as addressed in 1 Cor. 1, is reversed or transformed in the kingdom of God. The weakness of God's force lies in its refusal to resort to military or institutional or systemic "power" that coerces, oppresses, and abuses those without a voice in the system, and to function, instead, as a seemingly weak, gentle, noncoercive force of forgiveness, justice, hospitality, and love that welcomes and "empowers" even those without a voice. See *Weakness of God,* 268, 267–77.

The voice of René Girard echoes the importance of imitating Christ as we live our kingdom lives in his works cited above (*The Scapegoat; Things Hidden Since the Foundation of the World; I See Satan Fall*).

In their work *Saving Paradise*, Brock and Parker believe that the obsession and focus on paradise and eternal life after this life rose to popularity in the 10th and 11th centuries in response to the seemingly unending violence in the European empires. For the early church, paradise was this earth, this life, in the kingdom of God—what we would call the kingdom of God (xv).

On the topic of love, the following works were extremely helpful:

Leonardo Boff, *Jesus Christ the Liberator: A Critical Christology for Our Time*, trans. Patrick Hughes (Maryknoll, NY: Orbis Books, 1978), 27.

Paul Fiddes, "Creation out of Love," in *The Work of Love: Creation as Kenosis*, ed. John Polkinghorne (Grand Rapids: Wm. B. Eerdmans Publishing Co., 2001). Paul Fiddes comments that infinite love is a part of God's character and, as a result, God overflows with an excess of love, which finds its satisfaction in loving others.

John D. Caputo, *More Radical Hermeneutics* (cited above).

John D. Caputo, *Against Ethics* (also cited above). For Caputo, love is not a duty; it is the natural outflow of a life loved by God and in love with God.

John D. Caputo, *On Religion* (cited above). Caputo stresses that there are many ways to love, ways often not counted as authentic love by the worldly conceptions of love, such as heterosexual love and homosexual love in religious monogamy within the bounds of marriage/union. Hatred, however, ravages these types of love. In fact, Caputo cautions against a too-innocent, simple, and schmaltzy conception of love. He knows that we are capable of killing in the name of love, and we are capable of ominous hatred in the name of love. His notions of love, therefore, like the kingdom, justice, forgiveness, and hospitality, turn on a poetics, a poetics that indicate and demand praxis, but praxis with our eyes wide open and our ears cocked toward the continual coming of the kingdom, justice, forgiveness, hospitality, and love (also based upon an e-mail conversation, November 7, 2005).

Huston Smith, "Reasons for Joy," *Christian Century*, October 4, 2005, 11. Smith writes that "the only power that can effect transformations of the order we have described [in the Gospel stories] is love."

Further Reading

Beauchemin, Gerry. *Hope beyond Hell: The Righteous Purpose of God's Judgment.* Olmito, TX: Malista Press, 2007.

Camp, Lee C. *Mere Discipleship: Radical Christianity in a Rebellious World.* Grand Rapids: Brazos Press, 2003.

Caputo, John D. *On Religion.* New York: Routledge, 2001.

Chalke, Steve, and Alan Mann. *The Lost Message of Jesus.* Grand Rapids: Zondervan Press, 2003.

Crossan, John Dominic. *God and Empire: Jesus against Rome, Then and Now.* San Francisco: HarperOne, 2008.

Gulley, Philip, and James Mulholland. *If Grace Is True: Why God Will Save Every Person.* San Francisco: HarperSanFrancisco, 2003.

Holloway, Richard. *Doubts and Loves: What Is Left of Christianity.* Edinburgh: Canongate Books, 2005.

Hughes, Richard. *Christian America and the Kingdom of God.* Chicago: University of Illinois Press, 2009.

Kearney, Richard. *Anatheism: Returning to God after God.* New York: Columbia University Press, 2009.

McLaren, Brian. *The Last Word and the Word after That: A Tale of Faith, Doubt, and a New Kind of Christianity.* San Francisco: Jossey Bass, 2005.

Seibert, Eric. *Disturbing Divine Behavior: Troubling Old Testament Images of God.* Minneapolis: Fortress Press, 2009.

Wright, N. T. *Evil and the Justice of God.* Downers Grove, IL: IVP Books, 2006.

Yoder, Perry. *Shalom: The Bible's Word for Salvation, Justice, and Peace.* Nappanee, IN: Evangel Publishing House, 1998.

Questions for Study and Reflection

INTRODUCTION

1. What images of hell have you held throughout your life? Have those images changed during your life? If so, how?
2. How have these thoughts troubled you, comforted you, or worried you. Why?
3. What do you think about studying hell and trying to find biblical answers to your questions?

CHAPTER 1: THE LANDSCAPE

1. In what ways do you resonate with Lisa, or Brooke, or Eric? Why?
2. After reading the quotes on hell and God's attitude toward it, what are your thoughts? Which of the theologians describe hell according to the way you've been taught? Which descriptions troubled you the most? Why?
3. Which of the seven troubles associated with traditional doctrines of hell strikes you as most significant? Why?

CHAPTER 2: THE IMAGE OF GOD

1. In your thinking, have you tried to harmonize the image of God as loving and compassionate, who desires the redemption of all people, with the image of God as punishing sinners, assigning most people to hell for eternity? How?
2. When you read the Old Testament, which images of God do you focus on? Why?
3. Which theory used to justify God's violent behavior in the Old Testament do you resonate with most? Why?

4. Have you ever felt that God requiring the death of an innocent man in order to forgive sin was unfair? Why or why not?

CHAPTER 3: THE JUSTICE OF GOD

1. What are some of the images of God that disturb you? Why?
2. How have you always understood divine justice in the Bible?
3. How do you primarily understand God: as wrathful or as loving? Why do you think you understand God in the way you do?
4. In what ways have you understood the work of Jesus on the cross? If someone asked you to explain it, what would you say?
5. Can you think of certain instances in which your view of God or your interpretations of the Bible influenced your actions?

CHAPTER 4: THE FORGIVENESS OF GOD

1. What does it mean to forgive someone? Does God require certain conditions to be met before forgiving your sin? Why or why not?
2. If you were to describe forgiveness based upon the story of the Prodigal Son alone, how would you describe it?
3. Which theory of atonement most resonates with you? Why? What view of forgiveness does this theory offer?
4. How do you forgive others: with conditions or without? How do you hope/think God forgives? Why?

CHAPTER 5: RETHINKING THE VIOLENCE OF GOD

1. Why is it important to learn about the culture that the biblical writers lived in? How can knowing the culture help us interpret the Bible?
2. How do you think God feels about killing innocent people? How do you think God feels about killing enemies? Why?
3. Which do you think God prefers: violence or peace? How then do you think God acts in the world toward God's enemies? Why?
4. How would you harmonize the violent images of God with the peaceful images seen especially in the life and teachings of Jesus?

5. What are your thoughts about the author's attempt to harmonize these images? Why?

CHAPTER 6: RETHINKING THE IMAGE OF GOD

1. How does the view of God in this chapter compare with the view of God we've seen in the first four chapters? Which most resonates with you? Why?
2. Think of the one thing or person that is most precious to you. Could you burn that thing to ashes or see it suffer destruction forever? The Bible indicates that you are many times more precious to God than that one thing or person.
3. Which of the biblical images of God portrayed in this chapter is your favorite? Why?
4. Why is reading the Bible through Jesus-colored glasses a valid method for discovering the character of God?

CHAPTER 7: RETHINKING THE JUSTICE OF GOD

1. What are the differences between retributive and restorative justice? Which form of justice do you prefer for yourself?
2. Which form of justice do you think Jesus taught? Why?
3. Which types of actions does restorative justice include or exclude? Which types of actions does retributive justice include or exclude? Why is it important to explore the actions resulting from justice?
4. Why is determining the character of divine justice important?
5. If God's primary form of justice is restorative, how might that affect God's dealings with humans after they die?
6. How do justice and love harmonize?

CHAPTER 8: RETHINKING THE FORGIVENESS OF GOD

1. What is forgiveness? What do you think the Bible teaches about forgiveness?
2. How does restorative justice work hand in hand with forgiveness?

3. After reading the parable of the Prodigal Son, how do you think God forgives: conditionally or unconditionally? Why? How is your answer now different from your answer to chapter 4's question 4?
4. How are you supposed to forgive others?
5. Do you feel as though you have received God's unconditional forgiveness in your life? Explain.
6. How does unconditional forgiveness repair the past and transform the future? Do you feel that is true in your life?

CHAPTER 9: THE FIRE, THE WICKED, AND THE REDEEMED

1. What did you learn about fire? Why is the discussion on fire significant for thinking about hell?
2. How do you feel about Otto and his experience with God? Why? Which form of justice did God serve? Which form of forgiveness?
3. How do God's wrath and God's love interconnect and harmonize?
4. If you have loved ones who died outside of Christ, how does this view of hell resonate with you?

CHAPTER 10: OUTER DARKNESS, GNASHING OF TEETH, AND THE LAKE OF FIRE

1. Can you think of any metaphors, expressions, or words that only someone from your own context would understand? What are they?
2. Which view of "eternity" most resonates with you: eternity as "forever" or eternity as explained in this chapter? Why?
3. Why is viewing hell as a purification process in God's fiery presence significant?
4. How does this alternative view of hell harmonize with God's justice and forgiveness?

CHAPTER 11: THE SAVIOR

1. Why is it important for our Christian tradition to keep reinterpreting the Bible and the tradition?

2. Can you think of some areas in which we have reinterpreted the Bible and tradition in the last hundred years?
3. Which atonement theory are you most familiar/comfortable with? Which forms of justice and forgiveness does that theory espouse?
4. What is the connection between *kippur* and God's purifying fire?
5. What might offering your body to God as a living sacrifice look like in everyday life? How might it be lived out? Have you offered your life to God as a living and holy sacrifice?

CHAPTER 12: HOW THEN SHALL WE LIVE?

1. How can the alternative view of hell be useful in talking to others about Jesus?
2. Why is your salvation important to you?
3. In what practical ways should loving others be obvious in your life?
4. After reading this chapter, what do you believe is the good news?

Index of Scripture

Index of Subjects and Names

green press INITIATIVE

Westminster John Knox Press is committed to preserving ancient forests and natural resources. We elected to print this title on 30% post consumer recycled paper, processed chlorine free. As a result, for this printing, we have saved:

18 Trees (40' tall and 6-8" diameter)
6 Million BTUs of Total Energy
1,723 Pounds of Greenhouse Gases
8,301 Gallons of Wastewater
504 Pounds of Solid Waste

Westminster John Knox Press made this paper choice because our printer, Thomson-Shore, Inc., is a member of Green Press Initiative, a nonprofit program dedicated to supporting authors, publishers, and suppliers in their efforts to reduce their use of fiber obtained from endangered forests.

For more information, visit www.greenpressinitiative.org

Environmental impact estimates were made using the Environmental Defense Paper Calculator. For more information visit: www.edf.org/papercalculator